LIMITING RESOURCES

LaDAWN HAGLUND

LIMITING RESOURCES

Market-Led Reform and the Transformation
of Public Goods

The Pennsylvania State University Press
University Park, Pennsylvania

Library of Congress Cataloging-in-Publication Data

Haglund, LaDawn, 1968–
    Limiting resources : market-led reform and the transformation of public goods /
LaDawn Haglund.
        p.   cm.
Includes bibliographical references and index.
ISBN 978-0-271-03718-9 (cloth : alk. paper)
1. Water resources development—Costa Rica.
2. Water resources development—El Salvador.
3. Electric power—Costa Rica.
4. Electric power—El Salvador.
5. Public goods.
I. Title.

HD1696.C8.H34   2010
333.793'2097284—dc22
2010007381

In memory of JOLIE RICKMAN,
stronger than your average superhero

Although Central America has had no political unity . . . it has had a certain "economic unity" as a result of its subjection to common external influences [which] have filtered through domestic institutions to affect each economy in slightly different ways. Thus, the region exhibits both conformity and diversity and the problem facing an author is to see the one without losing sight of the other.

—VICTOR BULMER-THOMAS,
The Political Economy of Central America Since 1920

CONTENTS

FIGURES AND TABLES

Figures

Tables

As this book went to press, the global economy was experiencing its worst crisis since the Great Depression. One could look just about anywhere and find bad news, even in the supposedly healthy U.S. economy: from a collapsing financial system resulting in multi-billion-dollar taxpayer bailouts to burst real estate bubbles and foreclosures at record highs. Unemployment and underemployment plagued the working poor, while the "misery index," that is, the sum of the unemployment and inflation rates, was rising fast. Increasingly intense hurricanes fueled by global warming wrecked coastal cities—and oil spewed into our waters—as we fumbled around, hopelessly inadequate to the task of reducing our dependence on fossil fuels.

Moments like these bring Karl Polanyi to mind. In his 1944 book *The Great Transformation*, Polanyi referred to land, labor, and money as "fictitious commodities." Applying excessive market rationality to these realms, he argued, distorts the substantive relationship between the economy and society in ways that create insecurity and threaten the social fabric. What we are experiencing is the predictable result of a societal restructuring that made market exchange the key organizing principle in places it did not belong, a rich-country version of the market fundamentalism that was thrust on the developing world by Washington in the 1980s and 1990s. Conservatives from Ronald Reagan on sought to

> change how America is governed—to strip from government all its functions except those that reward their rich and privileged benefactors. They are quite candid about it, even acknowledging their mean spirit in accomplishing it. . . . Grover Norquist has famously said he wants to shrink the government down to the size that it could be drowned in a bathtub. More recently, in commenting on the fiscal crisis in the states and its effect on schools and poor people, Norquist said, "I hope one of them"—one of the states—"goes bankrupt." So

much for compassionate conservatism. . . . And what happens once the public's property has been [drowned]? Privatize it. Sell it at a discounted rate to the corporations. . . . It is the most radical assault on the notion of one nation, indivisible, that has occurred in our lifetime. (Moyers 2003)

This fundamentalism led to the deregulation of the financial system, the removal of safeguards against speculation and greed, the dismantling of social safety nets, the easing of environmental regulations, and, increasingly, the privatization of risk. The exception in our drive toward a market society, of course, was fiscal austerity policies that forced developing countries to limit deficit spending—the United States did not hold itself to those same pesky standards, especially when it came to spending on warfare.

Given the terrible consequences for humans and the earth, it was particularly perplexing that market fundamentalism went so far for so long. Part of the explanation, as I argue in this book, was a distorted understanding of public goods at the core of economic thinking. In contrast to popular understandings of "public goods"—where education, health care, water, and infrastructure are ensured by government, with an implicit social agreement to promote well-being and justice for the people—economists were trained to evaluate public goods devoid of social content. "The public" (you and I) was reduced to prisoner's dilemmas and collective action problems, while state intervention was incorporated mainly as a last resort to remedy market "failure."

One result of this thin understanding of the full social significance of public goods was a turn to markets wherever possible, through unbundling, contracting, granting concessions, and privatizing. At the same time, taxes were reduced to levels that could not sustain robust social programs. The resulting excessive reliance on markets diminished the pool of resources considered "public" and precluded important nonmarket alternatives, in developed and developing countries alike. The effects of "free" markets in money, land, and human beings (Polanyi's "fictitious commodities") were just as visible in the United States—meager responses to environmental threats and an abysmal health care system—as they were in supposedly "undeveloped" countries.

So complete was the hegemony of markets that even with the neoliberal model collapsing all around us, people were still clamoring for market solutions and were panicked about state intervention. The public was dismayed and distrustful of the state, just as intended. But eventually something will have to give: "business as usual" is likely leading to a breakdown in our financial, ecological, and human systems. As we watch the financial world in meltdown, we must wonder what kind of double movement, perhaps unimagined by Polanyi, will save us now. Perhaps the magnitude of the current crisis and new leaders in Washington will awaken people to the real changes needed to turn this ship around. Will we place limits on the destructive power of markets and market actors, or will we continue to believe that the pursuit of self-interest will save the world?

ACKNOWLEDGMENTS

After writing an entire book, it seems the acknowledgments should be easy. Yet as I look back and see how much guidance and support I received from mentors, colleagues, friends, activists, and complete strangers over the years, I am awed and humbled. Perhaps it is best to start at the beginning.

I sincerely thank Steven Lukes, Neil Brenner and Eric Hershberg for their generous feedback and encouragement, as well as Troy Duster, and Ann Morning and the International Center for Advanced Studies at New York University for their support. I would also like to thank Butch Montes, Ha-Joon Chang, Ashwini Deshpande, Paulo Gala, Maria Angela Parra, Codrina Rada, and all the scholars and participants of the Cambridge Advanced Program on Rethinking Development Economics and the Annual Conference for Development and Change for helping me to deepen my understanding of development issues. The Latin American Social Sciences Faculty (FLACSO), and in particular Carlos Sojo and Juan Pablo Pérez Sáinz at FLACSO Costa Rica, were excellent interlocutors and instrumental in supporting my field research. I was aided and inspired by a number of activists during the data collection stage, including Adrian Jaen, Jolie Rickman, Marcela Sojo, Burke Stansbury, the Sindicato de Empresa Trabajadores de ANDA (SETA), and the Committee in Solidarity with the People of El Salvador. Keep up the good fight!

I would like to express my gratitude to the faculty and staff at Arizona State University's Faculty of Justice and Social Inquiry, especially Marjorie Zatz, as well as Jill Fisher, Jeff Juris, and Torin Monahan, for their help in navigating the publication process and in some cases with reading parts of the book manuscript. I owe a special debt of gratitude to Miranda March for generously reading the final proofs—Ack!—as well as for just being a wonderful friend in general. Thanks also to my terrific editor, Sandy Thatcher, as well as two anonymous reviewers, whose comments undoubtedly improved the final text. Obviously, all flaws that remain are my responsibility alone.

I am also grateful for a number of colleagues and friends who, though perhaps not involved directly with this project, have made my life more interesting and enjoyable over the years of its production, including Robert Bailey, Dorith Geva, Vanna Gonzales, Cecilia Guerrero, Phil Josselyn, Andy Kafel, Vera Lopez, Bill Mazza, Bernie McAleer, Cori Plachy, H.L.T. Quan, Heather Strong, and Monica Varsanyi. I would also like to acknowledge my family for their love and support, despite some puzzlement regarding exactly what it is I do for a living. Finally, to my best friend, Michelin Riley—thank you for always, always being there. While my heart and head seek justice, it is you that keeps me grounded.

General

CAFTA — Central America Free Trade Agreement
CEDAW — United Nations Convention on the Elimination of All Forms of Discrimination against Women
CESCR — United Nations Committee on Economic, Social, and Cultural Rights
IADB — Inter-American Development Bank
IFIS — international financial institutions
IMF — International Monetary Fund
ISI — import substitution industrialization
NAFTA — North American Free Trade Agreement
NGOS — nongovernmental organizations
SAPS — structural adjustment programs
SOES — state-owned enterprises
USAID — United States Agency for International Development

El Salvador

AES — AES Corporation, a U.S. multinational energy firm which controls 85 percent of electricity distribution in El Salvador
ANDA — The National Aqueducts and Sewers Administration
ANEP — National Association of Private Business (Asociación Nacional de la Empresa Privada)
ARENA — National Republican Alliance (Alianza Republicana Nacionalista)
CAESS — Electrical Lighting Company of San Salvador (Compañía de Alumbrado Eléctrico de San Salvador)
CDC — Center for Consumer Defense (Centro para la Defensa del Consumidor)
CEL — The Lempa River Executive Hydroelectric Commission (La Comisión Ejecutiva Hidroeléctrica del Río Lempa)

FISDL   Salvadoran Social Investment Fund for Local Development
            (Fondo de Inversión Social para el Desarrollo Local)
FMLN   Farabundo Marti National Liberation Front (Frente Farabundo
            Martí para la Liberación Nacional)
FUNDE   National Development Foundation (Fundación Nacional para
            el Desarrollo)
FUSADES   Salvadoran Foundation for Economic and Social Development
            (Fundación Salvadoreña para el Desarrollo Económico y
            Social)
PDDH   Human Rights Defense Attorney (Procuraduría para la
            Defensa de los Derechos Humanos)
SIGET   General Electricity and Telecommunications Superintendent
            (Superintendencia General de Electricidad y
            Telecomunicaciones)

Costa Rica

ANEP   National Association of Public and Private Employees
            (Asociación Nacional de Empleados Públicos y Privados)
ARESEP   Public Services Regulatory Authority (Autoridad Reguladora de
            los Servicios Públicos)
AYA   Costa Rican Institute of Aqueducts and Sewage Systems
            (Instituto Costarricense de Acueductos y Alcantarillados)
ICE   Costa Rican Electricity and Telecommunications Institute
            (Instituto Costarricense de Electricidad y
            Telecomunicaciones)
PAC   Citizen Action Party (Partido Acción Ciudadana)
PLN   National Liberation Party (Partido Liberación Nacional)
PUSC   Social Christian Unity Party (Partido Unidad Social Cristiana)
SNE   National Electricity Service (Servicio Nacional de Electricidad)

Over the past twenty-five years, extensive programs designed to encourage private participation in the provision of public utilities have been implemented globally. In Latin America, where fiscal austerity and divestiture in state-run firms became a condition for access to development loans, privatization was particularly widespread. Citing problems of corruption and inefficiency in state-owned enterprises, economists and advisors in the region promoted market solutions, even in sensitive utility sectors: "In 1993, the World Bank approved policies that stressed the need for sound commercial practices, independent regulation, and extensive private sector participation in the energy sector. These policies extended to the power sector a process that had first begun with the oil and gas sector in 1983. . . . The orientation towards introducing competition and the private sector was extended to all infrastructure sectors after [1994]" (Albouy 1999).

El Salvador was one country that took World Bank prescriptions to heart. The Salvadoran government "realized early on that without significantly changing the way the public sector operates; providing a credible framework; and involving increasingly the private sector in service provision, it [would] be difficult to maintain the high levels of growth needed to reduce wide spread poverty, particularly in the rural areas."[1] A massive transfer of assets and activities from the state to the private sector, nongovernmental organizations, and local government occurred during the

1. World Bank, "World Bank Finances Modernization of El Salvador's Public Sector," press release, 3 September 1996. Quotation from Harold Fuhr, task manager, Technical Assistance Loan (the subject of the press release).

1990s. The international rating agency for private investment, Fitch New York, was so impressed by these structural reforms that it granted El Salvador high investment ratings but warned that "further privatization and prudent liability management [would] also be necessary to limit the deterioration of the government's balance sheet."[2]

Despite the praise and guidance of international investors and economists, however, the promise of privatization and other forms of marketization fell short for ordinary Salvadorans. In rural sectors, rate increases following electricity privatization took a serious toll, with the additional burden of rising costs for energy-dependent services, such as deep-well water pumps. In poor sectors that consumed less electricity, rates increased up to 47 percent, while high-usage customers paid 24 percent more. Meanwhile, few improvements in service quality or coverage were evident in the years following privatization (Structural Adjustment Participatory Review International Network [SAPRIN] 2001). Labor groups expressed particular disaffection for the "impressive" gains made by privatization, mainly due to shifting social relations that left workers with little power: "Over the past two weeks, the Salvadoran Right-wing government fired [numerous] public sector workers, many of whom had over 20 years of service and the majority of whom were rank-and-file union members. . . . Salvadorans have been protesting in the streets and marching together with the demands that the government stop the firings, reinstate the workers, stop privatization of state owned services, and stop raising the cost of living."[3]

Accounts of early bank privatizations mirror this theme of shifting social relations by focusing on the elite side of the equation: "In El Salvador, privatization, implemented as it was without taking into account relationships of power, was used by [elite] groups . . . to appropriate for themselves most of the banks. . . . The outcome of these privatizations was different than anticipated because the country's power relations were not understood or taken into account."[4] A similar set of privatization policies—accompanied by similar shifts in social relations and patterns of resistance—was seen in other countries of the region. In May 2008, for example, more than a dozen people were injured in Sardinal, Costa Rica, by flying stones, sticks, and tear gas in clashes over the construction of a

2. Reported in *Business Wire*, 16 August 2001, www.businesswire.com.
3. Reported by the Committee in Solidarity with the People of El Salvador (CISPES), 15 January 2002, www.cispes.org.
4. Roberto Rubio, FUNDE (Fundación Nacional para el Desarrollo), El Salvador, in a report to the Structural Adjustment Participatory Review Initiative (SAPRI), http://www.worldbank.org/research/sapri/fgfmeth.htm.

privately financed and publicly built aqueduct.[5] Water company representatives held that, although the government should have explained the project better to the community, the degree of unrest was not due to any genuine threat the project posed but to special interest groups, such as free trade opponents.[6] Protesters disagreed, complaining that the government had granted the concession to assist a group of private hotel developers without considering the impact such a project could have on their community.[7] They cited drought conditions and contamination in other areas from tourism and plantations to justify their resistance.[8] There was a strong sense of urgency to the protest and anger at residents' exclusion from discussions: "Nobody said anything to us about the aqueduct. We realized what was happening only after it was already partly completed."[9] Some government officials also expressed concern about the project. Municipal president Claudio Rivas suspended its permit, charging that the project—initially approved because it promised improvements to the existing aqueduct—was being designed to carry water to tourism projects outside the area.[10] The national Public Interest Office criticized the project as well, arguing that the public water company would be obliged, because of the design of the system, to cater to private interests rather than public welfare.[11]

In the narratives presented here, and in others like them throughout the developing world, we see the contentious and unpredictable nature of market transformations in public goods sectors (Green 2003; Olivera and Lewis 2004; Balanyá et al. 2005). These transformations highlight latent conflicts between public and private sectors; among competing industries, such as tourism, agribusiness, and industry; and among different stakeholders, such as citizens, investors, and the natural environment.[12] Given the proliferation of privatization and marketization policies since 1980, as

5. "Turba vapuleó a policías en protesta por acueducto," *La Nación*, 20 May 2008.

6. "Gobierno dice que falló al explicar obras en Sardinal," *La Nación*, 29 May 2008.

7. "AyA perforó pozos en Sardinal sin estudios," *La Nación*, 13 May 2008; "Estudio de UCR advierte problemas en nuevo acueducto de Sardinal," *La Nación*, 3 June 2008.

8. "Vecinos de Sardinal dispuestos a frenar construcción de acueducto," *La Nación*, 23 May 2008; Víctor Hugo Murillo S., columnist, "Aguas turbias," *La Nación*, 3 June 2008; "Desorden amenaza reservas de agua en la costa del Pacífico," *La Nación*, 3 February 2008; "Gran expansión piñera eleva ingresos y causa denuncias," *La Nación*, 31 December 2007.

9. "Vecinos de Sardinal dispuestos a frenar construcción de acueducto" (quotation from resident José Alberto Bustos), *La Nación*, 23 May 2008.

10. "Municipio suspende obras de acueducto en Sardinal," *La Nación*, 28 May 2008.

11. "Contraloría revisa actuación de AyA sobre acueducto" [Defensoría de los Habitantes], *La Nación*, 16 June 2008.

12. On protests in Colombia, see Mario Novelli, "Workers Protest Privatization in Cali," *Colombia Report*, 8 January 2002, http://www.colombiareport.org/colombia98.htm.

well as conflicting evidence regarding their costs and benefits, there is a pressing need to examine these policies more closely. It is not simply a matter of economics: the principles underlying different models of service provision—public, private, or mixed—circumscribe and define available public goods policy alternatives at a time when states and communities need more, not fewer, options for addressing urgent public health, social justice, and sustainability issues.

The Human Right to Basic Goods

Human health and well-being depend on access to basic goods. Yet more than 1 billion people in the world do not have safe drinking water, and more than double this number do not have sufficient sanitation (WHO 2002). The World Health Organization estimates that more than 2 million children die every year from drinking contaminated water. In Latin America alone, more than 50 million people still lacked improved water sources by 2004, and nearly 125 million lacked adequate sanitation. In addition, approximately 1.6 billion people worldwide do not have electricity (International Energy Agency 2002). The situation is worst in rural areas of developing countries, where residents are mainly dependent on traditional fuels—wood, dung, and crop residue—as well as on inefficient technologies. This leaves many without access to basic goods, such as nutrition, warmth, and light, much less energy for productive uses. Of course, the burden of insufficient electrification, water, and sanitation falls disproportionately on women.

This is an issue of great importance to numerous international organizations, such as the United Nations (UN), as well as governmental and nongovernmental organizations. The right to adequate housing—including water, electricity, and sanitation—appears repeatedly in international conventions and treaties, such as the United Nations Convention on the Elimination of All Forms of Discrimination Against Women (CEDAW 1979), which stipulates that "states parties shall take all appropriate measures to . . . ensure women the right . . . to enjoy adequate living conditions, particularly in relation to housing, sanitation, electricity and water supply, transport and communication" (Article 14). Closely linked is the Declaration on the Right to Development (UN General Assembly 1986), in which development was articulated as an "inalienable human right by virtue of which every human person and all peoples are entitled to participate in, contribute to, and enjoy economic, social, cultural and political development, in which all human rights and fundamental freedoms can be fully realized" (Article 1, Section 1). Sustainability became an increasingly important aspect of this right with the Rio Earth Summit (1992), the International Conference on Population and Development (1994), the World Summit for Social Development (1995), the Conference on Human Settlements (Habitat II, 1996), and the Beijing Declaration on Renewable Energy for Sustainable Development (2005).

In 2000, the UN General Assembly unanimously passed the Millennium Development Goals, thus reaffirming the commitment of member countries "to strive for the full protection and promotion in all our countries of civil, political, economic, social and cultural rights for all" (UN General Assembly 2000, Section V, No. 25). With regard to water specifically, countries vowed "to halve the proportion of people who are unable to reach or to afford safe drinking water [and] to stop the unsustainable exploitation of water resources by developing water management strategies at the regional, national and local levels" (Section III, No. 19). In 2002, the UN Committee on Economic, Social, and Cultural Rights (CESCR) went even further with the "General Comment on the Right to Water," advocating its protection as a social and cultural good under international human rights law, rather than an economic commodity (CESCR 2002).[13] The UN recently proclaimed 2005–15 as the Decade of Water for Life, reaffirming the human right to water and a commitment by governments to develop water and sanitation services.

These documents and declarations put forward a view of human rights that encompasses both freedoms—such as "the right to maintain access" or "the right to be free from arbitrary disconnections or contamination"—and entitlements, including "the right to a system of . . . supply and management that provides equality of opportunity for people to enjoy the right." Entitlements, by definition, imply state obligations. According to CESCR (2002), states have three primary obligations:

1. *To respect*: i.e., refrain from interfering directly or indirectly with the enjoyment of a right
2. *To protect*: i.e., prevent third parties (individuals, groups, corporations, etc.) from interfering with the enjoyment of a right. Where third parties operate or control services (such as piped water networks, water tankers, or access to rivers and wells), states must prevent them from compromising equal, affordable, and physical access

---

13. "General Comments" elaborate on rights specified in existing covenants, conventions, or treaties, spelling out more clearly states' obligations for compliance.

to sufficient, safe and acceptable service; preventing such abuses requires an effective regulatory system.

3. *To fulfill*: i.e., take positive measures to assist individuals and communities to enjoy their rights; to ensure that there is appropriate education concerning, for example, the hygienic use of water, protection of resources, and methods to minimize waste; and to provide goods when individuals or groups are unable to realize their rights by the means at their disposal.

International financial institutions have also been called on to respond to the needs of citizens for basic services, especially "when it is clear that States acting alone cannot meet their human rights obligations" (Kothari 2001, 23). Accountability and participatory mechanisms, to which citizens can turn when the need for public goods goes unmet, are also stressed. With regard to water and accountability, CESCR (2002) stipulates that "each State should ensure that persons whose right to water has been denied have access to effective judicial or other appropriate remedies at the national level, and should be entitled to adequate reparation" (Section V, No. 55). In terms of inclusion and development (UN General Assembly 1986), "the human person is the central subject . . . and should be the active participant and beneficiary of the right to development" (Article 2, Section 1).

The principles embodied in these texts are widely recognized at both the international and the national levels. Although no state has been able to ensure all rights enshrined in international law, most countries have ratified key human rights treaties, indicating at least a rhetorical acceptance of the core standards embodied therein. This is reiterated at the national level through protections embodied in constitutions worldwide. Despite real and important disparities between officially binding norms and actual practice, an acceptance of the centrality of certain public goods to health and well-being is apparent. But just how are nations to reach these lofty aspirations? While there is little controversy regarding the goals themselves, heated debates continue regarding how best to achieve them. This book contrasts one of the more contentious approaches to promoting public goods, marketization, with historical efforts at state-led development and the emerging interpretation of basic goods as human rights. To set the stage for the empirical analysis that forms the book's core, I will present a brief historical review relevant to the study of public goods, as well as a theoretical framework for understanding the basic requirements for adequate public goods provision.

Postwar Development Strategy and Public Goods Infrastructure

The history of twentieth-century social policy attests to the wide variety of available alternatives for promoting public well-being. Interventionist approaches to economic and social welfare, such as Keynesianism, corporatism, and "embedded liberalism" (Ruggie 1982), proliferated as responses to the shortcomings of nineteenth-century laissez-faire (Polanyi 1944). In the postwar period, strong and sizable public sectors in Europe, Canada, Australia, New Zealand, and Japan actively participated in reconstruction and development efforts. State intervention in developing countries also grew after World War II, as countries attempted to achieve economic independence in an unstable world and promote development. In Latin America, the United Nations Economic Commission for Latin America encouraged state action through such policies as import substitution industrialization (ISI), which was designed to wean economies from an overreliance on a few primary commodities by promoting manufacturing and infrastructural development.

Public ownership, central planning, and protective measures for workers and citizens were often part of the new "developmentalist state" in Latin America (Cardoso and Faletto 1979). ISI produced new coalitions of industrialists and urban working classes demanding access to services. Citizens began to make claims for access to education, health, water, and public housing, while emerging business interests demanded better electricity, communications, and transport infrastructure. States nationalized services throughout the region, driven by the inadequacy of private sector provisions in terms of coverage, cost, and quality. State provision of basic services was a key strategy for populist incorporation of poor, urban masses (Casteñeda 1996). Even under authoritarian governments, electricity, health, and water services grew. Meanwhile, the Cuban revolution and its promise of social justice gave new urgency to development policy, inspiring the foundation of President John F. Kennedy's Alliance for Progress. The Inter-American Development Bank was created as a source of funding for Latin American countries seeking to build roads, telephone networks, and electricity, water, and sewage infrastructure. In a large number of countries, and with varying degrees of success, the state took a proactive role in providing essential goods.

Pressures for development were apparent even in Central America, despite deficiencies in formal political democracy. Urban middle classes and trade unions fought for and won social and economic benefits, with gains most widely and generously distributed in Costa Rica. Costa Rica and Honduras were also successful in incorporating rural sectors in development strategies (Bulmer-Thomas 1987), which may partly explain the lack of rural unrest as experienced elsewhere in the region. Although ISI was not as widespread in Central America as in other Latin American countries, many elements of the state-led development strategy affected infrastructural expansion. States assumed the task of providing goods and services that private firms had not adequately fulfilled. High commodity prices and increased taxation on agriculture in the immediate postwar period afforded considerable resources for public investment, including the establishment of hydroelectric plants. Thereafter, access to international credit allowed states to give priority to social infrastructure. Thus, "the supply of electricity, in particular, increased notably, with installed capacity more than doubling in all republics (except Honduras) between 1953 and 1960 and virtually all the increase coming from plants in the public sector" (Bulmer-Thomas 1987, 168).

Crisis and the Decline of State-Led Development

The oil crisis of the 1970s set the stage for one of the greatest turning points for economic policy in Latin American history. High world prices filled banks in industrialized countries with oil revenue, leading to a lending binge and a massive flow of petrodollars into both public and private sectors. States across the region took advantage of this freely available credit to finance economic development. Although this debt-based financing in Central America "was not irresponsible" before 1978 (Bulmer-Thomas 1987, 218), a series of external shocks thereafter—declining terms of trade, rising interest rates, declining trade credits, capital flight, and world recession—made borrowing a more risky strategy and created pressure for structural adjustment. Following huge interest rate hikes by the United States, countries suddenly found themselves with crippling debt. Service on the accumulated debt, rather than state expenditures per se, was at the root of the crisis. When controlling for interest payments, the fiscal imbalances in the region statistically diminished or disappeared (Duménil and Lévy 2001). In Costa Rica, the deterioration in the current account deficit from 1978 to 1981 could be almost entirely explained by a fall in the value of coffee prices (27.3 percent), an increase in oil imports (33.5 percent), and an increase in debt service (39.3 percent; Bulmer-Thomas 1987).

It is important to note that, the debt crisis notwithstanding, "a spectacular rise in the rate of capital formation" (Bulmer-Thomas 1987, 216) accompanied state borrowing in the precrisis period. By 1980, the ratios of investment to gross domestic product (GDP) were more than 25 percent in Costa Rica and Honduras. Despite labor repression and exceedingly unequal property ownership in El Salvador and Nicaragua, investment-to-GDP ratios in infrastructure rose to 20 percent just prior to the onset of civil war. It is undeniable that state actors were at least moderately successful at expanding infrastructure when they set their minds (and their policies) to it. ISI enhanced state capacity in the region by encouraging the development of public sector functions and policy instruments. Planning processes, though imperfect, led to genuine improvements in human resources, information gathering, and national long-term planning, with greater resources channeled into infrastructure projects. This type of capacity building, we will see, is a critical feature of successful public goods sectors. Moreover, it can be undermined by market-friendly policies that starve state institutions of financial and human capital.

Marketization and the Transformation of Public Goods

What followed the debt crisis in Latin America is well known: stabilization and structural adjustment policies advocated and sometimes demanded by international financial institutions (IFIs). The relative progress made under ISI and the largely exogenous causes of the debt crisis did not shield interventionist policy from the coming assault. As the International Monetary Fund (IMF) in particular began to impose loan conditionalities, macroeconomic policy moved forcefully in the direction of strict budget controls. State-led development, which had been widespread even among relatively liberalized economies, was recast as irresponsible and futile. Retraction of public spending and privatization figured prominently in efforts to service debt and control deficits. State intervention gave way to a belief in markets as a solution to deficiencies in basic services. This policy shift directly affected public goods infrastructure in Central America. Extensive programs designed to encourage private sector participation in public utilities were formulated and implemented, while public investment projects were cut back, slowing down long-term capital accumulation in public sectors and initiating a process of dismantling state-owned enterprises.

Critiques of state-centered development driving these new policies had at their root an important insight regarding the dangers of political interference in state firms that could lead to rent-seeking and productive inefficiencies. Privatization—rather than improvements in public accountability or state capacity to provide services—was presented as the solution to these problems. This deep concern with state failure was coupled with an oftentimes sincere belief that market failures were less problematic and more easily rectified. Economists and advisors at the IMF, Inter-American Development Bank (IADB), the World Bank, and the United States Agency for International Development (USAID) were not always unified in their emphases and recommendations; however, they were nearly unanimous in maintaining that greater private sector participation in the management and provision of public goods would be necessary. Many Latin American governments also embraced privatization, in part to meet loan conditionalities and in part because sales of state holdings could bring in immediate capital and temporarily alleviate claims on already thin resources.

Heterodox economists and other critics of this "neoliberal" turn argued that obsession with state failure closed off a range of once-successful policy options, resulting in a one-size-fits-all policy regime.[14] Far from providing development-enhancing solutions, they argued, these policies simply redrew state boundaries to include actions that aided strong market actors and limited activities designed to help weaker actors, thereby redefining whose claims could be addressed legitimately by the state (Chang 2003a). Privatization was particularly criticized for shifting power from the state and local communities to the more privileged participants in the global economy, the owners of capital, and for allowing private profit making to take precedence over social and environmental goals. From this perspective, neoliberal reforms went too far by presenting obstacles to state intervention even where it had been relatively successful. The new policy regime was further criticized for failing to account for cultural, historical, and institutional realities that might render market-friendly policies inappropriate in many developing countries (Evans 2004; Portes 2006).

Gains from marketization have been mixed at best, forcing even its most enthusiastic proponents to qualify policy recommendations that once seemed unimpeachable. Not only has corruption in privatization processes occurred in several countries, such as Bolivia, Argentina, Brazil, and Peru

---

14. "Neoliberalism" refers to a set of policy prescriptions—including trade and capital account liberalization, fiscal austerity, reduced government expenditure, privatization, and deregulation—in which markets are the preferred mechanism for economic management.

(Rose-Ackerman 1997),[15] but private firms have also proved to be disappointing providers of basic services. Privatization in Latin America, especially of profitable state-owned enterprises, was generally unsuccessful at reducing fiscal imbalances (Pinheiro and Schneider 1995) and did not dramatically improve services or reduce rates (Bauer 1997; Loftus 2001; Wilder and Lankao 2006). Support for privatization among the public declined from 1998 to 2003, with only 21 percent of Latinobarómetro respondents strongly or somewhat agreeing that privatization had been beneficial to their country, down from 46 percent.[16] By 2007, opinions had improved somewhat, but a clear majority (65 percent) still disagreed that privatization had been beneficial.

Civil unrest resulted from privatization policies in many countries following price hikes, job losses, and deteriorating levels of accountability (Public Citizen 2001; North American Congress on Latin America 2003).[17] Of all the recommendations promoted under the neoliberal model, privatization arguably produced the greatest targeted resistance in Latin America. Explicitly antiprivatization protests occurred in Costa Rica, El Salvador, Nicaragua, Colombia, Peru, Ecuador, Bolivia, and Argentina and in several cases resulted in violent conflict. Intense opposition to market-friendly reforms also became an issue at the negotiating table and the ballot box. Although states varied in their response to privatization pressures, many governments chafed at lending requirements linking loans to private sector participation in areas previously handled by the state (World Bank 2001). In recent years, an increasing number of Latin American leaders were ousted by challengers campaigning on explicitly antineoliberal, antiprivatization platforms.

Despite this opposition, dialogue regarding the appropriate role of the state and private sector in providing essential goods continued, until recently, to be expert-driven or superficial among U.S.-dominated institutions, such as the World Bank and IMF, national governments, and local communities. Market-oriented reforms remained a policy priority in trade negotiations, loan agreements, and expert discourses. John Williamson, the "father of the Washington Consensus," himself argued that privatization should still be promoted in Latin America, regardless of the fact that

15. "Secret Deal That Kept Brazil in the Dark: Electricity Privatisation in Which Enron Had a Role Turned Out to Be a Disaster for the Government," *Financial Times*, 21 May 2003.

16. Data can be found at http://www.latinobarometro.org/.

17. María Suárez Toro, "Telecommunications as Public Service Threatened in Costa Rica," *Radio Internacional Feminista*, 1 March 2000; Justin Podur and Manuel Rozental, "A Snapshot of Colombia: Occupation in Cali, the Peace Process, and Cauca," *ZNet*, 16 July 2006.

"it is clearly not politically popular" (Williamson 2004).[18] It is unclear whether this disconnect between Washington and the populations that development policy is designed to serve will shift under a new U.S. administration or as a result of the global economic crisis that began in 2007. But it continues to be a subject of concern for those interested in promoting true openness, cooperation, and democracy in the hemisphere.

Limiting Resources: Public Goods and Shrinking Policy Space

This is where our story begins. The dramatic shift toward market-friendly policy and an emphasis on the cost of providing basic goods contrasts sharply with the postwar history of state-led development and more recent concerns regarding the human right to essential services. This book explores the contours of these potentially contradictory policies and priorities by examining conceptual shifts, institutional structures, and political struggles that have accompanied privatization and marketization in public goods sectors. It localizes the analysis by examining how two different nations and multiple subnational groups have addressed demand for public services, as well as their relationship with developed country governments, multinational bodies, and one another. It evaluates the claims and interests of various actors, situating seemingly neutral economic policies in the context of struggles over their implementation. Given the conflicting beliefs about the desirability of marketization as a remedy for shortcomings in basic services, this analysis is especially important.

Two puzzles in particular drive this study, both involving deeper issues of political economy and the sociology of knowledge:

- Puzzle 1: Why was the effort to promote privatization so widespread throughout Latin America, regardless of institutional and political context, and regardless of evidence of its shortcomings? Was it because "there is no alternative," as Margaret Thatcher famously argued, or a natural outcome of state failure and the effectiveness of markets, as IFIs implied (Kessides 2004)? Or were there more calculating forces at work?
- Puzzle 2: If privatization and marketization provided better solutions, as proponents claimed, why was there so much resistance? Was it

18. The term "Washington Consensus" refers to "liberalization policies as they were" disseminated throughout Latin America starting in the 1980s (Williamson 1990).

because collective action problems and coordination failures among potential beneficiaries prevented them from overcoming entrenched interests, as some theories argued (Nelson 1990; Haggard and Kaufman 1992; World Bank 2004)?[19] Are there alternative explanations regarding what drove resistance?

The argument that I develop is that, notwithstanding claims by reformers that privatization was simply a technical solution to problems of strained budgets and poor service, it involved real-world power and interests that transcended public goods provision and profoundly shifted political and social relations. Advocates of marketization—for example, multinational corporations seeking access to scarce resources and local elites, aided by international financial institutions—stood to gain a great deal from these policies. Moreover, they had greater access to media, personnel, and resources to carry out legitimating research and to discredit opponents, as well as political leverage to preclude alternatives. The ideological and institutional strategies employed by these actors to justify and facilitate the dominance of markets over other governance mechanisms did not go unchallenged. Those who raised their voices against marketization policies did so not simply as "interest groups" seeking to retain special privileges. Many did so as concerned citizens who believed they had much to lose. They sought to open spaces in which differing interpretations of the role of the state, the meaning of "public," and processes of accountability and exclusion could be mediated and in which new understandings based on reciprocal exchange of ideas could emerge.

In the process of exploring these questions, this book also addresses two theoretical issues about the transformative effects of market-oriented reforms on inherited sociopolitical landscapes:

- Isomorphism: Was there policy convergence or institutional isomorphism among countries in the long run as a result of reforms? What were the prospects for constructing alternatives?
- Path dependence: How were similar market-oriented reforms "indigenized" as they traveled (Haney 2000)? Specifically, how was it possible for Costa Rica to resist privatization on so many fronts, despite multiple pressures to liberalize its public goods sectors? What are the

19. The World Bank has a Web page entitled "Addressing Sources of Resistance," dedicated to resources for overcoming the collective action problems that they see impeding reform. It can be found at http://www1.worldbank.org/publicsector/civilservice/epublish docs/rightsizing/rightsizingChallenges3.asp (accessed 11 May 2008).

long-term prospects for the continued existence of such alternative models of public goods provision? What effects could be seen in El Salvador, where state capacity was sorely lacking? What are the long-term prospects for ensuring the right to basic goods in such contexts?

Although these two theoretical issues seem potentially in conflict—the former implying institutional and political homogeneity, the latter implying heterogeneity—I argue that they occurred simultaneously. Both processes and outcomes were path dependent and combinatorial (Ragin 1989), resulting not only from inherited policy structures but also from the interaction between political and supranational forces operating in a particular historical moment.

Some convergence among contexts was evident in how the role of the state was reshaped to support mainly market-oriented activity and to remove restrictions on market actors. The overall effect of this push toward market-led reform was that it not only failed significantly to improve public services, It also undermined democratic institutions and processes, reproduced authoritarian relations of power, and suppressed alternatives made possible by increasing democratization and a global acceptance of the importance of economic and social rights. These changes will leave lasting institutional legacies within which future policy makers will be obliged to operate. Yet national political and institutional landscapes clearly influenced how politicians, bureaucrats, and society at large adopted, adapted, and/or rejected policies. These place-specific struggles and clashes served to drive back and alter the neoliberal push and revived the hope that democracy could limit the power of capital in Latin America.

Comparative-Historical Analysis of Electricity and Water in Costa Rica and El Salvador

The original fieldwork for this book was carried out from 2002 to 2006 and consisted of collecting archival, governmental, and private sector data on energy and water-related utilities and reform in Costa Rica and El Salvador since 1980. Media reports and nearly one hundred "key informant" interviews augmented these data. The interviews were indispensable for understanding relations among state agencies, between agencies and non-state organizations, and among individuals, as well as struggles over policy. Interviewees were chosen on the basis of their direct involvement in—or resistance to—reforms in the water and electricity sectors and were drawn from international nongovernmental organizations, major lending institutions (the World Bank and the IADB), USAID, national and local governments, business and labor groups, civil society organizations, and local communities.

The water and electricity sectors were chosen for this analysis for several reasons. First, these sectors form natural monopolies in which start-up costs and entry barriers are high and majority ownership affords great decision-making power. This interferes with competition, the key mechanism that purportedly makes markets superior to public ownership and management. The regulation needed to protect consumers and industries from market failure requires advanced institutional capacity, and the attendant transaction costs can be substantial. Second, water and energy provision is central to both economic and human development, and it is widely agreed that their supply must be assured by the state, even if the goods themselves are provided by the private sector. But precisely because these goods are essential, market failure in their provision can have serious consequences for human suffering, exclusion, and social unrest. The most impressive resistance in recent developing-country history involved struggles over control of essential resources, which distinguishes these goods from the production of, for example, concrete or beer. Third, the transformation of public utilities directly affects more than just workers and unions; it crosses over into groups and communities that may not be organized or protesting. This raises questions about the meaning of "civil society" and whether only organized voices can be validated as claimants of social and economic rights. Finally, these sectors have a compelling spatial dimension, as regional integration and development plans stimulate cross-border sectoral coordination and expansion. Concretely, this often means privatizing land and resources and jockeying among multinational corporations for control over these resources. At present, states are ill equipped to mediate the conflicts that result, especially in ways that remain accountable to affected communities.

Two primary methodological strategies were employed to analyze the puzzles introduced earlier: case studies in a "most likely/least likely" design (Goldstone 2003) and comparative-historical analysis in a "most dissimilar cases" design (Przeworski and Teune 1970). Costa Rica and El Salvador were the case studies used to test two arguments from the literature on state reform: one regarding the causes and the other regarding the consequences of marketization. The causal argument—that privatization arose from the fact that state-owned enterprises "did not function well

[and] it was next to impossible to make them function well" (Nellis 2002, 4)—was tested for Costa Rica, where it was "least likely" to be true. The consequential argument—"that governments perform less well than the private sector" (World Bank 1995, 1)—was examined for El Salvador, where it was "most likely" to be true. In the subsequent analysis, these rather different cases (in terms of public goods sectors) were compared to explore the deeper institutional and political dynamics of marketization.[20]

Case Studies and "Most Likely/Least Likely" Design

Costa Rica is a good site in which to test claims that failed states and more efficient private sectors were what drove privatization policy, as it is a context in which such arguments were "least likely" to be true. For many decades, Costa Rica operated under a developmental paradigm that embraced elements of intervention and social democracy. The Costa Rican Constitution of 1949, coupled with processes of nationalization carried out through the 1940s, placed the provision of public goods firmly in the hands of the state. Enterprises in the health, water, electricity, telecommunications, insurance, and banking sectors served largely social ends under a model of solidarity. This, in turn, contributed to a marked improvement in the quality of life for the average citizen, faith in public institutions as equalizing mechanisms, strong support for social equality, and high expectations regarding democratic inclusion. For these reasons alone, Costa Rica is interesting as a developing country case study. If economic theory were correct, this would be the *least likely* place for marketization policy to emerge. Yet despite relatively efficient and nearly universal government services, marketization *did* emerge. Thus, more analysis is required to explain the emergence of privatization policy.

El Salvador is a good site for testing the argument that private provision is superior to public provision, as its notoriously ineffective and unresponsive public sector makes this argument very likely to be true. Throughout the twentieth century, peasant and urban uprisings alternated with brutal repression by a military-backed oligarchy, setting a sour tone for El Salvador's social and political relations. Although El Salvador was formally a democratic society, before the Peace Accords of 1992, political rights were virtually meaningless for most citizens, civil rights were blatantly violated, and public goods were patchy, especially in rural areas. The devastating

---

20. For a more detailed explanation of the methodology used herein, please see the appendix.

civil war of 1980–92 left few resources for public investment, and state intervention was minimal. Elements of the electricity and water sector were already private, and the capacity of regulatory bodies to monitor and control these left much to be desired. Salvadoran economic reforms, which started in the 1980s, were the most liberal in the region, following closely the advice of Washington. El Salvador, like Costa Rica, is interesting purely as a case study of institutional, political, and social transformation under liberalization. It also provides a good context for testing theoretical claims that privatization would improve conditions of public services in cases where states proved inadequate to the task, as it is a case in which such arguments were "most likely" to be true.

Beyond the Case Studies: Comparative-Historical Analysis

These two countries are excellent candidates for a comparative "most dissimilar cases" methodological design. The strength of this strategy is the ability to examine two very different macro-social systems (the public goods sectors of Costa Rica and El Salvador) as similar reforms are applied to them and trace the consequent structural, institutional, and political effects (Ragin 1989). As discussed earlier, Costa Rica is truly exceptional among Latin American countries, with its actively interventionist state and impressive planning, regulation, and public administration capabilities. Coverage rates are high, as is satisfaction among the general population with public services. Services in El Salvador, by contrast, are similar to other Central American countries: uneven coverage, unstable quality, and low user satisfaction.

Yet despite these unique starting points, the challenges these countries face are quite similar: both have undergone isomorphic processes of institution-building to meet challenges wrought by globalization, fiscal crises, and declining infrastructure (DiMaggio and Powell 1983). International financial institutions and the U.S. government have presented both with demands regarding how to meet those challenges. Both are parties to the recently negotiated Central America Free Trade Agreement, which features a contentious agreement on "trade in services" that precludes state monopolies in many key sectors and requires new institutional capacities to implement. Multinational corporations increasingly operate in the regional markets that link these countries, creating the need for cross-border regulatory capacity, coordination mechanisms, and corporate accountability, especially in ecologically sensitive sectors. Global rules and international pressures similarly constrain state autonomy, yet in ways that differ from the era of ISI.

Privatization processes as well followed a similar logic and provoked similar responses from the populace. Both countries had problems balancing calls for structural adjustment with accusations "from below" that they were ignoring popular sentiment by privatizing public utilities, and both experienced massive antiprivatization demonstrations. Although the Costa Rican state had a longer tradition of democratic institutions, the Salvadoran Peace Accords of 1992 brought with them emergent expectations regarding democratic inclusion, as well as the institutionalization of opposition forces. Rights claims were a driving force behind resistance movements in both countries, with high expectations regarding citizenship, political accountability, and voice. It is these similarities, as well as their political and institutional differences, that will allow me to compare institution-building and other efforts to ensure basic services, to assess market-oriented transformations, and to delineate requirements for capable and effective action in a changing global environment.

Theoretical Grounding: Polanyi's Instituted Economic Processes

If we are serious about "making services work for poor people" (World Bank 2004), we must adopt a "thick" view of state and societal institutions (Chang and Evans 2005), examining not only whether reforms promote better services but also whether they are equitable, environmentally and politically sustainable, and well integrated with other social and developmental goals. States are better able to facilitate such goals if they are not constrained by interests that run counter to these goals (i.e., have *autonomy* from actors that would obstruct projects) (Skocpol 1985), have sufficient *capacity* to implement development plans (Evans 1995; Grindle 1996), and are held *accountable* to those for whom policies are designed to benefit (i.e., maintain ties to the citizenry). These issues are linked intimately with practical policy concerns: not only which model of service provision will be promoted but also how programs for institutional capacity building will be designed and implemented (Graham 2002; United Nations Development Programme [UNDP] 2002b; World Bank 2004) and whether citizens will be included as key stakeholders with a legitimate interest in policy outcomes (UNDP 2002a). Market transformations in water and electricity sectors are thus analyzed within a larger institutional and sociopolitical context.

This approach is designed to answer Polanyi's (1957) call to social scientists to recognize that "the study of the shifting place occupied by the economy in society is . . . no other than the study of the manner in which the economic process is instituted at different times and places" (250). His economic anthropology of substantive conditions in traditional societies reveals that "the capitalist market economy is only one form of organising economic activity and should not be used as a transhistorical model for interpreting other economies" (Jessop 2001, 214). This is in contrast to the approach of economists at the end of the nineteenth century, who shunned substantive readings of the economy in favor of an undersocialized interpretation, with abstract models of scarcity, competition, and exchange as the central ruling principles. This "starkly utopian" vision represented a significant break from economic thinking throughout human history, where economic activity had been embedded in and subordinated to society.

"Embeddedness" connotes a deep, transhistorical claim that social relations permeate and constitute markets, and that moves toward a self-regulating market system violate basic principles of human organization by attempting to separate economics from politics (Polanyi 1944, 1957). This definition transcends the use of the term in much of economic sociology (e.g., Granovetter 1985), which focuses more narrowly on the embedding of economic actors in networks that create stability and predictability through reciprocal interdependence among individuals. It also goes beyond definitions that focus on the internal cohesion and adaptability of organizations, their operational unities and independence, and their interdependence with other organizations (e.g., Grabher 1993). Although Polanyi's discussion of haute finance and cooperatives revealed mechanisms analogous to these, he was not concerned with interpersonal or interfirm relations per se. The key for Polanyi was to recognize that the economy itself is not a static entity based solely on economic exchange but rather a *process* that involves procuring and transferring substantive resources through institutions, both economic and noneconomic, to meet human needs. Decisions about how this movement occurs are based on more than market logic: they are based in the social, political, and even religious parameters set by a given society (Krippner 2001).

Polanyi (1944) criticized attempts to institute a self-regulating market system, in which even noncommodities (land, labor, and money, referred to as "fictitious commodities") were managed via markets. Applying market rationality to these realms, he argued, distorted the substantive relationship between the economy and society in ways that created insecurity and threatened the social fabric. Polanyi's analysis underscores the ideological nature of liberal economics. Its vision strives to redefine and restructure society in ways that make market exchange the key organizing principle. Of course, markets can never be disembedded from society or the state (Block 2003), but as economic policy liberalizes, institutional patterns of embeddedness are more responsive to market than nonmarket logics. Society survives the disruption caused by attempts to institute a self-regulating market system with a collectivist countermovement that reembeds market forces in social institutions by subjecting them to various forms of extraeconomic regulation, such as legislation or restrictive associations. This protective "double movement" tempers the harmful effects of liberalization by reintroducing noneconomic norms and values from other social realms to economic activity, creating a bulwark against destructive market forces.

A key way this embedding is accomplished is by protecting fictitious commodities, a process that often entails harnessing the state to ameliorate negative externalities (i.e., negative consequences of market activity) and achieve positive externalities (i.e., positive but perhaps unintended consequences of market activity) (see table 1).

Public goods constitute a crucial realm where protective moves designed to embed fictitious commodities in societal norms and expectations are prevalent. Yet Polanyi left open the question of what instigates a double movement and did not elaborate on the different forms the double movement may take according to context. This book theorizes the nature of embeddedness of public goods under neoliberalism in relation to other possible forms of embeddedness, demonstrating how and why shifting articulations of market and social principles in institutional form provoke responses from state and societal actors. It further explores the manner in which context shapes the stylistic approach of groups attempting to patch

Table 1   Examples of embedding mechanisms for fictitious commodities

	Embedding mechanisms
Land	Tariffs, rent control, use regulations, environmental protection, "constitutional orders" (e.g., water districts)
Labor	Safety nets, unions, cooperatives, labor laws, labor rights, collective bargaining
Money	Control of inflation and exchange rates, reserve requirements, capital controls, state or community banks, credit unions

the holes ripped in the social fabric by market liberalization. At the core of the explanation is the nature of institutional and political clashes that occur as a result of deeper value conflicts. As we will see in the next chapter, several sets of principles guide the formulation of public goods policy, each reflecting different assumptions, norms, and values. Institutional blueprints embodying these norms and values may clash with inherited institutional contexts and their underlying values; moreover, existing structures of power may transform them in ways that are unexpected and sometimes undesired (Portes 2006).

It is my hope that this work will contribute to a growing productive debate on the reasons for continued shortcomings in water and electricity sectors and on what is to be done. International financial institutions continue to argue that state failure is the root cause and that markets, as well as certain types of market-oriented institution building, must be part of the solution. The answer put forward in this work is that even if state failure is a problem, market failure is no less serious. When markets are transferred indiscriminately to ill-prepared settings, much-needed state capacity building, autonomy from restrictions on state action, and accountability to citizens tend to be sidelined. Alternatives to radical liberalization, moreover, often comprise quite successful models for furthering economic progress in less-developed countries (Stallings 1995). Although this book does not deny that markets work well in some sectors of the economy, it provides evidence to substantiate what opponents of liberalism have long suspected: that neoliberal policies can actually harm development and that markets are not only inadequate but often inappropriate mechanisms for managing essential services.

THEORIZING PUBLIC GOODS:
THE ROLE OF ORGANIZING PRINCIPLES

What is a public good? Popular understandings of the term assume a central role for the state in education, health policy, water, sanitation, and electricity, with an implicit social agreement that such goods should promote the well-being of the general populace. This is especially true in OECD (Organisation for Economic Co-operation and Development) countries, where public goods served an explicit social welfare function after World War II. Yet, paradoxically, policy discourses and practices that emerged and spread globally during the 1980s from these same OECD countries—most notably Prime Minister Margaret Thatcher's Britain and President Ronald Reagan's United States—increasingly introduced markets where states once reigned. Concurrently, the social content evident in the common vernacular of public goods was subordinated to the more simplistic framing of classical economics. This chapter critiques this conceptual framing for failing to encompass the full meaning of public goods and for excluding a range of criteria with which actual societies determine their public importance. The alternative interdisciplinary perspective that I propose draws from sociology, political economy, political philosophy, and geography to incorporate concerns about justice, inclusion, and sustainability. It highlights the distinct organizing principles that influence the construction of public goods, underscoring synergies and inconsistencies among approaches based on markets, social and economic rights, and environmental protection. In later chapters, I will build upon this analysis by evaluating how these organizing principles interact and/or clash in concrete institutional and political environments. I will then show how neoliberalism, by choosing a narrow view of public goods, promotes policies that shrink the pool of resources considered "public" and that preclude several important nonmarket alternatives.

When Markets Fail: An Economic Approach to Public Goods

The field of economics frames goods provision primarily in reference to markets rather than to the public or state. Markets are deemed the most efficient mechanisms for distributing goods and services so that nobody can be made better off without someone else made worse off. Public goods are those that markets are unable to provide efficiently because of the characteristics of the goods themselves. In these cases, state intervention is justified to remedy or prevent "market failure." Two criteria used to distinguish public goods are rivalry and excludability (Musgrave 1969). Rivalrous goods are those that, once taken or consumed by one person, are not available for use by another, such as goods sold in supermarkets or fish in common waters. Nonrivalrous goods are those that are available regardless of how many people use them, such as policing and lighthouses. Excludable goods are those that can be denied to people without a great deal of difficulty, such as most goods bought and sold for a market price. Nonexcludable goods are those for which it would be costly or impossible to exclude users, as with common land or military protection. Although many goods we consume are "private" in this rendering (both excludable and rivalrous), our most essential goods are generally "public" (nonrivalrous and nonexcludable) or "semipublic," or "mixed" (either rivalrous or excludable but not both) (see table 2).

Table 2 Classical typology of goods

		Excludability	
		Yes	No
Rivalry	Yes	"Private" saleable goods, charity, international aid	Common-pool resources: fishing areas, water supplies, forests
	No	"Club goods" (excludable entry, nonrivalrous once admitted): membership organizations, from local-level sports clubs to international organizations like NATO	"Pure public goods," or collective goods: policing, military, education, roads, lighthouses, traffic signals

This classic modeling of public goods clarifies how market failure operates. Free-rider problems arise when users cannot be easily denied access to a good for refusing to contribute to its reproduction or to abide by certain rules of usage, as with nonexcludable goods. With nonrivalrous goods, this leads to undersupply because of muted demand, as people are less likely to express a preference for a good if they can get it without paying. Regarding rivalrous goods, this can lead to a "tragedy of the commons" (overutilization, destruction, erosion, and exhaustion), as people use resources or contribute pollution without accounting for the costs to others (Hardin 1968).[1] Free-rider problems can be overcome when people feel it is in their interests to cooperate toward a common end. But a second problem, the prisoner's dilemma, makes cooperation difficult, especially under the conditions assumed by the model of atomized individuals making one-time decisions with insufficient information.

The crux of the prisoner's dilemma is not knowing how others will behave when the possibility for cooperation exists. This uncertainty leads people to choose suboptimal outcomes instead of outcomes that would have been achieved through cooperation. An example of water conservation during a drought will help illustrate this point: If everyone were to conserve, there would be less of a scarcity problem. Person A can choose to conserve or not. If she conserves and nobody else does, she will be worse off because there will still be scarcity, and she will have been inconvenienced by having to cut down on her normal water usage. If everyone else conserves and she does not, she will be less inconvenienced and better off, as she alone will not exacerbate scarcity. If everyone fails to conserve, everyone is worse off, because water scarcity affects all users. The incentive for a single individual acting in her self-interest is not to conserve, for at least she will not be inconvenienced. Setting aside for a moment the problematic assumptions regarding the conditions under which real people make such decisions and the criteria they use, information deficiencies in this scenario create a tendency toward noncooperation. Because free-rider problems and prisoner's dilemmas undermine collective action, the theory goes, states must intervene to ensure the adequate provision of commonly shared goods.

However, market-based management of essential goods can create problems beyond those involving collective action. For example, though

---

1. Commons scholars have debunked many of Hardin's claims regarding the "tragedy" of the commons, such as his confusing "common property" with "open access" conditions, or his assumption that all commons situations are plagued by free-rider problems or prisoner's dilemmas. See Ostrom et al. (2002).

not considered a "market failure" by most economists, market processes can greatly exacerbate inequality. In the private sector, the price mechanism moderates supply and demand for excludable goods. When more users demand a good, the price rises and a larger quantity of the good is generally produced. When prices rise, some people are priced out of the market and demand decreases. Eventually, the market for that good reaches equilibrium: supply meets demand at a certain price. For nonessential goods, higher prices and unequal access is unfortunate but not critical. But for marketized essential services, inequality in access can have profound social and political consequences, especially in areas with low levels of economic development. Water, for example, is not a good that people can simply choose not to consume. At subsistence levels of consumption, prices can rise without a concomitant drop in demand, thus creating pressures for the poor to spend a greater percentage of their resources or to turn to contaminated sources for access. The wealthy and powerful do not face the same stark realities, as they are able to access private sources when public ones prove inadequate. Thus, without state action, markets reproduce and intensify inequality in ways that are directly detrimental to the health and well-being of the most vulnerable members of the population.

Regardless of rivalry and excludability criteria, there may also be costs (or, less frequently, benefits) that fall on third parties or society as a whole due to market activity. These "externalities" are especially critical in sectors involving essential goods, which are often linked to health and environmental outcomes. Private firms have incentives to externalize costs, for example, by dumping waste in rivers rather than properly disposing of it or by using cheaper but dirty technologies that pollute the air and water, thus imposing "costs" on affected communities. Without government intervention, that is, taxes, penalties, subsidies, or the enforcement of standards in affected areas, markets alone would perpetuate the damage. An added problem is sectoral concentration, especially in natural monopoly sectors, such as water and energy, where large initial investments, high sunk costs, and exclusive, nontransferable assets limit entry. Antitrust legislation, price regulation, and competition policies are often the only way to limit the damage caused by monopolies and cartels.

This analysis undergirds a neoclassical definition of public goods: states shall be allowed to intervene when markets, the preferred allocative mechanism, fail to produce optimal outcomes. A range of policy options exist to address shortcomings in market allocation of goods (and "bads"). Usage regulations, incentives for conservation, and information dissemination have been applied to common pool resources, while universal provision, based on political deliberation about desirable levels of supply, have been applied to collective goods. Finally, governments and communities have employed techniques, including state provision, subsidies, and transfers, to address inequality and to meet basic needs of excluded populations (see table 3). This underscores the centrality of the state in any approach to public goods. However, as we shall see, the degree and type of state intervention considered permissible will vary depending on the philosophical perspective of the evaluator.

Why Markets? Organizing Principles Underlying Market-Friendly Policy

Although the rivalry/excludability dichotomies are helpful for describing how and why markets fail, and for pinpointing "pure" public goods, they neither offer guidance regarding other legitimate spheres of government provision of essential goods nor explain real-world government intervention (Pickhardt 2006). Empirically, public goods may fit a certain category because of decisions regarding how they are to be managed, not necessarily because of inherent characteristics, as the model implies. Forests, for example, may be club goods (national parks with fees), public

Table 3 Public approaches to addressing problems in market provision of goods

| | | Excludability | |
		Yes	No
Rivalry	Yes	Problems: Inequality, externalities Solutions: Public provision, subsidies, minimum salaries, welfare transfers for basic needs	Problems: Externalities; free-rider problems + prisoner's dilemmas → "tragedy of the commons" Solutions: Usage regulations, incentives for conservation of common-pool resources
	No	Problems: Inequality, externalities Solutions: Solidarity approach for goods determined to be important (through political deliberation)	Problems: Externalities, free-rider problems → undersupply of goods Solutions: Universal provision based on political deliberation regarding desirable supply of collective goods

goods (protected areas with no fees but public access), private property, or *res nullius* (nonprotected common access) goods (Humphreys 2006). The assumption behind the framing of classical economics is that goods should be allocated by markets when possible and that governments should intervene if and only if these market mechanisms are not fully functional. But why are markets considered to be superior allocation mechanisms to states? The answer: they are thought to promote both efficiency and justice. I will deal with each argument in turn, as well as discuss how these arguments support the political purpose of suppressing possible alternatives.

Markets and Efficiency

The efficiency argument rests on three central concepts: monitoring, incentives, and competition. Monitoring state-owned enterprises (SOEs) is particularly difficult, the argument goes, because the "agents" (administrators and workers) of SOEs are insulated from "owners" (government overseers and citizens). In private firms, there is also separation between ownership (of shareholders) and control (of managers), but private agents are supposedly more responsive to profit maximization than public agents are to the welfare maximization expected of state firms. The key mechanism by which this "principal-agent problem" is thought to be overcome is through incentives: without the proper incentives, agents will not act on principals' interests in public *or* private firms. Private companies are exposed to competition, and thus potential failure, which provides incentives for internal efficiency. State firms are not allowed to fail or they receive subsidies, so such incentives are undermined. Even in competitive environments, the reasoning goes, public owners cannot provide as effective an incentive structure as private owners. First, "the public" has many and conflicting goals and definitions of welfare, which may lead to scattered efforts and mission drift. There is no such problem when profit maximization is the singular aim. Second, company performance, as reflected in the stock market, enhances or reduces private managers' career possibilities, which may have a disciplining effect on private agents, while public employees face no such concern. Finally, the threat of takeover or bankruptcy is also said to discipline private managers.

A closer examination of these arguments, however, raises a number of theoretical and empirical doubts. First, profit maximization is not the only route to organizational coherence. Real-world SOEs have proved capable in overcoming conflicting mandates and increasing efficiency (Corona

1996), given the proper institutional conditions, such as the existence of meso-level "nodal agencies" guided by "strategic rationality" and broader state goals (Chibber 2003). Second, the main feedback mechanisms managers use to determine customer satisfaction—exit and voice—are not always available. In sectors with only one provider, such as water, electricity distribution, and sanitation, there may be no exit options, and mechanisms of "voice" are scarce. Well-designed public institutions are more likely to incorporate formal accountability mechanisms than are private firms in monopoly sectors, which have no incentive to allow intrusions into their business practices. Third, stock prices are unlikely to provide the feedback required by the model of efficient markets. Even when customers are able to exercise exit, capital markets do not necessarily reflect underlying management efficacy or even customer preferences. Instead, they may reflect lies, information deficits, or manipulation (as with the overvaluation of Enron shares before its collapse in 2001 or, more recently, of mortgage-backed securities). This is even truer in underdeveloped capital markets such as those found in poor countries. Worse, capital market discipline may create perverse incentives for empire building by large firms, asset speculation, and short-termism due to ever-increasing drives to maximize profits (Chang 2003b).

Incentives facing public and private managers are not inherently as different as market theory predicts. Most people—even bureaucrats—do not wish their enterprises to fail. Failure can mean not only bankruptcy but also failure to meet clearly established standards. If they do well by such standards, the "job marketability" of personnel increases, while the threat of being fired for doing a poor job has a disciplining effect. Further, governments often bail out troubled private firms, especially in key sectors, thereby reducing the disciplining effect of bankruptcy. Even when bankruptcy occurs, the harshest punishment seems to fall on workers rather than managers (again, the Enron case is instructive). In sum, monitoring and incentives improve the efficiency of private firms less than the discourse would have us believe and, moreover, can be built into state operations. In monopolistic environments, especially, public ownership may be preferable because of regulatory challenges under these conditions. The monitoring gap between regulators and managers of private firms can be just as wide as between regulators and administrators in public sectors and the difficulty of collecting accurate information even greater (Salamon 2002). It is not private ownership per se, but the introduction of managerial accountability that improves efficiency.

What of the argument, so prevalent in discussions of the public sector since the 1980s, that competition should be introduced to promote efficiency whenever possible, even in areas dominated by public entities? There is no denying that competition can force firms to cut costs in order to survive. But that begs the question of whether cutting costs in public goods sectors, especially in poor countries where people are desperate for services and the environment is increasingly threatened, is the most important objective. Such cost cutting can seriously threaten service quality. Competition may also cause overcapacity and inefficient redundancies in the economy as firms vie for market share with overlapping services. This problem has led to soaring health care costs in the United States, with 25 percent of health care expenditures used to cover overhead (compared with 15 percent in universalized Canada; Sclar 2000). Further, promoting competitive markets can debilitate the development of strong sectors, as energy companies in OECD countries have discovered (Von Ungern-Sternberg 2004). Without consolidation, firms are vulnerable to takeovers and are unable to compete with energy giants from elsewhere. This can lead to a loss of local control over resources and instability in key sectors. Finally, in natural monopoly sectors, mechanisms designed to create competition can undermine economies of scale, pervert planning and conservation goals, and even lead to consolidation of whole industries in the hands of a few private multinational corporations (Beatty 1999). In such cases, the argument that competition creates efficiency becomes difficult to sustain.

Even more problematic than claims to efficiency is the collateral damage caused when these arguments are allowed to dominate policy-making decisions. Boom and bust cycles that worsen with laissez-faire market management punctuate the history of capitalism. The drive of investors and corporations to search the globe for the highest profits and, supposedly, most efficient allocation of resources has only increased speculation, global instability, and suffering for those left in the wake of collapse. These periodic crises can be devastating: when "credit systems break down, real economies and their inhabitants suffer huge losses of production, employment, and capital accumulation" (Hahnel 2005, 13). In water and electricity sectors, dramatic fluctuations in market prices can also cause severe hardship, while the instability caused by turnover in ownership creates an ever-moving target for citizens and communities fighting for services.

Deregulation and the increasing rule of markets are also associated with greater inequality and concentration of ownership. Throughout the history of capitalism, firms tried, when possible, to increase their sphere of influ-ence. Yet with loosening capital controls and increasing globalization, firms were able to expand their operations incomparably, eliminating com-petitors worldwide through mergers and acquisitions (Dicken 1998). Financial crises and IMF conditionalities aided these drives, which forced a number of countries to tighten their money supply to prevent capital flight, driving credit out of reach for domestic enterprises. Crippled by lack of capital, these were often acquired at fire-sale prices by competitors (Hahnel 2005). Although there were countertendencies to this process of conglomeration, "free competition . . . as a description of the normal stage of capitalist economy" was "merely a myth" (Kalecki 1939, 252). A sys-temic feature of capitalism, then, is that liberalized markets not only fail to meet more robust "social efficiency" criteria (Lefeber and Vietorisz 2007) but also cause serious harm to society, as financial crises of current and previous eras aptly demonstrate.

Markets and Justice

The efficiency argument regarding the superiority of markets as allocation mechanisms rests on deeper assumptions about human nature, social jus-tice, and the meaning of freedom. Three philosophical traditions in partic-ular—utilitarianism, classical liberalism, and libertarianism—see market organization as positively linked to social justice. Utilitarianism measures justice according to welfare gains or losses that accompany social arrange-ments. It uses current and potential distribution as the justice metric: whether anyone can be made better off without others being made worse off. If changes would not improve the situation, it is said to be "Pareto optimal." Just policies are those that promote *subsistence* (people are ensured access to resources created through their labor), *security* (property and tenure are protected), *abundance* (policies promote the productive use of resources), and *equality* (distribution promotes the greatest happiness for greatest number; Bentham 2005). The first two factors possess an inherent priority, being "objects of life itself," while the latter are mere "ornaments of life." These criteria indicate that utilitarians value market processes, property rights, and hard work as routes to general prosperity, while leaving open the possibility of government intervention to promote human welfare. However, though redistribution might be justified and certain rights—to personal security, to property, and to "receiving aid in case of need"—may be granted, state action should not interfere with pri-vate ownership or destroy incentives for individual productivity, for "if the lot of the industrious was not better than the lot of the idle, there would be no longer any motives for industry" (Bentham 2005, 99).

Classical liberalism also has a clear preference for market mechanisms, even though the term "liberal" encompasses a variety of economic and political viewpoints. In this, it has a great deal in common with (right) libertarianism, a less widely held but still influential theory. Classical liberals and libertarians share with utilitarians a concern for the security of property rights, yet both are much less willing to allow states to act beyond providing "pure" public goods, believing instead that a society ordered by the "invisible hand" of market forces, driven by the self-interested transactions among market participants, is the essence of freedom. They are deeply concerned about what is termed "procedural justice," especially the establishment of individual rights against arbitrary coercion or encroachments by the state (Hayek 1944/1976). Redistribution, for example, through progressive taxation, is distasteful to classical liberals and out of the question for libertarians, as the pattern of rewards and benefits that arises from the free play of market forces is already considered to be just (Nozick 1974). If inequality arises from a historically just (i.e., "free" market) process, there is no injustice, for it is market processes and security of property that propel productivity, capital accumulation, and growth in society. Classical liberalism encompasses a slightly broader range of options for state intervention than libertarianism but still emphasizes limiting state action as much as possible.

The "minimal state" and focus on individual property rights and capital accumulation envisioned by libertarians and classical liberals reduce available policy options for providing public goods. This orientation constrains the ability of state actors to raise funds for public aims, to limit private prerogative for planning or conservation, and to redirect resources toward creating universal access to essential goods. It also fails to deal effectively with prevalent issues in many developing countries, such as communal or other forms of property ownership, severe inequality in initial resource distribution, and extreme deprivation that limits the capacity of individuals to participate meaningfully in a market society. These theories also tend to ignore historical injustices wrought by colonialism, imperial domination, and multinational corporations' overwhelming power over local communities and even nation-states. More important, the institutional mechanisms created to put these ideas into practice increase the constraints on states and further limit alternatives. The "freedom" arising from these ideas is not freedom for the weak to "live lives they have reason

to value" (Sen 1999, 293) or freedom for state actors to redress social or
economic injustices comprehensively.

Utilitarianism permits more leeway in dealing with the issues mentioned earlier but still suffers from some debilitating features. Although
"welfare" is the metric used to measure justice, the fairness of the initial
distribution from which Pareto optimality is calculated is not challenged.
Like libertarianism and classical liberalism, utilitarianism cannot deal adequately with inequality, much less the colonial, exploitative history of most
developing countries. Utilitarians are ostensibly egalitarian; however,
when the security of property holders is threatened by measures to promote equality (which is usually the case), utilitarians prioritize security
(Bentham 2005). Few options are available for improving the lot of the
most vulnerable members of society under such constraints. This focus
on efficiency without an attendant commitment to fairness leaves us with
a situation considered just, "even when some people are rolling in luxury
and others are near starvation, as long as the starvers cannot be made
better off without cutting into the pleasures of the rich" (Sen 1970, 22).
The overriding concern with security of property also debilitates state and
community capacity to address ecological problems. This is exacerbated by
the focus on "abundance," which prioritizes productive uses of land and
resources over conservation, thus undermining the sustainability that has
become a central concern in public resource management.

Market Theory and the Suppression of Alternatives

Although most economists believe in the efficiency of markets, not all
of them adopt the same position on philosophical matters. Similarly, the
international financial institutions are not homogeneous in their policy
recommendations. Yet despite this variation among economists and institutions, since the 1980s the options preferred by the major development
agencies for managing public goods have been few, in part because of
the limited range of political philosophies most mainstream economists
consider as relevant to development issues. The influence of utilitarian,
classical liberal, and libertarian ideas in particular is implicated in this
narrowing of policy options. A view of human nature that assumes atomized individuals acting in their self-interest characterizes these approaches.
Citizens are reduced to consumers, concerned mainly with securing their
personal well-being and the well-being of those close to them. Moreover,

these characteristics are seen as "good," allowing the free hand of the market and self-interest to produce optimal outcomes and advance human freedom. Faith in collective processes or altruism is seen as naïve.

Unfortunately, the models that arise from this view are inadequate for explaining how public policy is managed in the real world (Green and Shapiro 1994). For example, people do not act solely out of selfishness; they also act out of an aversion to inequality (Klasen 2008). In their ten-year examination of compliance with environmental rules and proenvironmental behaviors, Syme et al. (2006) found that, although the influence of self-interest increased as decisions became more central to the personal life and livelihood of citizens, people were unwilling to allow self-interest to prevail at the expense of the common good. Moreover, they saw intergenerational and intragenerational fairness as complementary, not in competition. In a component study of perceptions of fairness in water-allocation decisions, Syme, Nancarrow, and McCreddin (1999, 51) concluded that "self-interest is tempered by pro-social motivations" and that the public was capable of participating in decision making that involved relatively complicated judgments on multiple dimensions.

Rather than self-interest driving market outcomes, I argue that market rules and policies foster and reward self-interested behavior while undermining altruism and collective processes. Economists censure states for investing in "sociopolitical" objectives, such as employment creation or regional development (as opposed to "neutral" economic objectives, such as macroeconomic balance). State investment in areas that could potentially attract private funding is criticized by international financial institutions and used to restrict loans for public investments in basic services. Politicians who seek to direct monies toward targeted investments in the economy are accused of bias toward "special interest groups." This illustrates the style of rule associated with "advanced liberalism" (Rose 1993) that depoliticizes social issues by claiming that rational, technical calculations can adjudicate among contesting and opposed interests. However, the calculus that equates social welfare with efficiency is peculiar. Why should we assume that a good society is always "efficient"? As Sen cogently states, "a society can be Pareto optimal and still be perfectly disgusting" (Sen 1970, 22). This question is not simply rhetorical: it has real consequences for the lives of citizens, especially those living at the margins of society, who depend heavily on how well public goods are provided for their well-being.

To summarize, I have discussed a range of *market-based organizing principles* that have been increasingly influential over the past few decades in framing public goods policy. These include "laws of the market," such as pricing, supply, and demand; efficiency through competition and incentives; profit maximization; individualistic pursuit of self-interest; property rights; and capital accumulation. This delineation of principles can be used to clarify the moral basis on which policy decisions are based. In upcoming sections, I expand this conceptual pool to include a wider range of organizing principles that encompass both equality and environmental protection. In public goods sectors, especially, this sort of broad theoretical framing is crucial to ensure the development and implementation of strategies that address the full implications of public goods provision, including social justice, human rights, and ecological sustainability.

Beyond Utility and the Minimal State: Incorporating Rights and Social Justice

One obstacle to a broader vision of public goods is objections by economists and scientists that decisions regarding managing such goods should be made based on objective technical and scientific criteria, rather than subjective political criteria. A key point of this book is that these claims are at best shortsighted and that policies that follow from these claims suppress alternatives that might better solve crises in public goods provision. Although it is true that qualitative public evaluations are not constrained by the same evidential requirements as scientific claims, this is in part because uncertainty permeates the evaluation of potential risks and benefits. Under these circumstances, value-based decision making becomes crucial (Power and McCarty 2006). Economic models are riddled with even more uncertainty and, at times, wishful thinking about the performance of markets. Technical analyses are insufficient because, although they may meet self-referential standards, they do not ask the right questions from a public interest point of view. Even though scientists and economists play an important role in providing information, they cannot identify or adjudicate among uncertain courses of action. Public deliberation that includes legal, political, and social perspectives is therefore necessary. The "loss of objectivity" that technocrats fear from this public input "is more apparent than real," as even science "is neither objective nor neutral" (Power and McCarty 2006, 21).

What other principles relevant to public goods might be included in such deliberations? To answer this question, I turn first to human rights approaches to basic services. The connection between public goods and rights is complicated and varies by context. One of the earliest and most widely cited framings of human rights comes from the work of T. H. Marshall (1949), who distinguishes three types of citizenship: civil, political, and social. Civil citizenship includes individual "bourgeois" rights, such as freedom of speech, equality before the law, the right to work, and the right to own property. Political rights comprise mainly suffrage, which became increasingly widespread (in law if not in practice) during the twentieth century. These two rights dominate classical liberal and libertarian theories, which reject the concept of social rights. Social rights refer to access to goods and services that support "the right to live the life of a civilized being according to the standards prevailing in the society" (Marshall 1949, 72). Historically linked to one another, though by no means universal, "the three elements of citizenship parted company [and] were soon barely on speaking terms" (74). This separation, largely due to the influence of nineteenth-century liberalism, created a disconnect among what are actually complementary categories of rights. The exercise of civil and political rights requires resources, a realization that led to a greater emphasis on social rights in human rights discourse. Meanwhile, channels of accountability, brought by struggles for civil and political rights, made it possible to demand that social equality be considered part of citizenship.

In recent years, international nongovernmental organizations (NGOs), in conjunction with local organizations, have increasingly supported rights-based approaches to development. The switch "from a focus on basic needs to one on fundamental rights is based on new understanding of poverty linked to the lack of economic, social and cultural rights" (Rowden and Gass 2003, 4). Even though full rights realization remains elusive, globalization has led to a wider dissemination of information and ideas and to a shrinking of space and time between people, aided by technological advances, which has facilitated the growth of human rights as imagined goals. Public goods are key components of this imagination. Debates regarding public goods that adopt a rights-based discourse are plentiful. Examples include gender and water privatization (WEDO 2003), international environmental justice and poverty (Harper and Rajan 2004), and indigenous rights and dams.[2]

Not everyone agrees that the notion of social and economic well-being should be considered a "right." Libertarians and classical liberals, in particular, argue that, to achieve social rights, an unacceptable burden would be

2. Gustavo González, "Ralco Dam: The Dark Story Behind the Biggest Source of Light," *Inter-Press Service News Agency*, 28 September 2004, ipsnews.net/interna.asp?idnews = 25651 (accessed 1 July 2009).

placed on individual economic freedom. On this view, state planning and intervention almost inevitably conflict with individual liberty (Hayek 1944/ 1976), while the taxes used to promote economic and social rights threaten other rights, such as property rights (Barry 1990). Although it is undoubtedly true that some limits on liberty are necessary for human beings to coexist, the empirical evidence appears to confound the fears of liberals that "increasing the scope of government programs and policies would wreak great harm to individual liberties and ultimately even threaten the survival of democratic institutions. . . . Indeed, evidence suggests that the relationship just might be the inverse. It is in the mature democracies, which have the largest governments measured by their role in the economy, that civil and political liberties are most secure" (Dahl 1999, 919).

Evidence for Latin America also bears out this observation, although the three types of citizenship were not necessarily established in the manner Marshall discussed. In some countries, social citizenship was limited to populism and patron-client relations before widespread political and civil rights were granted (Roberts 1995). In early democratic states, such as Chile, Uruguay, and Costa Rica, social rights were widespread from an early stage. It was in the most brutally authoritarian states like El Salvador, Nicaragua, and Guatemala, as well as in the Andean countries, that repression was widely used to silence calls for social and economic justice. Thus, ample evidence suggests that a lack of political freedom correlates with the *suppression* of economic and social rights, not their pursuit.

As Sen (1999) argues, freedom is intimately connected to social justice. Human rights have not only intrinsic importance but also shape values and priorities to encourage broad-based social policy. Even if rights are not fully institutionalized, they are still legitimate ethical claims; and even if there is no specific responsible party, rights can still be meaningfully and coherently "addressed to all those who are in a position to help" (230). Like Marshall, Sen believes rights discourse can inspire and mobilize actors to force *someone* to respond. A growing number of scholars, practitioners, and policy makers accept social and economic rights as valid citizenship claims and support taxation or other forms of redistribution as necessary and valid means to create wider societal equality. The implications can be radical. Citizenship based in social rights differs from utilitarian designs to promote welfare, as it challenges the social bases of inequality. Egalitarian citizenship conflicts with the unequal class relations inherent to capitalism, shaping and challenging them: "Social rights in their modern form imply an invasion of contract by status, the subordination of market price to social justice, the replacement of the free bargain by the declaration of rights" (Marshall 1949, 111).

One of the most influential theorists to incorporate rights into a theory of social justice was John Rawls. In a Rawlsian society, everyone would have access to a set of "primary goods" that would help them promote their own well-being, such as "rights, liberties and opportunities, income and wealth, and the social bases of self-respect" (Rawls 1971, 54). His concept of "original position" emerges from a thought experiment in which members of society, who are ignorant of the position they hold in the social hierarchy or of their own entitlement, design a "fair" social contract (Rawls 1971). Because the initial distribution of goods, services, and power would not be determined by self-interest, society would be characterized by equality of opportunity and the absence of exploitation. Even in the absence of perfect equality, justice would be sought by promoting the welfare of the least well off. This is clearly a more interventionist doctrine than those discussed earlier, as promoting well-being is seen as an active duty of society. Rawls allows for the use of markets as allocative mechanisms but warns against overly relying on them for determining the institutional structures (property rights, structural opportunities, wealth distribution, etc.) within which markets operate. Distribution at the outset must be fair, as must the structure of the market. In this respect, Rawls moves beyond the individualized, atomized actors in previously discussed theories to account for structural impediments to justice. Rawls bridges the divide between economic and political rights by insisting that the concentration of wealth and power must not be allowed to interfere with equality of opportunity and political liberty.

Critical legal studies (CLS) scholars are critical of rights talk, arguing that it depoliticizes citizens by making them overly reliant on the state as the guarantor of rights. Conflicts between groups over different sets of rights obscure real possibilities for social change (Schneider 1986). These critiques are important in stressing the need for inclusive mechanisms to adjudicate among conflicting claims and to help societies interpret and institute rights-based norms. Yet they underestimate how social movements use human rights discourse to pry open institutional and political spaces for access to social goods, as well as how the assertion of rights can advance political struggle by politicizing need (Fraser 1989) and creating counterhegemonic narratives and strategies (Hunt 1990). In developing countries, "juridical rights" as laid out in international treaties remain an essential leveraging tool in the fight for essential services (Vilhena 2007). The argument favoring the use of rights discourse for securing social and economic rights in developing countries thus mirrors the argument of critical race theory (CRT) and critical race feminism regarding rights claims for women of color: "Although CRT endorses the CLS notion that legal rights are indeterminate, we vehemently disagree that rights are therefore not important. Indeed, the struggle to attain human rights remains critical for American minorities who have never had the luxury of taking such rights for granted" (Wing 2000, 4).

The capabilities approach, first explicated by Amartya Sen (1970, 1999; see also Nussbaum 2003), is another approach to social justice gaining currency in development policy circles. Although Sen's approach resembles that of Rawls in arguing that a just society must care for its most vulnerable members, and that people must have freedom to choose among real options for their well-being, Sen focuses on the capabilities that people have to function fully as human beings, rather than income and "things" that they possess. Evaluating capabilities means seeing how people are actually able to live and what substantive freedom they have that gives them a chance to live lives they have reason to value. A great strength of the capabilities approach, as with Rawls, is that there is no need to base societal outcomes on untenable propositions about self-interested actors. The issue is no longer "the achievement of interest fulfillment" but rather "the availability of freedom (no matter whether the freedom is aimed at self-interest or at some other objective)" (Sen 1999, 118). It is not personal choices that make a society optimal; it is the useful options people have to choose from and their freedom to do so.

In this section, I have discussed a range of *organizing principles based on social justice* that differ significantly from the market-based principles discussed earlier. These social principles include human rights, needs, and capabilities; support for human and social reproduction; and equity and distributive justice. Rights-based and capabilities approaches provide useful metrics for measuring progress in bridging the divide between human rights ideals and global realities, despite claims that their focus on individuals as the objects of social policy underestimates the influence of structures and social relations on individual life chances. Indeed, many "rights-based development" projects (United Nations Development Programme [UNDP] 2003) emerged from the conviction that earlier programs focused unduly on macroeconomic and governance reforms while discounting structural constraints that kept poor countries in a "poverty trap." Liberal approaches in the tradition of Rawls and Sen, though seemingly individualized, have been adapted to deal with such complexities. How well they do so, however, is a matter of politics. In the next section, I address these issues by reviewing the role of states in reaching socially minded ends, providing analytic strategies for recognizing how structure and power affect public goods management, and discussing political strategies for overcoming the influence of exclusionary forces.

Power, Process, and Politics: Establishing Public Goods Policy

Given the complexity of needs and the variety of conflicting philosophical positions of actors involved in public goods discussions (e.g., economists, bureaucrats, scientists, unions, social justice activists, and environmentalists), decisions about public goods management are deeply political. States may act as arbiters of clashes among organizing principles, as well as producers of mechanisms by which values are instituted. Interests of state actors may in turn be molded by institutions and interactions with societal forces. As neoclassical and neoutilitarian thinkers rightly point out, the state can fail to adjudicate effectively among competing ideas and interests, either because it has contradictory interests of its own or because it is "captured" by rent-seeking groups at the expense of the larger society. However, even if problems with state intervention are as pervasive as the discourse suggests, it does not follow that the role and discretion of the state must (or can) be reduced. Benefits of self-preservation also accrue to states and to state actors that successfully provide for their citizens. As we will see, states are integral to public goods development regardless of the values in which public goods policies are "embedded."

For states (at the national or subnational level) to meet public interest or other goals, they require certain institutional and political capabilities. State theory tells us that states more easily facilitate development if state actors have *autonomy* to pursue policies of their choosing (Skocpol 1979; Mann 1984), if the bureaucracy has sufficient *capacity* to implement plans (Evans 1995; Grindle 1996), and if there is *accountability* to the wider public (UNDP 2002a). The first of these, autonomy, is a multifaceted condition that comprises both relational and structural dimensions. It can be understood *relationally* by accounting for the direct or indirect influence of dominant classes; the ways states address or confront subordinate groups through remediation, co-optation, or repression; the relative strength of classes and alliances, both within and outside the state; and ties among national and international elites, associations, and grassroots organizations. *Structural* factors, such as the control of economic resources by groups inside or outside the national territory, the state's position in the international political economy, and the state's unity and cohesion, also affect state autonomy. Because constraints on autonomy are both structural and relational, we would also expect autonomy-enhancing factors to operate on both levels. State capacity (which is also both structural and relational) and alliance building are two enabling factors that can strengthen autonomy for the full realization of state projects.

State Capacity for Development

State capacity entails the ability—based on institutional factors, human competence, and social relations—to devise coherent social and economic policies and carry them through to completion. It can be conceived as comprising institutional, technical, administrative, and political aspects (Grindle 1996). *Institutional capacity* is having authoritative and effective rules in place regarding the regulation of economic and political action. *Technical capacity* means managerial competence in directing economic policy and the use of technically driven policy criteria. *Administrative capacity* refers to the presence of basic state bureaucratic functions to promote development and social welfare. Finally, *political capacity* comprises responsive state actors and effective channels of interest representation and mediation. Some factors that contribute to capacity are centralization and unity within and among agencies or committees; the number, training, competence, and level of experience of government staff; and meritocratic promotion and long-term career prospects, which supposedly encourage norms that reduce state actors' incentives to pursue predatory or patronage policies.

This schema simplifies an admittedly complex reality. Bureaucratic rule following in a Weberian state does not necessarily lead to effective policies and, in fact, "is perfectly consistent with inter-ministerial deadlock and bitter inter-agency rivalries" (Chibber 2002, 959). Overcoming conflicts among bureaus and bureaucrats may require special strategies for channeling plans through mid-level coordinating bodies (Chibber 2003). The ability of states to implement policies and exercise control over a national territory (its *infrastructural power*) will also partially determine the effectiveness of policy implementation (Mann 1984). Moreover, the kinds of rules considered inviolable at any particular time will lead to different state activities. Rules stressing distributive justice, for example, prioritize different policies than rules promoting procedural justice. The protection of private property will likewise entail different state actions than the promotion of collective goods. Technical capacity will vary depending on the "technically driven" criteria used. The technical expertise required for fiscal austerity and inflation targeting, for example, is distinct from that needed to create jobs or stimulate savings. Finally, capacity does not necessarily require responsiveness to all or even most sectors of society. It is perfectly conceivable that a government has great capacity but relies on repression, fear, neglect, or docile compliance to accomplish its goals.

As this discussion clarifies, variation in state goals will necessitate different capacities, and not all types of capacity are needed for all tasks. In general, states must have the ability to gain revenue, which is often achieved through taxation. They must also possess some degree of managerial capacity, especially in directing the economy. Specific policies such as subsidies require the ability to coordinate investment into broadly beneficial, shared projects and the ability to regulate. Disciplining business has its own set of state capacity requirements, such as the ability to set and monitor performance standards, to establish and maintain clear communication, and to devise accountability mechanisms like sanctions (Schneider 1998). They also must be able to obtain and process information that will allow them to revise regulations and policies. State capacity is not, and cannot be, static: "States (modern or otherwise) never finish enhancing their ability to function. States are never 'finally' built; they change and adapt over time. State-building is an iterative process, it is shaped by elite interaction, and by state-society relations" (Whaites 2008).

The cases in this book illustrate this dynamic process of building (and destroying) capacities through marketization of public goods and the effects of these transformations on two very different inherited institutional and political landscapes.

Capacity Building and Embeddedness

States can improve their capacities by forming alliances with business, civil society organizations, and international institutions or groups, as well as by linking goals and activities among state institutions. This "positive coordination" is integral to corporatist and developmental state structures, as well as sectoral planning (Jayasuriya 2001). Alliances with business are widely seen as central to the success of state projects (Amsden 2001; Chibber 2003; Evans 1995). Embeddedness in networks of communication and coordination with selected firms facilitates policy implementation, allows the state to utilize the expertise of market actors, and gives the state more leverage with which to secure the cooperation of business. State-sponsored trade associations, development councils, and tripartite, corporatist bargaining structures are examples of embedding mechanisms that facilitate alliances with business. Capacity can also be enhanced through outsourcing to consultants from the private sector (e.g., Goldman Sachs; Donaldson, Lufkin & Jenrette; Merrill Lynch), the Inter-American Development Bank, and the Organization of American States (among others), who offer services in areas as wide ranging as privatization (MacLeod 2005), decentralization, corruption control, and even democratization, all former areas of state prerogative.

Capacity building through alliances with domestic or international elites is consistent with many policy and regime types, including economic liberalization, corporatism, and authoritarianism. The question is whether it is consistent with further democratization. Can the state be deeply enmeshed in elite enterprises while maintaining accountability to popular or marginalized groups? This question is even more salient during periods of economic liberalization, when states are expected to encourage private investment in public goods sectors just as democratization pressures states to ensure the adequacy of public goods and protect economic and social rights. Democratic embedding, that is, creating accountability mechanisms that ensure the continued responsiveness of public goods to community concerns, is sorely needed in many developing countries. Although existing societies have designed institutional spaces to promote participation (discussed in chapter 2), many challenges to transparent, inclusive deliberative processes still exist.[3] Traditional opposition groups—organized labor, strong associations, or newly empowered classes—may serve as counterweights to business, though they may not be truly representative. Even these groups, however, receive little attention in the development literature, perhaps because alliances between states and subordinate groups are somewhat contradictory (Hamilton 1982). Goals that diverge from the goals of dominant elites are likely to face intense opposition. Further, states interested in stimulating business activity often must simultaneously control subordinate groups, and this social control may undermine popular-state alliances. Finally, state actors generally seek to maintain the status quo of power, while the goal of social movements is to alter it. Thus, without institutional spaces where rival values and interpretations of truth can be continually evaluated and weighed, powerful elites tend to dominate policy discussions.

3. See Fung and Wright (2003), Avritzer (2006), Cornwall (2008), and Levine and Torres (2008) for recent work on emerging participatory spaces and the promise for—and obstacles to—overcoming elite-dominated policy making.

Structure, Power, and the Challenges of Inclusive Social Policy

Efforts to create consensus and participatory mechanisms, newly popular with the World Bank and development organizations, are unlikely to succeed, despite the best intentions, without an analysis of broader structural dynamics and relations of power. As Sandbrook (2000) warns, traditional channels of interest representation are disappointing mechanisms for resolving conflicts over policy priorities: "We all embrace democracy, open discussion of issues, and the hope that reason will prevail. But to abstract these attractive features from power relations by focusing on individual actors . . . offers a false promise to the poor and excluded" (1079).

States, though perhaps not mechanically promoting the interests of capital, are largely excluded from control over surpluses and production processes and thus must depend on revenues outside their control (mainly taxation of private income and profits) for survival. This creates an imperative "to secure the social conditions in which market forces can operate to maximize capital accumulation in the long-term" (Jessop 1990, 185). Other social systems (e.g., political, educational, health, or welfare) tend to adjust to the logic of capital accumulation rather than vice versa (Jessop 2001) because of capital's greater exit options in time (e.g., discounting, insurance, risk management, and futures) and space (e.g., capital flight, relocation, and extraterritoriality). As market actors gain control over public goods, market hegemony rooted in asymmetric relations between capitalism and other orders can creep into public goods priorities. International financial institutions from the Global North further constrain states with restrictive fiscal, monetary, and labor policies designed for implementation in the Global South, where local communities have little opportunity to question the priorities embedded in them.

Even when state policy is used to protect citizens, it may favor some groups over others, as with preferential treatment of union versus non-union labor under "embedded liberalism" (Ruggie 1982). As power relations and distribution of material resources strongly influence who makes allocation decisions (Swyngedouw and Heynen 2003), public goods outcomes reflect existing cleavages of class, gender, ethnicity, and citizenship. Relational inequalities such as these, and not inherent scarcity, are one of the key reasons for the persistence of poverty and lack of access to essential goods (Baldry 2006). Within the state, moreover, the behavior of various actors and agencies (the executive, legislature, judiciary, ministries, agencies, regulatory bodies, etc.) may work at cross-purposes. In fact, democracy itself can be contradictory. Democratic processes do not always lead to enlightened public policy, and the electorate may be complicit in undermining the state's ability to provide goods or embed markets. This is especially true in this era of globalization, where corporations insist on reduced taxation in return for investment. Under these conditions, the fiscal burden shifts to increasingly resentful individual taxpayers, major parties compete over who will cut taxes most, lower tax income restricts state expenditures, and the citizenry finds itself with inadequate services for which they understandably do not wish to pay more taxes (Crouch 2000).

Given these thorny problems, how can structural dynamics and power inequities be usefully analyzed? Public choice theory and other liberal traditions see power as the ability of groups, through individual action, to secure their own interests and thus look for power in favorable political decisions. But the political system does not give equal weight to all wants (Bachrach and Baratz 1970). Outcomes are also influenced by the "mobilization of bias" in communities, namely, "a set of predominant values, beliefs, rituals, and institutional procedures . . . that operate systematically and consistently to the benefit of certain persons and groups at the expense of others" (43). This suffocates alternatives before they are voiced, kills them before they reach the decision-making table, or distorts or destroys them during implementation. To detect such mobilization, analysts can look at alternatives that are *not* decided in the political realm, that is, "nondecisions." In the analysis that follows, I trace both decisions and nondecisions through the political process to examine how market-friendly forces in consequential institutional realms stifled what had once been deemed viable alternatives.

Although this "second face of power" moves beyond the facile assumptions of the liberal perspective, its exclusive focus on observable conflict— overt or covert—among interested parties "gives a misleading picture of the ways in which individuals and, above all, groups and institutions succeed in excluding potential issues from the political process" (Lukes 1974, 21). Measurable "preferences," the key unit of analysis in public choice and political process theories, are susceptible to influence by a "third face" of power (Lukes 1974, 2004b). In this reading, interests transcend the smaller subgroup of perceived choices. For example, when facing a fait accompli, social actors may "voluntarily" limit their desires to the range of options they see as achievable, rather than those that might serve them best (Lukes and Haglund 2005). Beliefs about one's own interests may also be shaped by "influences that subvert or trick or dominate or, in the extreme case, control [one's] conscious will" (59). In the area of public goods reform analyzed later, "experts" with a market-oriented bias sought to limit policy choices through control over knowledge production, information dissemination, and interpretation of viable alternatives.

Power also operates through institutions and structures in ways that may undermine policy alternatives. Strange's (1988) work proposes strategies for analyzing structural power, defined as the ability "to shape and determine the structures of the global political economy within which other states, their political institutions, their economic enterprises and (not least) their scientists and other professional people have to operate" (25). Three realms of structural power are particularly relevant to public goods: control over production, credit (finance), and knowledge, beliefs, and ideas (ideology). Geopolitical mapping strategies can reveal the operation of structural power obscured by agent-centered approaches.[4] I use these strategies in the case studies that follow to trace the evolution of neoliberal policies as they transform production, financing, and knowledge of public goods. For instance, institutional arrangements that shielded the haves from the have-nots (e.g., fees for access to public goods, private property protections) created barriers to inclusion and redistribution. Monopoly power of transnational corporations was identified through ownership patterns in electricity and water sectors. Institutional power arose also from "rules of the game" that favored certain interests over others, for example, under the Central America Free Trade Agreement regime. In the design, implementation, and management of trade policy, corporations and states were included as legitimate negotiating partners, while community, environmental, or social justice organizations had no official role. Moreover, trade rules, once in effect, had the force of law and were closed to further public deliberation short of renegotiation. Individual agents benefit when their personal interests are institutionalized in this way, as it obviates the need for more crude exercises of power (Searle 1998).

"Double Movements" and Political Inclusion

Societal groups may attempt to harness the state to overcome structural impediments to alternative visions or to create a bulwark against powerful interests. Just as welfare state analysis (Esping-Andersen 1990; Orloff 1993) argues that decommodification arises as workers struggle to institutionalize their version of a good society, this book supports the view that

---

4. For example, the mapping of commodity chains and the distribution of resources among various "nodes" (Gereffi and Korzeniewicz 1994) reveal interesting power dynamics in production. Tracing financial flows and their distributive effects (Zysman 1985) or mapping the knowledge structure (Bourdieu 1977) are other useful examples.

social struggles over the principles underlying different visions of "public goods" shape organizational outcomes in public goods sectors. Karl Polanyi (1944) called measures taken to protect society from market overexposure "double movements." Double movements can be understood as struggles between different organizing principles, which, in Polanyi's time, were "the principle of economic liberalism, aiming at the establishment of a self-regulating market . . . using largely *laissez-faire* and free trade as its methods; [and] the principle of social protection aiming at the conservation of man and nature . . . using protective legislation, restrictive associations, and other instruments of intervention as its method" (132). The double movements of this earlier period foreshadowed recent institutional and political clashes over privatization and marketization that occurred because of deeper value conflicts between neoliberalism and other possible economic and social orders.

This is not a question of individuals vying for their "self-interest." Contrary to the predictions of libertarian or classical liberal theories, people are more likely to forgo their own desires to achieve community goals if the procedures are fair and the authorities are deemed legitimate representatives of the larger whole (Tyler and Degoey 1995, 1). This is true regardless of whom final allocations favor. Perceptions of fairness that arise from a concern with "procedural justice" (usually the protection of private property and due process) are very different from this community-minded concern for fair processes. Where states have been unresponsive or unconcerned about including nonelites in policy discussions, more radical double movements have emerged in the form of protest. This does not mean that injustice always spurs resistance. Rather, resistance arises in cases where the injustice violates perceived values of the population, and where the state does not take action to remedy what they see as their legitimate needs—whether solidarity, human rights, sustainability, or inclusion.

A clash of principles was at the root of many recent popular double movements. Principles of ownership and control over natural resources often conflict with calls for market efficiency through privatization, which, in turn, may conflict with principles of environmental conservation. It may matter a great deal to a group, region, or nation whether they retain control over their water, oil, natural gas, or other resources, even when alternatives are not deemed "efficient" from an economic standpoint. This explains, in part, the vehemence of resistance to privatization of gas pipelines and water in Bolivia, oil exploration on U'wa land in Colombia, and other protests worldwide. Indigenous communities are often at the forefront of such protests; as U'wa spiritual leaders explained, they would rather "walk off a cliff" than permit oil exploration to threaten "our home, the animals and plants we eat, the water we drink, and our culture, which is based on the forest."[5] The organizing principles that these communities have used for centuries to manage resources conflicted with the modernizing logic of corporate globalization.

This is not simply about individuals fighting for their rights to particular goods or services. A more solidary logic underpins such action, where groups of citizens or workers or marginalized communities push back against structural or ideological constraints to their vision of the public good. The objective is to create a wider political and social milieu through collective action, in which options for expanding capabilities and demanding individual and group rights become possible. Institutional actors alone may not be capable of accommodating multiple values and principles or guarding against power relations and structural impediments within nations and in the global political economy. There is far more social struggle to the story than the public goods literature suggests. Rights are rarely granted freely, and battles for them are generally hard-fought and only occasionally won. Activists throughout history have overcome structural constraints and entrenched interests in the fight for justice, long before the emergence of human rights theory and "development as freedom." The philosophical foundations of social justice go back at least to the ancient Greeks and can be found in all major religious traditions. Social justice in practice has meant intense struggle by workers, women, environmentalists, indigenous communities, and other marginalized groups for a "social contract" that includes an equitable distribution of resources; the cessation of persistent abuse and exploitation of people and the earth; support for women and families in their reproduction of human society (for which public goods serve a crucial function); and the promotion of *systematically* fair outcomes.

In sum, given that the construction of public goods is a political process, several political factors will be relevant to decisions about how such goods are managed. These *political organizing principles* include state capacities required for providing, monitoring, and funding public goods; ownership, control, and distribution of resources; procedural justice (security of property, inclusion, voice); accountability; and relations of power and structural impediments to justice. We have yet to address a

5. Quoted in Laura Carlsen, "Indigenous Communities in Latin America: Fighting for Control of Natural Resources in a Globalized Age," Americas Program: Citizen Action in the Americas, 2002, http://americas.irc-online.org/citizen-action/focus/0207indigenous.html (accessed 9 July 2009).

pressing global issue: environmental sustainability. In the following section, I discuss the kinds of principles entailed by a concern with sustainability, as well as the challenges of incorporating these principles into human-focused decision-making processes.

Beyond Human Communities: Incorporating Environmental Concerns

Addressing ecological problems and promoting equity often mean interventions in which some human beings must give up material benefits. Advocates for marginalized human communities may participate in such policy decisions, but the environment has historically gone underrepresented, and environmental concerns have commonly lost out to other considerations, such as job creation and capital accumulation. Although human welfare and justice are important moral concerns, they do not exist independently of the health and well-being of the environment. It is no longer possible to ignore the requirements of the natural world for reproduction without also compromising long-term sustainability and creating greater scarcity. The absence of a wider ecological perspective exacerbates distributional conflict and can lead to overallocation, as with water in the American West, or outright plunder, as with natural resources in many poor countries. Indeed, sometimes untouched or unpolluted resources are themselves desirable ends for existing communities, future generations, and even nonhuman beings. Thus, we must improve our ability to integrate environmental and ecological justice concerns into decision-making processes.

Actions that promote growth, market activity, or other immediate economic ends can cause long-term ecological harm that affects future generations (Sandler 1999). Competition, the profit motive, and corporate consolidation tend to work against conservation and sustainability. Competition, when present, forces firms to reduce costs in the short term to prevail over other firms in the market. The mandate for maximizing shareholder value written into corporate law provides further incentives for cutting current expenditures. Although reducing labor costs is one possible solution open to managers, cutting corners on the environment and nonhuman species, which have no voice, is often politically safer. The incentive naturally arising from the short-term thinking of market actors is thus exploitation, not conservation. As public monopolies are unbundled and forced to compete with the private sector, these incentives proliferate. Markets also do not respond appropriately to the natural time frame of renewability. Some resources are nonrenewable (such as petroleum), others regenerate slowly or at an unknown rate (such as river basins and forests), and others can regenerate quickly (such as radio airwaves). Greater "production" (i.e., extraction) of natural resources—to meet demand or to ensure profits—can have difficult-to-reverse consequences that include dropping water tables, increasing scarcity, and environmental degradation.

As mentioned earlier in this chapter, another consequence of marketization in natural monopoly sectors has been corporate consolidation. Despite Herculean efforts and substantial resources directed toward making markets competitive, the sheer scale of providing goods such as water, energy, and sanitation undermines competition, especially in small countries where the size of the market cannot support multiple firms. The result often is *private* monopolies or oligopolies, as large firms are able to set prices below their long-term costs and drive out smaller firms. Once private firms have monopoly control, the difficulties of state environmental regulation grow dramatically. Some environmental economists, with their steadfast faith in markets, propose market solutions to these and an array of other ecological problems. By reducing costs and increasing incentives for environmental protection for the private sector, individual self-interest and good environmental policy will supposedly converge. "Externalities," they argue, occur because there are no markets for "environmental goods," such as clean air and virgin forests. With proper pricing and marketization, conservation would result. The mental acrobatics involved in "pricing" the environment will not be covered here (see Bellamy Foster 2002 for a fascinating account), but some of the mechanisms designed to assist marketization bear mentioning: tax incentives or subsidies, users' fees, creation and enforcement of private property rights, and tradable credits, such as in carbon pollution.

As with all realms of social policy, relying on narrow economic understandings of environmental conservation may actually make matters worse. Besides the economic inequities discussed earlier, market-based management of natural resources has caused serious environmental imbalances between people, nations, and generations (Syme et al. 2006). This is because the organizing principles that answer to the needs of the natural world are quite distinct from market principles, which destroy nature to promote profit (Polanyi 1944). Nature needs more than commodification to reproduce itself; sometimes it requires being left alone or actively shielded from exploitation. Moreover, marketization creates incentives for people to view nature only as an economic good and, therefore, to privilege avarice over other human attributes, such as reverence for nature and respect for future generations. The intrinsic value of nature, which is incalculable and transcends its market value, is not taken seriously by market-oriented policy. Even in "natural capitalism" (Hawken, Lovins, and Lovins 2000), the underlying conditions and incentives created by profit, competition, and monopoly remain, yet the appearance of protection is added, actually decreasing real, institutionalized protections (Bellamy Foster 2002). Nature does not "accumulate" like capital under market conditions, and markets have no way of evaluating the true value of nature.

Marketization policies alter strategies for protecting the environment in water and in electricity sectors, as the cases in this book demonstrate. The problems mentioned previously require a different reckoning of incentives and alternate mechanisms for supplying public goods than management based on market signals, individual self-interest, or even human rights. These *ecological organizing principles* comprise a distinct set of value orientations that shape the meaning of public goods: recognizing and addressing the reproductive needs of the natural world, including the time frame of renewability; determining the optimal scale of sectoral activities; mitigating the long-term consequences of policies in terms of ecological and intergenerational justice; and acknowledging and respecting the benefits of unperturbed nature. Although tackling these problems does not necessarily require public ownership—planning and coordination might be managed by the government, by a common property regime, or as regulated private property (Ostrom et al. 2002)—national development and environmental protection entail broad-based planning. Coordination problems can be surmounted if firms and resources are managed under a single, coherent framework. For large-scale strategic activities, such as creating an institutional infrastructure to address problems of scale, temporal inefficiencies, and renewability, a strong case can be made that "public interventions are superior to market mechanisms" (Boyer 2000, 275). Although these ecological principles cannot replace economic and social principles, they provide an important corrective to historically anthropocentric approaches to public goods.

Organizing Principles and the Struggle for Embedded Social Policy

As in "the golden age of liberalism" of the late nineteenth century, a reemergence of market principles as the primary referent to organize the economy characterized the late twentieth century. Polanyi (1957) reminds us that we cannot grasp the ramifications of such liberalization, "unless the social sciences succeed in developing a wider frame of reference to which the market itself is referable" (270), that is, grounded in the substantive understandings of the economy. Figure 1 shows the multiple organizing principles that ground public goods policy in substantive concerns: market principles, social principles, ecological principles, and political principles.

This heuristic device pinpoints the assumptions, norms, and values at the root of the institutionalization of markets, politics, social relations, and environmental policies in different contexts. It is important, however, not to reify these categories. These principles are continually contested and

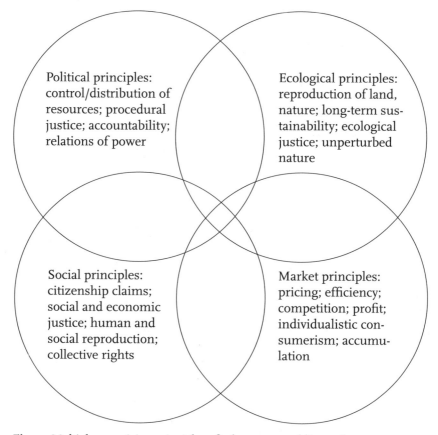

Fig. 1   Multiple organizing principles of relevance to public goods

reformulated, and these realms are mutually constitutive. Market organization, for example, reflects certain conceptions of justice and power relations and not others. Similarly, prevailing market principles and social norms reproduce or challenge conceptions of appropriate mechanisms of control over resources. Finally, social values, such as beliefs about citizenship entitlements, vary depending on conceptions of "efficiency" and level of acceptance of inclusion as a political principle. The organizational principles that hold sway in any given context depend on the relative power of social groups and their ability to advocate for framings that correspond to their conception of "the good." This is one reason discursive space (e.g., media, associations, political groups) is important. The predominance of certain principles in a given society, however, does not mean that those principles are, by definition, fully implemented in practice. Political outcomes are always approximations of ideas.

Although market, societal, environmental, and political organizing principles may coexist—albeit uneasily—on the conceptual level, the risk of clashes becomes greater when institutional mechanisms by which principles can be translated into practices are created (or destroyed). States that have given up their role in protecting "fictitious commodities" because of outside pressures, internal choices, or simply neglect are finding themselves faced with double movements of a sometimes disruptive nature. The goal of this book is to move beyond abstract models of market efficiency that recommend retrenchment to explore place-specific institutional arrangements devised to address substantive needs. The key insight is that there is no ready definition of public goods: the "public" character is partly in its constitution and partly in a political rendering of the good, that is, what a given society *decides* should be public (Malkin and Wildavsky 1991; Kaul 2003). At the root of such choices are differing ways of valuing: for some, a higher value is placed on social and economic rights than on efficiency or property rights; for others, market principles are foundational for optimal societal outcomes. For such valuation to be valid, societies must define their own version of "optimality." The categories delineated previously can help make explicit the multiple principles that communities and policy makers may consider when formulating public goods strategies, rather than having the assumptions hidden behind supposedly neutral economic models.

What follows is a more detailed explication of how particular societies institutionalize electricity and water provision according to various organizing principles. I will contrast a "neoliberal," or "market-oriented," model

based on Washington Consensus principles of efficiency, market allocation, and individual choice, with a social and economic rights-based model
rooted in principles of solidarity, equity, and accountability. The goal is to
demonstrate how concepts are (albeit imperfectly) put into practice
through institutions, and how this process can favor some societal actors
and disfavor others. As we will see, the global spread of neoliberal ideas,
whether bearing closer resemblance to the liberalism of Friedrich Hayek
or the libertarianism of Robert Nozick, has made citizenship-based models
of public goods provision more difficult to secure.

2

"FOR THE PEOPLE":
CONSTRUCTING THE "PUBLIC" OF PUBLIC GOODS

States and communities have employed a variety of strategies for linking economic activities with desired socioeconomic outcomes. From socialism to social democracy to "embedded liberalism," societies have built "cooperative institutions" to protect people "from market forces, exploitation, and domination" (Chase-Dunn 2002, 50). In both the developed and the developing world, examples of institutions that "embed" economies can be found: corporatist structures, social welfare policies, public forums, and formal social dialogue. In public goods sectors as well, a range of delivery systems are available for instituting the principles discussed in chapter 1. Despite the strong criticism of states in recent reform efforts, many national and subnational actors, even in poor areas, have attempted to put public goods values into practice through policy choices. This chapter explores such institution-building efforts. The purpose of comparing Costa Rica and El Salvador in these terms is not to argue that they have created equivalent public goods delivery systems—they clearly have not—but to highlight the divergent policies that can emerge despite initial adherence to similar goals and to emphasize the importance of political factors in these divergent outcomes.

The Institutionalization of Organizing Principles

The ideational axis of this analysis centers on rights-based principles underlying attempts at public goods provision.[1] Although the social democratic

1. This chapter focuses on social and political (as opposed to ecological or market) ethics outlined in chapter 1. Environmental issues at the time were not given as much

basis of the Costa Rican state contrasts starkly with the authoritarian history of El Salvador, the conceptual foundation of public goods in the rhetoric of social and economic rights—such as access to housing, water, and electricity—is, in fact, surprisingly similar. The constitutions of both Costa Rica and El Salvador acknowledge international norms regarding social and economic rights and stipulate that the state play a central role in ensuring them. Both countries are parties to the International Covenant on Economic, Social, and Cultural Rights (CESCR 1976), as well as the United Nations Convention on the Elimination of All Forms of Discrimination against Women (CEDAW 1979) and the Millennium Development Goals (United Nations 2000). Despite the questionable commitment of El Salvador's postwar governments to these principles, both countries claimed overtly to stand by them. What renders their public goods sectors so different is the efficacy (or absence) of institutional mechanisms created to meet the goals of seemingly similar principles and hold policy makers accountable to those principles.

In Costa Rica, the Constitution of 1949 affirmed the interventionist and social democratic characteristics of the state, despite its liberal foundations. State institutions have served a wide array of development goals, including addressing social and economic rights in both the electricity and the water sectors. There is agreement, even among proponents of privatization, that a strong, active regulatory apparatus must be employed in public goods sectors and that natural resources themselves must remain public property. The similarities in governance between Costa Rica and El Salvador are admittedly few. Costa Rica's long century of peace—interrupted only briefly, and only before 1950—contrasts starkly with the brutal repression and subsequent armed resistance of Salvadorans during much of the latter half of the twentieth century. But even in El Salvador, social and economic rights were officially recognized with the implementation of the CESCR in 1976, and the constitution stipulated the state's central role in providing public services (Centro de Estudios para la Aplicación de Derecho [CESPAD] 1991). As early as the 1980s, the Christian Democratic Party had recognized the destabilizing effects of social inequities and had attempted to institute a mixed economy with heavy state involvement to address them (Segovia 2002). Finally, the demands of guerillas during the civil war included social and economic rights as foundational for any lasting resolution to the conflict.

---

urgency as they are in the contemporary reform discourse, and they are thus treated here as emerging problems to be incorporated in forward-looking policy strategies, discussed later in the book. The emergence and institutionalization of market principles are discussed in chapters 3 and 4, respectively.

The Peace Accords of 1992 brought with them great expectations regarding a resolution of the social and economic problems that were at the root of the twelve-year civil war. The cease-fire alleviated, at least temporarily, the deep mistrust that had characterized much of the twentieth century. Declarations made on both sides of the negotiations process expressed the hope that prevailed (quoted in Spence 2004, 7):

- The FMLN's Shafik Handal: "We have embarked on the course . . . to shape a politically, economically, and socially pluralist country, as the foundation of a participatory and representative democracy."
- ARENA's Alfredo Cristiani: "We are committed to an integral promotion of human rights, not only political but also social and economic."

The language establishing the Office of the Human Rights Defense Attorney (PDDH) also brimmed with expectation. The PDDH was designed to protect "the civil, political, economic, social, and cultural rights, as well as third generation rights [to development, to a healthy environment, and to peace] considered in the Constitution; laws and treaties currently in force; as well as the content of declarations and principles approved by the United Nations, or the Organization of American States."[2]

Of course, even if principles regarding public goods are widely accepted, states vary in the degree to which they are able to provide the conditions for their realization, as well as how hard they try. This variation is evident in the two cases presented here. However, the point is that, as in Costa Rica, peace negotiations in El Salvador led to an overt acknowledgment of the responsibility of the state to ensure that public goods were provided equitably and well and mandated the creation of institutions that could monitor these goals accountably. Early democratization in Costa Rica and recent processes in El Salvador both awakened expectations regarding accountability, voice, and the right to public goods and led to the development of institutions designed to meet these goals. In the remainder of the chapter, I explain institution building, generally speaking, for providing, regulating, and financing electricity and water, as well as describe the emergence of public institutions created for these purposes in Costa Rica and El Salvador. I also discuss mechanisms designed to increase public accountability for social and economic policy.

2. Ley de la Procuraduría para la Defensa de los Derechos Humanos, 1992.

State and Community Intervention in Public Goods Sectors

States can meet their obligations "to respect, protect, and fulfill" the human right to essential goods, as stipulated in CESCR (2002), in a number of ways. At a minimum, states must have regulatory bodies capable of monitoring either public or private firms and protecting users. The scale of the investments required for viable electricity, water, and sewage sectors often requires public support of finance, either direct (state investments) or indirect (state guarantees for private investment). Finally, states often create public utility firms designed to ensure access, to keep prices affordable, and to plan in sensitive sectors, where holistic approaches to environmental or developmental goals are desired (see table 4).

Public Utilities: Justifications and Precedent

Despite criticism of state-owned enterprises (SOEs), many states chose to create public utility firms because of sectoral characteristics that make private provision and monitoring difficult. SOEs in water and electricity sectors can overcome a number of technical and social problems, as well as

Table 4   State- and community-led institutionalization of public goods

	Relevant actors	Tasks contributing to adequate public goods provision
Public utilities	Electricity, water, and sewage firms	• Coverage • Affordable pricing • Cross-subsidies • Sectoral planning
Regulatory agencies	Bodies charged with regulation of markets or public providers, environmental protection, and state planning objectives	• Price regulation and financial oversight • Antimonopoly • Monitoring providers • Protecting system reliability • Holistic planning • Impact assessment • Disciplining noncompliance
Public or semipublic finance	Public utilities IFIs, banks Central government Other	• Investments from profits • Subsidies from profits • Loans, esp. for infrastructure • Taxation • Other financial instruments

provide indirect benefits (Chang 2003a). For example, the scale of investment may be too large for the private sector to undertake, or natural monopoly characteristics and volatile markets in subsectors may make private provision difficult or undesirable. Monitoring public utilities is easier for the state, as private firms have the incentive and capacity to withhold needed information for pricing and investment decisions. Public firms, moreover, have no incentive to charge monopolistic or oligopolistic prices, or to distort supply, as occurred with private electricity generation firms in California (thereby contributing to the electricity crisis of 2000–2001). In addition, local capabilities and technologies can be fostered with SOEs, creating upward and downward linkages to other sectors of the economy. Finally, public firms are more able to direct funds to "socially desirable" ends. Equity considerations, for example, can be handled through pricing policy rather than markets. Cross-subsidies reduce information gathering and monitoring costs that accompany taxation and external targeting schemes designed to ensure access.

Another advantage of public providers of particular relevance to water and electricity sectors is that they can directly protect ecological resources and promote holistic development planning in sensitive sectors. In Central America, dams—the main source of electricity in Costa Rica and an important one in El Salvador—tend to be state owned, as do most water resources. There have been moves to privatize in both countries, but these sectors are especially resistant because of their sensitivity and the need for integrated planning in hydroelectric sectors. As one respondent noted, "For strategic reasons, for questions of security, a service so vital and essential to the life of a country as electricity generation should not be left to the laws of the market."[3] Geothermal and thermal generation also raise important environmental and strategic questions.

Once SOEs have been created, there can be drawbacks to marketization that might discourage countries from using policies such as privatization and public–private partnerships. Depriving sectors of funds and then hoping private investors will make up the shortfall, as has been done in Central America, is risky. As Jeffrey Sachs argued in a May 2003 World Bank seminar, "if public-private partnerships are a means to get the private sector to do work that only the public sector can pay for, it will be a sad experiment."[4] In addition, "there have been problems of corruption in the

3. Norman Quijano, deputy of the Salvadoran Legislative Assembly, ARENA (National Republican Alliance), interview with the author, 25 August 2003.
4. Quoted in Tim Kessler, "Review of the 2004 World Development Report 'Making Services Work for Poor People,'" *Network IDEAS*, http://www.networkideas.org/themes/human/oct2003/hdo8_Tim_Kessler.htm (accessed 5 July 2008).

process of privatization in a number of cases" (Williamson 2004), an outcome that is averted when ownership remains public. Most important, from the point of view of social and economic rights, users can more effectively make claims to essential services as organized citizens than as atomized consumers. Constitutional protections against governmental abuse do not apply to contractor abuse in the same industries. The more services are contracted, the more dispersed the lines of accountability.

Costa Rica was a pioneer in the creation of SOEs in water and electricity sectors in Central America. In the nineteenth century, uncoordinated participation of both private companies and state and community projects characterized these sectors. Various businesses, both national and foreign, established electrical grids and generation plants in diverse locations, especially after 1884, when the first public lighting grid was inaugurated in the city of San José (and with it, the first hydroelectric plant). The central government and municipalities granted businesses permission to use water for electrical generation, as well as to provide electrical service to users across their distribution networks. Law No. 14 of 1910 transformed the electrical industry with the nationalization of hydropower, giving the state a decisive role in administering water for electrical generation. This did not yet entail the creation of a public monopoly over the use of such forces, but it did mean that the state was obligated to exercise control and to protect water concessions for electrical generation.

Eventually, control over the electrical sector began to concentrate in the hands of one U.S. firm, Electric Bond and Share Company (EBASCO). Little by little, EBASCO consolidated its private monopoly by buying plants and by obtaining electricity generation concessions. Services were deficient and onerous for most consumers because of the low level of capital investment realized by the industry, their targeting of wealthy customers and neglect of less lucrative sectors of the population, and the high costs of regulation by the state. Failure of the private sector to provide adequate electrical service eventually prompted nationalization: "When Bond and Share of New York, which was the firm that controlled distribution in Costa Rica, reached the heights of negligence, of inefficiency, and of disaster, what happened? A state institution was created to provide services in its place."[5] In 1968, the Costa Rican Electricity and Telecommunications Institute (ICE) eliminated EBASCO's private monopoly by acquiring its stocks.

ICE is the most important public utility in Costa Rica today. Its founders conceived it as a mechanism to solve a power crisis that affected the

5. Vice president of CADEXCO, the Costa Rican Chamber of Exporters, interview with the author, 27 January 2003.

country in the 1940s due to unprecedented growth. ICE was to plan, to execute, and to coordinate the national electrification program. Law No. 449 of 1949, the Law Creating the Costa Rican Electricity Institute, established the legal framework; in the late 1960s, telecommunications was also incorporated into its mission. During its sixty-year history, ICE has been a revenue-generating public monopoly that also funds other social projects. There are dozens of hydroelectric power plants (85 percent of the electricity in Costa Rica is generated by renewable hydroelectric power), and the country is totally self-sufficient in its energy needs, except for oil. Today, ICE is one of the most important—and most profitable—firms in all of Central America, public or private.

ICE is a vertically integrated firm, from generation to transmission to distribution, with one subsidiary, the National Power and Light Company (CNFL). The electricity transmission subsector forms a natural monopoly administered by ICE, while the structure of the generation and distribution subsectors could be described as mainly monopolistic (more than 80 percent controlled by ICE and CNFL), with some horizontal decentralization. Before Law No. 7200 was passed in 1990, which opened up the generation subsector to private firms, there were already two municipal companies (the Cartago Electrical Service Administration Board [JASEC] and the now-privatized Heredia Public Services [ESPH]) and four Rural Electrification Cooperatives (in Guanacaste, Los Santos, San Carlos, and Alfaro Ruiz) that relied on local generation plants for their energy supply (see table 5). These agents were responsible for distribution, and in each case, the concession areas formed natural mini-monopolies.

Table 5 Electricity distribution by source, Costa Rica

Source	Percentage of electricity provided by source
ICE	39.7
CNFL	40.2
JASEC	5.8
ESPH	5.8
Cooperatives	8.5
Total	100.0

SOURCE: ICE (2006). "Datos relevantes sector electricidad."

NOTE: CNFL = National Power and Light Company; ESPH = Heredia Public Services; ICE = Costa Rican Electricity and Telecommunications Institute; JASEC = Cartago Electrical Service Administration Board.

In the Costa Rican water sector, public entities also retain monopoly control over resources. As table 6 shows, national and municipal public and communal bodies mainly provide water, with very little private sector participation.

The Institute of Aqueducts and Sewage Systems (AyA) was created in 1961 to address the poor municipal service, which was beleaguered by deficits in human, financial, and institutional capacity. The objective of Law No. 2726, which created AyA, was "to provide direction, establish policies, create and apply norms, realize and promote planning, financing, and development, and resolve problems related to water provision and the collection and disposal of sewage and liquid industrial waste" (AyA 2002, 80). AyA, like ICE, has proved relatively efficacious. Coverage of water and sewer service is high, although infrastructure declined during the 1990s because of low investment levels resulting from fiscal austerity policies. This has caused some problems in quality and environmental protection, as well as undermined the stability of supply.

In terms of efficiency, AyA has a slightly higher number of employees (5) per 1,000 connections than firms elsewhere in Latin America (3–4 per 1,000; AyA 2002), and there are some capacity deficits in business administration, finance, and marketing. AyA also has many institutional strengths, including the ability to gather detailed, nationwide information on the sector; access to credit (though not always permission to obtain it) from numerous multilateral banks and national sources; technical and

Table 6   Water provision by source, Costa Rica

Source	Percentage of water for human consumption provided by source[a]	Percentage of potable water provided by source
AyA	43.2	42.0
Municipalities	17.1	10.6
ESPH	4.7	4.7
Rural aqueducts and users' associations	24.4	13.5
Private or communal wells	9.0	5.0
Total	98.4	75.8

SOURCE: Institute of Aqueducts and Sewage Systems (AyA 2002). "Análisis Sectorial de Agua Potable y Saneamiento (ASAPS)."

NOTE: ESPH = Heredia Public Services.
[a] "Potable water" is distinguished from "water for human consumption," which is lower quality.

financial support from entities, such as the Pan-American Health Organization and the World Health Organization; and institutional support for its goals from several other Costa Rican state entities, such as the Health Ministry (MINSALUD), the Environment and Energy Ministry (MINAE), the Ministry of National Planning and Economic Policy (MIDEPLAN), the Public Services Regulatory Authority (ARESEP), the Support and Advisement Institute for Municipalities (IFAM), and the National Subterranean Water, Irrigation, and Drainage Service (SENARA). Although the rights and responsibilities in the sector are not always clear, there is without question a high degree of state capacity to carry out sectoral goals.

In El Salvador, the government created the Lempa River Executive Hydroelectric Commission (CEL), the main public electricity entity, and the National Aqueducts and Sewers Administration (ANDA) during the period of import substitution industrialization (ISI) to promote industrial activity, as well as meet demands for services in newly urbanized areas. For more than fifty years, CEL was the only company in El Salvador that handled all aspects of electricity provision. Since 1996, when CEL was unbundled and partially privatized, it has competed successfully with private generation plants and has continued to manage the transmission lines of the country. In 2003, CEL received international accreditation for its efficiency and high-quality service from the Spanish Society for Normalization and Standardization (AENOR), a group whose mission is "to contribute to the improvement in quality and competitiveness of companies, and to environmental protection."[6] The factors that influenced its efficiency qualification were its operations, communications, human relations, and security of service. The autonomous institution was the first electricity company in the region to receive this qualification.[7] Despite the many institutional problems of the Salvadoran state, CEL maintained low costs, high-quality service, and efficiency. Even in this unlikely case, state-owned enterprises can be effective.

There are great disparities between these countries regarding the extent to which state-owned enterprises permeate utility sectors and their effectiveness. Costa Rica's social democratic paradigm was institutionalized in public goods sectors through nationalization processes carried out to remedy inadequacies of private provision. Unlike many other countries in the region, however, the infrastructural and resource development that followed was dramatic. ICE, AyA, and numerous municipal and community

---

6. See http://www.aenor.es/desarrollo/aenor/quees/quees.asp.
7. "Certifican calidad de operaciones de CEL," *La Prensa Gráfica*, 15 August 2003.

public works promoted the extension of services to the majority of the population, contributing to impressive indicators for coverage, quality, and price. Although not every state-owned enterprise in Costa Rica was problem free, those in the water and electricity sectors functioned quite well, embodying not only the duty to provide but also the values of solidarity and universality. This "solidary model" is central to understandings of citizenship for many Costa Ricans. A political agreement over the desirability of these principles provided a fertile ground for their institutionalization.

In El Salvador, however, elite sectors opposed to Costa Rican–style interventions blocked attempts to institutionalize state duties, resulting in underdeveloped capacities in public goods sectors. There were some improvements in water and sewer development during the postwar period, as well as advances in hydroelectric energy, and CEL has proved to be an excellent provider. But El Salvador's devastating civil war, quarrels between Christian Democrats and business-friendly elites over economic models, and a decline in government and international financial institution (IFI) support for public projects in the 1980s compromised state-building efforts in public goods sectors. Thus, the state and private sector are both implicated in the mediocre performance of public goods arising from a lack of commitment to social principles and neglect of infrastructure investment.

Regulatory Mechanisms

One way to ensure that utility firms are socially responsive is through effective regulation. Regulatory agencies charged with monitoring markets and alleviating market failure, protecting vulnerable populations and precious resources, and coordinating sectoral policies are central to any model of service provision, whether public, private, or mixed. This is especially true in ecologically sensitive sectors, such as power, water, and sanitation, where there are serious risks, especially with privatization. These sectors are either natural monopolies (water and sewage, electricity transmission and distribution) or lend themselves to monopoly structures (electricity generation). Unregulated or poorly regulated monopolies and oligopolies can control prices and outputs to their own advantage. Strong regulation allows states to monitor prices, ensure inclusion of poorer customers, protect the environment, and safeguard countries "against the strategic power of big investors and their resulting market power" (HERA 2002, 17). Even competitive sectors linked to strategic goals—such as industrial development (which requires electricity), tourism (which requires both electricity and water), and ecotourism (which requires preservation of natural water-ways and river basins)—as well as equity targets (which require a reinvest-ment of profits into nonprofitable areas) require regulation to ensure goals are met in a holistic, efficient, and adequate manner.

Societal principles that can be institutionalized through the creation of regulatory agencies are universal service, prohibitions on price discrimina-tion, and a balance between efficiency and externalities (e.g., environ-mental protection, safety). Some examples of regulatory mechanisms are quality standards, accompanied by penalties or incentives; coverage tar-gets; and price regulation (cost-plus regulation or price caps).[8] The kinds of regulation used will depend on sectoral structures (e.g., competitive, oligopoly, or monopoly), as well as the explicit and implicit goals of the state (e.g., promoting competition, fair pricing, universalism, or conserva-tion). In competitive situations, regulation can moderate competitive pres-sures that might lead firms to cut corners. In monopolistic situations, regulation can inhibit the tendency to use monopoly power only for max-imizing profits at consumer expense. In publicly owned monopolies, this kind of supervision may not be as important as maintaining a direct link between policy and service. Governmental monitoring can lead to "positive coordination": the transmission of nonprice information among institu-tions so that policy can be adjusted to meet sectoral goals and increase internal coherence of policy (Jayasuriya 2001).

In the water and sanitation sectors in particular, regulators must insist that firms internalize health and environmental externalities, as well as ensure that consumption is not excessive (Johnstone, Wood, and Hearne 1999). Environmental regulation faces particular challenges due to fiscal constraints, conflicts between environmental protection and certain types of development strategies, and low levels of consciousness about the importance of protecting natural resources. Yet it is clearly part of any rights-based strategy for public goods provision, for reasons related to human health and community well-being. Pollution and resource deple-tion cause problems not only for citizens and communities but also for businesses that depend on natural resources for profit (Vlachou 2004). Air pollution causes damage to productive equipment and infrastructure, while air and soil pollution hurt agriculture. All types of pollution despoil natural attractions and outdoor art and sculpture, which may negatively affect tourism and recreation. Even insurance firms have begun to resist

8. For more on the pros and cons of various types of regulation, please see Foster (1992); HERA (2002); Johnstone, Wood, and Hearne (1999).

environmentally unsound policies based on the future damage climate change is expected to cause. A conflict also arises when the cost of compliance with environmental regulations is passed on to consumers or workers. Finally, as mentioned in chapter 1, a strong argument can be made for protecting the environment as an end in itself. The state plays a key role as arbitrator in environmental conflicts, as various groups call on state institutions "to mediate their access to nature" (Vlachou 2004, 926).

At the World Summit on Sustainable Development, held in Johannesburg from August 26 to September 4, 2002, the governments of Central America affirmed their commitment to environmental protection.[9] They agreed on the importance of reducing water contamination, promoting integrated water management, raising consciousness regarding the value of water, and increasing coordination at the regional, national, and local levels to meet these goals. In energy, they pledged to support efficient, diversified, renewable sources and technologies; to avoid using dirty technologies and overexploitation of resources; and to educate consumers about conservation and environmental protection.[10] Finally, they vowed to create spaces for civil society organizations (e.g., business, NGOs, community organizations, and educational institutions) to participate in dialogue on these issues. Given previous affirmations of Central American governments regarding still-unrealized goals for social and economic rights, these pledges may sound empty. Yet institutional mechanisms that provide leverage for concerned actors to ensure governmental compliance accompanied these affirmations. For example, the Permanent Forum on Civil Society of the Central American Commission on the Environment and Development actively promoted including indigenous groups, farmers, communities of African descent, women, and business in environmental sustainability issues. The Johannesburg conference also generated the Central American Plan on Health and the Environment and the Central American Action Plan for the Integrated Development of Water Resources, which coordinated policy on river basins, resources, and crossnational challenges.

Although decades of neglect, war, and overexploitation had severely damaged the environment in places like El Salvador, these institutional developments were promising. The Salvadoran Legislative Assembly took

9. "Los compromisos ambientales en Centroamérica (I)," *El Salvador Proceso: Informativo Semanal*. Centro de Información, Documentación y Apoyo a la Investigación (UCA), San Salvador, año 23, número 1014, 4 septiembre 2002.

10. "Los compromisos ambientales en Centroamérica (II)," *El Salvador Proceso: Informativo Semanal*, año 23, número 1015, 11 septiembre 2002.

measures of its own that reflected the new environmental consciousness. In May 1998, they adopted the "Environmental Law," designed "to create norms for . . . environmental protection as a basic obligation of the State, the municipalities, and the general population" and to promote state capacity with regard to the protection, conservation, and regeneration of the environment.[11] The goals of the law were fourfold:

1. To slow the rapid deterioration of the environment and to bring the requirements for economic and social development into line with the sustainable use of natural resources and environmental protection.
2. To address environmental problems holistically, taking into account the various interrelated elements that the environment constitutes.
3. To ensure compliance with the Constitution regarding the protection, conservation, and betterment of natural resources.
4. To ensure compliance with international environmental agreements and internally to operationalize international norms on the environment.

Although past Salvadoran governments simply denied funding to projects and laws they saw as interfering with powerful interests, the Environmental Law had its own source of funding, the Environmental Fund, as stipulated in Article 11(f). Groups such as the Salvadoran Investigative Program on Development and the Environment (PRISMA) were hopeful that the law would inspire "a new dynamic, since it has institutional weight behind it" (Gómez 1997, 2), and groups such as the Salvadoran Ecological Union (UNES) used it as leverage in challenging urban development projects that they felt threatened water sources.

Unfortunately, there remained a lack of coordination or a clear idea of which body is the final arbiter in water issues in El Salvador. The only entity in the water sector that acted as a regulator, ANDA, was also a provider. It was difficult for the enterprise to be impartial in rulings regarding violations when acting as both "judge and jury." Institutional development and capacity building were sorely needed in this realm, but there was precedent for the task. In the 1990s, the Salvadoran government, at the urging of the World Bank and the Inter-American Development Bank, created the General Electricity and Telecommunications Superintendent (SIGET). The mandates of this entity included ensuring compliance with sectoral laws

11. Ley del Medio Ambiente, Decreto Legislativo No. 233, República de El Salvador, 4 May 1998.

and regulations; approving rates; determining technical standards; mediating conflicts among providers; policing violations of competitive rules; publishing statistical information; coordinating with environmental authorities; and setting wage levels in accordance with private sector wages.[12] Although heavily oriented toward promoting and protecting competition, SIGET was modeled on advanced legislation in other countries and ostensibly embodied "best practices" from these regulatory frameworks.[13] There were still problems—for example, superintendents changed with each new government, and there was very little political will to depoliticize regulation[14]—but SIGET was a step in the right direction.

Although SIGET was a recent development, the Costa Rican regulatory agency existed in some form for more than seventy-five years. Regulation emerged in response to the deficiency of electrical service and the threat of monopoly consolidation. On July 27, 1928, a group of concerned citizens called the Civic League pressured the state to pass Law No. 77, creating the National Electricity Service (SNE), the country's first regulatory body. Its purpose was to ensure coordination among electric companies, to investigate consumer complaints, to keep a record of municipal and other proceedings, to grant hydroelectric concessions, and to review county-level briefings and motions posed by directors (Rodríguez Argüello 2000). Later laws—No. 21 (1930), No. 55 (1936), No. 258 (1941), and the Ley de Aguas (1942)—granted additional powers to SNE, strengthening its authority and establishing various penalties for people or businesses that violated Law No. 77 and the state monopoly it created to exploit electrical energy. The SNE was one of the pillars of the legal and regulatory framework of the electrical sector until 1996, when Law No. 7593 transformed SNE into the Public Services Regulatory Authority (ARESEP).

The goals of ARESEP were "to fix rates and prices and ensure compliance with norms of quality, quantity, confidence, continuity, opportunity, and optimal provision" (AyA 2002, 5) in the water, electricity, and telecommunications sectors, as well as provide consumer support. With SNE's dismantling and its replacement by ARESEP, the mission of the regulatory entity changed somewhat. The economic crisis of the 1980s led to

12. Ley General de Creación de la SIGET, Decreto Legislativo No. 808, República de El Salvador, 12 September 1996.

13. Raúl Moreno, economist, Center for Consumer Defense, interview with the author, 16 July 2003.

14. "Expertos aconsejan a candidatos sobre economía," *La Prensa Gráfica*, 24 November 2003. The experts quoted are Arturo Zablah, economist and businessperson, and William Pleitez, economist and general coordinator for Human Development for the UNPD in El Salvador.

increased animosity toward SNE on the basis of the perceived need to privatize state-owned enterprises (e.g., CODESA, national banks); reformers saw SNE as an obstacle to this "deregulation." Reforms were intended to roll back its role mainly to address "technical" issues, as well as to establish its independence from politics and executive power. The language creating ARESEP was a strange mix of social democratic discourse laced with market-friendly rhetoric: "We must permit the greatest level of competition and let the market establish its own regulations, based in free competition and the diversity of services on offer; but there must exist an entity with sufficient strength, and legal and moral authority to intervene in the regulation of this market, avoiding abuses of some [firms] over others or avoiding oligopoly or monopoly situations and defending and protecting the rights of the consumer" (Rodríguez Argüello 2000, 228; quote from Lic. Antonio Alvarez Desanti).

In the water sector, ARESEP was to monitor rates but not serve a leading role in planning or resource management. A variety of (sometimes conflicting) entities and legal mandates governed water management. This created a "common agency" problem, with a number of regulatory agencies or ministries involved in the operating conditions of the utility and insufficient coordination between them (Johnstone, Wood, and Hearne 1999). Although there was a great deal of consciousness in Costa Rica regarding the need to view water as a totality and protect the integrity of river basins, the conservation and protection of water resources lagged. Extensive, poorly planned growth in the Central Valley (where the largest cities are situated), pollution, overuse of subterranean water sources, and an insufficient number of sewage systems have recently become problems that threaten the health of water basins.

The "Law of Costa Rican Waters" defined which water was in the public domain, including that in its territorial seas, lagoons, estuaries, beaches, naturally formed lakes, rivers and their tributaries, streams, and springs, as well as subterranean waters and rainwater that flows in riverbeds in the public domain. But incipient struggles among sectors making claims on water resources, particularly tourism and agriculture, added to the complexity of water management. Massive growth in tourism and diversification of export crops led to greatly increased rates of water usage and pollution, even in regions that did not receive a substantial amount of annual rainfall. In Guanacaste, the capacity of the Río Tempisque river basin was exceeded because of surface water concessions, and in the Nicoya Peninsula, one of the driest regions of the country, water scarcity and contamination reached alarming rates because of extensive tourist and other economic development. Under these conditions, there was a press-ing need for one clear authority with the final word in water resources management. A water reform bill to address a number of these issues was under discussion at the time of this writing.

In the regulatory realm, we see again attempts to include multiple organizing principles in the construction of institutions. An observation about these processes foreshadows the arguments to come: in each case, we see the emergence of institutional forms reflected in the political proc-esses and social values of included populations. In Costa Rica, regulation emerged as a call by citizens to protect citizens, and the institutional mech-anism answering this call was subsequently built on common ground. In El Salvador, regulation emerged as a "best practice" transposed onto Salvadoran reality by perhaps well-meaning outsiders, and the resulting institution, though well designed, sputtered without a commitment by local actors to the values it embodied. A regulatory structure without ade-quate support for the values it purports to uphold will be a hollow one.

Public or Semipublic Finance

Public or semipublic forms of finance are indispensable to state-led infra-structural and regulatory development. Funds for investments and subsid-ies often come from the profits of public utility companies, though private firms can be made to reinvest profits if these conditions are written into agreements at the outset and regulation is effective. Such "reciprocity" occurred frequently with industrial policy in East Asia (Amsden 2001) but is much less common in Latin America. In some cases, the central govern-ment transfers funds from general revenue to subsidize social ends, which requires a capacity both to tax and to gather information on recipients. Such transfers are unnecessary when public utilities are highly profitable and effective at utilizing internal cross-subsidies, as with ICE in Costa Rica. Funds may take the form of loans provided by state banks; interna-tional development institutions, such as the World Bank or Inter-Ameri-can Development Bank; and private banks. The state plays a key role in securing these finance sources, including guaranteeing loans and invest-ments that issue from the private sector.

For much of the postwar period, multilateral institutions funded infra-structure development. After these sources of finance dried up in the 1980s, states turned to creative new mechanisms to make ends meet. In Costa Rica, for example, trust funds channeling investment from citizens into particular projects were used to circumvent limits on spending and retraction of credit from IFIs without privatizing. Under this option, ICE created a trust mechanism through the National Bank with the to-be-constructed plant as collateral. The trust released bonds on the national bond market backed by payments that ICE made to the trust through the plant lease. Costa Ricans then bought bonds to invest in this trust. The trust then signed a contract with ICE to build the plant. This sort of mechanism had some market advantages while being completely publicly run and accountable:

> This allows projects to be completed in a very short time, with fewer expenses, which is advantageous; at the same time, it allows ICE to do it with its own labor force. It also forces ICE to be efficient and effective, because it has a contract with a set deadline; very demanding. And on the other hand, those expenses that ICE uses to pay the trust, that loan, are not entered as investment expenses, but current expenditures. . . . At base, everything is the same, but it is necessary to invent mechanisms, round-about ways, to get around the lack of authorization for becoming indebted.[15]

These financial acrobatics, though complicated, allowed ICE to continue funding state-led development in the electricity sector and to resist pressures to privatize.

International support was another way states worked around fiscal and capacity constraints without privatizing, as a water project supported by the Pan-American Health Organization and the World Health Organization in Costa Rica indicates. The Central American Bank for Economic Integration also provided funds for a program to provide potable water, rehabilitate distribution networks, protect river basins, and improve sewage systems in Costa Rica.[16] Recently, a Japanese loan with excellent terms was approved to repair, clean, and extend the existing sanitation system in four river basins.[17]

Even El Salvador found creative ways to finance development in an era of fiscal discipline. The Salvadoran Social Investment Fund for Local

15. Ing. Gilberto de la Cruz, director of CENPE, Centro Nacional de Planificación Eléctrica (ICE), interview with the author, 12 December 2002.

16. "Aprueban 68,5 milliones de dólares para agua potable en Costa Rica," La Nación, 27 May 2005.

17. Meeting with AyA president Ricardo Sancho and other members of AyA management, 9 August 2006.

Development (FISDL) was responsible for a range of development and capacity-building projects throughout the country. Besides promoting electricity, water, roads, and bridges, it provided technical assistance to municipalities for risk management, sustainability, and citizen participation.[18] Its funding came from the general budget, administered through the Treasury,[19] as well as from remittances by Salvadorans living in the United States (Terry and Wilson 2005). Much of FISDL's investment was in the poorest areas of the country, leaving richer markets to the private sector.

In sum, both countries created state institutions for funding essential services. A key difference is that, because of strong resistance to the logic of privatization in Costa Rica, the state sought and found multiple alternatives for financing public works. In El Salvador, by contrast, state elites felt little obligation to seek alternatives and instead embraced a model of marketization and public–private partnerships that allowed the private sector to invest in lucrative urban sectors and left unprofitable rural areas in the hands of the state.

An overview of the utility companies, regulatory bodies, and financial mechanisms discussed thus far appears in table 7.

These mechanisms discussed earlier were designed, in theory, to meet state obligations for public goods as reflected in the social principles discussed in chapter 1. As we have seen, state-owned enterprises are not inherently good or bad for development. To be successful in realizing the goals implicit in the rights discourse, each mechanism requires unique capacities, types of autonomy, and state–society ties to function responsively. Decentralized community development, for example, requires different institutional tasks than centralized, "developmental state" strategies, with distinct training, funding, decision making, and channels of accountability. At a minimum, however, public entities must have human and technical expertise, must be financially viable, and require enough freedom from political and fiscal constraints to act in defense of the principles they are designed to serve. But autonomy and capacity are not enough: institution building must be "embedded" in social objectives—such as regulatory and planning goals, expansion to underserved areas, quality control, and political inclusion—if they are to follow the spirit of rights-based approaches to basic goods. Political allies must also have the will to institutionalize service ideals conducive to reaching human rights goals.

18. "FISDL destina $338.8 milliones a desarrollo," *La Prensa Gráfica*, 20 Feburary 2004.
19. Representative, FISDL: Salvadoran Social Investment Fund for Local Development, confidential interview with the author, 28 July 2003.

Table 7   State support for water and electricity, Costa Rica and El Salvador

	Costa Rica	El Salvador
Public utilities and cooperatives	• The Costa Rican Electricity and Telecommunications Institute (ICE) • The National Power and Light Company (CNFL) • Municipal entities (JASEC, ESPH) • The Institute of Aqueducts and Sewage Systems (AyA) • The National Subterranean Water, Irrigation, and Drainage Service • Rural water and electricity cooperatives	• The Lempa River Hydroelectric Executive Commission (CEL) • Geotérmica Salvadoreña (GESAL) • The National Administration of Aqueducts and Sewage Systems (ANDA) • Asociación Nacional para la Distribución y Defensa del Agua Rural (ANDAR)
Regulatory agencies	• The Public Services Regulatory Authority (ARESEP; formerly the National Electricity Service [SNE])—electricity and water	• ANDA—water • General Electricity and Telecommunications Superintendent (SIGET)—electricity
Public or semipublic finance	• Trusts and other fiduciary mechanisms • Funds for basic services secured from external sources through government guarantees	• Social Investment Fund for Local Development (FISDL) • Funds from external sources through government guarantees

The Institutionalization of Public Accountability

Accountability mechanisms are the backbone of political will. Even well-meaning policy makers may not have enough political leverage to "do the right thing" without public pressure. Recent efforts to create responsive public goods sectors have focused on the enabling effects of "good governance" and political institutions that can promote social and economic rights. As the United Nations Development Programme (UNDP 2002a) argues, "just as human development requires much more than raising incomes, governance for human development requires much more than having effective public institutions. Good governance also requires fostering fair, accountable institutions that protect human rights and basic freedoms" (3).

Several political mechanisms can help communities determine the values they consider inviolable regarding essential services, as well as hold leaders accountable for instituting these principles in public policy (Smulovitz and Peruzzotti 2000). Horizontal accountability that creates a balance of power between the executive, legislative, and judicial branches of government can facilitate officeholder responsiveness and allow for appeals regarding policies that are unresponsive to rights-based social principles. Especially important for our later discussion of the advent of neoliberalism will be institutions such as constitutional courts, public accounting offices, public service commissions, auditors, and anticorruption bodies. Vertical accountability mechanisms that link citizens to representatives either directly (through elections) or indirectly (through political parties) can also contribute to demand representation and (at least ostensibly) hold representatives liable for unmet claims (O'Donnell 1999) (see table 8). When formal accountability mechanisms fail, more direct mechanisms for political control based on civil-society and citizen action are also available and increasingly utilized.

Formal Accountability Mechanisms

Like the service delivery entities discussed earlier, institutions of representative democracy require institutional, technical, and financial capacity to carry out the many tasks in their mandate. They also require political capacity, where state actors have effective channels through which to respond to demands and mediate among interests. The most stable democracies in Latin America (Costa Rica, Uruguay, and democratic Chile) can be explained by the existence of strong political parties and a substantial capacity to design agreements among factions (Torres-Rivas 1997). Another important factor in the success of state projects has been the ability to create ties between the state and business classes, while remaining true to state goals (Evans 1995). Although this "embedded autonomy" may create "attractive opportunities for rent-seeking," these can be tempered by "internal norms and a dependably rewarding system of long-term career benefits" for state officials (Evans 1996, 1126). However, it is not enough for democratic embeddedness for states and businesses to work together. Businesspeople "want the government to arrive at decisions on the basis of information and advice supplied by the interested industrialist group. What they propose is business intervention in government rather than government intervention in business" (Mosk 1950, 29).

To enhance the ability of the state to meet its obligations appropriately, linkages between the state and citizens must also be created. Such accountability mechanisms give states a degree of independence from

Table 8 State- and community-led institutionalization of accountability

	Relevant actors	Tasks contributing to adequate accountability
Horizontal accountability (balance of power)	Executive branch	• Policy making • Regulation
	Legislative branch	• Administrative oversight • Personnel appointments
	Judicial branch (e.g., constitutional courts)	• Judicial review
	Oversight agencies (e.g., auditors, public accounting offices, public service commissions)	• Enforcement power • Investigative power
Vertical accountability		
Electoral	Political parties with legislative representation	• Demand representation • Regulation • Policy making
	Citizens	• Voting • Referendums
Societal	Civil society and business associations, nongovernmental organizations, social movements	• Information dissemination, public awareness • Investigation by oversight bodies • Agenda setting • Lobbying • Mobilization, direct action
	Ombudspersons Consumer protection agencies	• Investigation • Information dissemination, public awareness • Litigation
	Media	• Investigation, public exposure • Agenda setting
	Other mechanisms	• Commissions, hearings • Working groups • Recall mechanisms

SOURCE: Table adapted from Smulovitz and Peruzzotti (2000).

businesses and corporations, allowing them greater freedom to carry out socially minded policies that might otherwise be resisted (Garrett 1998). Ties between the central state and local communities also encourage public legitimacy for state projects. When citizens trust that the state will follow through on its obligations, they are more likely to support state projects and respond positively to public policy (Evans 1996). For participation to be meaningful, however, the public must possess capacities for organization, political engagement, and awareness that effectively link demands with outcomes. Part of this capacity can arise from education and access to information, technology, and other knowledge-based resources often denied poor populations. Citizens also must have *autonomy*, in the form of human rights (freedom of speech and assembly, freedom from coercion, and freedom to form unions and petition the government).

Accountability mechanisms were integral to the Costa Rican model of social solidarity from its inception. Its impressive capacities for planning, implementation, and public administration were matched by equally impressive democratic processes. A relatively accessible congress, open commissions, and deliberative decision making strengthened state legitimacy, thereby enabling it to carry out policies with the consent and cooperation of large sectors of the population. Consequently, nonstate forms of claims making were fairly uncommon in Costa Rica until recently. The executive branch was historically prevented from carrying out sweeping economic reforms, in part because there were certain veto points that prevented radical action and increased broader accountability (Clark 2001). The main veto point was the Legislative Assembly, which is the strongest branch of government. Others included the Constitutional Chamber of the Supreme Court (Sala IV), the comptroller,[20] the attorney general, the ombudsperson, and the semiautonomous state institutions. The result was that reforms were slower and sometimes involved gridlock but were also relatively accountable and based on broad inclusion.

The Constitutional Court is an institution of the judiciary that rules on constitutional issues, based on existing laws, in situations that affect citizen rights. Its rulings are not open to appeal, and compliance is obligatory. Its rulings have redefined the water sector, especially in regard to the problems of institutional overlap (AyA 2002). The Sala IV has also acted to strike down a number of economic reforms as unconstitutional, such as certain contracts between state entities and private firms. The comptroller, for its part, has the authority to cancel corrupt contracts or those in which the contracted firm did not meet contract stipulations. It has been strict in disallowing projects to go through when contracted parties do not follow

---

20. The comptroller oversees several institutions discussed in the previous section, including ARESEP, AyA, MINAE, MINSALUD, ESPH, and municipalities.

proper procedure, frustrating neoliberals and private investors but upholding a vital protective role for Costa Rican society. The ombudsperson is charged with protecting the rights and interests of citizens and disclosing and publicizing those rights. The ombudsperson is an organ of the legislative branch but has functional, administrative, and discretionary independence, and acts regularly to defend specific citizen claims before public sector entities (AyA 2002). Finally, state-owned enterprises also possess some autonomy to resist executive reforms that functionaries see as damaging to the internal workings of their enterprises.

It is not difficult to find interesting cases of democracy at work in Costa Rica. For example, the Citizens Audit on the Quality of Democracy was carried out from 1998 to 2001, to identify where democracy was meeting citizen ideals and where it was falling short (UNDP 2002b). After a group of "notables" helped define a set of shared democratic aspirations, field research was carried out regarding how people evaluate democracy, and a citizens' panel then compared those results against the aspirations. They found great contrasts among different aspects of democratic life, with high ratings for the quality of the electoral system and constitutional review of public policies through the Sala IV. Respondents gave low ratings for local government, clientelism, bureaucrats' poor treatment of citizens, and lack of citizen participation in civic organizations. An important insight from this audit was that "citizens view democracy as a way of organizing society so that people do not suffer extreme inequalities that impede the exercise of their citizenship" (UNDP 2002b, 83). Democracy was deemed to be more than just elections; to these respondents, it was considered a multilevel process of participation in social and economic decisions. The audit led, among other things, to a proposal for administrative reform that incorporated the rights of citizens and aimed to improve bureaucratic handling of citizen claims. These experiments, as well as periodic processes of *concertación*,[21] demonstrate the relative robustness of Costa Rican democracy.

Through the last two decades of the twentieth century, more and more Latin American countries saw elected officials succeeded by other elected

---

21. The meaning of *concertación* is difficult to translate. Sometimes it is translated as "negotiation," but as David Escobar Galindo (poet, novelist, university dean, and language expert) argues, "negotiation happens between groups that, being immersed in a dispute over basic legitimacy and consequent legality, seek to develop understanding and common ground in ways that allow them to coexist peacefully." *Concertación*, however, "happens between groups that have the same rights and responsibilities, who try to come to agreement regarding something over which they compete" ("La necesidad de concertación," *La Prensa Gráfica*, 23 August 2003). Negotiation can bring peace; *concertación* is what sustains it. Rough equivalents are "reconciliation," or "harmonization" of interests, but I prefer to keep the original Spanish.

officials, human rights increasingly respected, and representative democracy seemingly functioning (Casteñeda 1996). The poor were more informed about human rights and increasingly demanded that they be respected. In El Salvador, for example, rights-based claims were central to opposition struggles. Resistance movements arose in part from union attempts to exercise their rights to organize not just workers but also recently urbanized peasants who lived under stark conditions in newly created shantytowns. Rural peasants, meanwhile, demanded higher wages and prices for sugarcane, as well as the right to own their land. Priests trained in liberation theology joined the fray to fight for social and economic rights, and many were martyred for their efforts.

Democratic reforms were more fragile than in Costa Rica, but they brought new legal institutions to the region "that allow[ed] citizens and collective actors to claim and petition for constitutional rights that they consider to have been violated" (Smulovitz and Peruzzotti 2000, 153). The Salvadoran Peace Accords incorporated many social movement demands, fostering expectations regarding both democratic and economic inclusion. Among the terms of the agreement were the restructuring of the military, which had been used to repress social claims, the establishment of the Office of the Human Rights Defense Attorney (PDDH), the incorporation of insurgents into the political machinery, and the creation of new means for representation and accountability. The polemical protest–repression cycle eased for a time, with protest limited to issues unresolved through institutional channels.

The PDDH was given a key role in defending and promoting economic, social, and cultural rights as stipulated in international agreements. It was designed to monitor the functionaries and offices of the state, "recognizing and respecting human dignity, defending rights, denouncing violations, safeguarding legitimate interests, spreading information about these rights, building citizen and civil society capacity to recognize and defend their rights, and preserving the established legal order" (Alvarez Basso 1992, 20). It served to force socioeconomic rights to the foreground as a public issue. Another small but important economic concession to come out of the accords was the Foro de Concertación, which was designed to address the economic inequality at the root of the war in negotiations among government, business, and unions. The agenda included a discussion of how the social costs of structural adjustment would be mitigated, as well as how "the economic and social problems that will arise due to the end of conflict" would be resolved (Wood 2000, 91). Unfortunately, the Foro operated with few resources, government and business willingness to discuss labor rights was lacking, and there was a disconnect between representatives and workers in the labor movement and distrust in the tripartite commission.[22] For a brief moment, the Foro created hope for participatory governance among some members of the polity; eventually, however, it simply dwindled away.

Another promise that came out of the Peace Accords was the Salvadoran government's pledge in 1992 to present a draft consumer protection law to the Legislative Assembly (CDC 1997). This proposal, along with one that the nongovernmental Center for Consumer Defense (CDC) submitted at the time, contributed to the formulation and approval of an important set of norms. For the first time, the state recognized consumers as subjects of rights and responsibilities vis-à-vis both public and private providers of goods and services, and established regulations designed to reduce fraud and market abuses. This law also established the Consumer Protection Office to ensure compliance with the law. There were some problems with lack of clarity regarding how contracts with private companies would be monitored, as well as how complaints should be filed, but this was a start. The CDC became involved in trying to resolve these lingering issues, as well as trying to improve the law. It also served an important role in pressuring for government action on behalf of consumers when these other mechanisms failed.

During uncertain transition periods, such as that experienced by El Salvador in the 1990s, actors have a greater degree of agency to create new institutions and reform existing ones. Unions championing social and economic justice, for example, joined former guerrillas to carve out a space in the postwar political sphere and spearhead resistance to the neoliberal policies implemented by the ARENA Party. Yet the difficulty of altering state practices and societal attitudes about the state tempered these transformative actions (Call 2003). The historical reality in El Salvador consisted of caudillo, civil, and military governments, with "power as an instrument of exclusion, not inclusion. There were no alternatives: either submit or be beaten. There was no space for cooptation, much less reconciliation" (Zamora 1997). Faith in the state to create conditions conducive to economic and social rights was difficult to come by under these conditions. At the same time, the peace process presented a rare opportunity to shift this equation: "The weakening or dislocation of state power . . . opens the door to institutional reform," in which "agency by national and international actors can pay off in the face of structural obstacles posed by culture, economic structure, and warfare" (Zamora 1997, 860–61).

22. "Débil acuerdo del FES," *El Salvador Proceso: Informativo Semanal*, número 558, 14 April 1993.

Yet this is only a window of opportunity, not a deterministic process. In El Salvador, accountability and community participation in the post–civil war period left much to be desired, thereby casting a shadow over otherwise dramatic institutional reforms. The peace agreement "was in essence a political compromise in which the Left agreed to a democratic political regime and a capitalist economy with only limited socioeconomic reform, and the Right agreed to the Left's participation in a democratic political regime along with some socioeconomic reform" (Wood 2000, 85). From the outside, it appeared that much had been accomplished, but to ordinary Salvadorans, the shortcomings were worrying. As one commentator argued, "much of the social instability of the country and the collective frustration is due, in large part, to institutional weakness, which leads to distrust and a retreat from institutions that appear to serve particular people or groups, and not citizens as a whole."[23] The district attorney, the General Accounting Office, and political parties all failed, by this account, to convert themselves into democratic institutions, and continued to reflect the authoritarianism from which they emerged. Transforming these and other institutions is one of the greatest challenges that remain for El Salvador.

Can positive synergies between the state and society be constructed? Path-dependent national characteristics, such as a lack of trust, low state capacity, and inequality, as well as resource constraints and hamstringing by IFIs, can certainly interfere (UNDP 2002b). Yet it is possible to address the lack of social capital endowments by finding ways to generate solidarity on a broader and more efficacious scale (Evans 1996). The mobilization of more "universalistic identities," such as those reflected in the human rights principles discussed in chapter 1, is one way to pursue this end. Robust public institutions themselves can foster democratic externalities "because they are capable of formulating more nuanced ways of distributing power and therefore of supporting decentralization and openness to local self-organization" (Evans 1996, 1126). When states are resource or capacity poor, institution building around public goods can create alliances, information exchange, and goodwill among states and citizens across a meaningful spatial territory, thus strengthening both state and society.

23. Editorial, *El Salvador Proceso: Informativo Semanal*, año 23, número 1006, 3 julio 2002.

Informal Accountability Mechanisms

Continuing problems with formal accountability, however, strengthen the appeal of more direct mechanisms for political control by citizens and civil-society organizations (Smulovitz and Peruzzotti 2000; see table 8). This "politics of societal accountability" is characterized by "the emergence of rights-oriented discourse and politics, media exposés of government scandals, and social movements organized around demands for due process," among other things (147). The increasing use of ombudsmen, consumer protection agencies, and citizen-based commissions contributes to the capacity of civil society to investigate complaints, litigate, expose wrongdoing, set agendas for change, lobby, and even mobilize for direct action. These alternative mechanisms of monitoring and agenda setting are growing in importance throughout Latin America as a means of overcoming democratic deficits.

Media that fosters informed debate, mobilizes civic engagement, and gives voice to a range of viewpoints is a vital input to a healthy democracy. Watchdog media in particular is extremely important for stimulating debate, monitoring elections, exposing rights violations or political corruption, and empowering excluded groups such as women or indigenous people. Growing press freedom allowed media to hold politicians' feet to the fire in both El Salvador and Costa Rica. The "Interview of the Day," a widely watched Salvadoran talk show, was a good example. The highly respected journalist (and now Salvadoran president) Mauricio Funes presented controversial topics each morning, which often formed the basis for public discourse on the street, in workplaces, and in other social settings. Channel 12, which hosted Funes's program, received an award in 2000 from the PDDH for outstanding work in education, diffusion of information, and protection of human rights in the country.[24] Funes was later fired without explanation, though his open criticism of the government's neoliberal economic agenda by guests on his program was a likely cause.[25]

---

24. "La declaración universal de derechos humanos, aquí y ahora." *El Salvador Proceso: Informativo Semanal*, año 21, número 931, Diciembre 13, 2000.

25. According to Funes, problems with the parent company, Mexican-owned TV Azteca, started in January 2001, "when the president of the company called me from Mexico to complain about our policy of informing the public [about social issues] that we had rolled out in the days after the January 13th earthquake." "Despido masivo de periodistas en El Salvador," *El Nuevo Diario* (Nicaragua), 22 February 2005.

But Funes and his unapologetic and pointed critiques returned with a vengeance with his bid for president in 2009, when for the first time in modern history, a progressive candidate was elected to national executive power. Although it is difficult to say with certainty the precise causes of this dramatic electoral victory, Funes's role as a trusted proponent of inclusive dialogue and public information was likely an important contributing factor.

An active media can contribute to government effectiveness by creating familiarity and trust, improving bureaucratic morale and "public-minded behavior" (Tendler 1997, 116), and enhancing the prestige of state actors implementing programs. People in power sometimes welcome an excuse to do the right thing, and the media can provide exactly this kind of pressure. When the media are biased, accountability must be sought through other means, such as independent media monitoring bodies, professional codes of ethics, official ombudspersons, and well-trained and aware journalists. Citizen mobilization can also serve this purpose. In El Salvador, for example, movements emerged calling for price controls in the privatized electricity sector and opposing water privatization. Two key players were the Center for Consumer Defense and the Salvadoran Ecology Union, both newly created groups that operated outside formal channels of representation but that had some success in influencing policy makers.

These approaches address an obvious deficit of blunt electoral democracy. When traditional channels of interest representation are not functioning, action by civil society can promote democratic policies and procedures in several ways. It limits state power by insisting on accountability via democratic political institutions; promotes political formation of citizens; fosters the collection and dissemination of information regarding rights and obligations; creates channels of interest representation outside of parties; and brings together a wide range of potentially intersecting interests, thereby mitigating polarization and promoting organization, solidarity, and compromise. Collective action can strengthen movements by increasing expectations and pooling resources. The vertical yet nonelectoral nature of "societal accountability" opens up possibilities for democracy through institutional (e.g., legal claims) and noninstitutional (e.g., social mobilization) means that lie between the atomized voter and the system of checks and balances, in the realm of organized civil society. Temporally, it operates between legitimate periods of vertical accountability (i.e., between elections) to comprise a continuous monitoring and agenda-setting force. Spatially, it can address any sector, policy, or state actor at any level of government. Its mechanisms encourage responsible citizenship rather than political apathy, a serious and growing problem, even in Costa Rica.

There are, of course, drawbacks to the "politics of societal accountability" approach, as a small but vocal minority may unduly influence policy to its advantage. Misuse of the media can also be dangerous, as the burden of proof for someone accused of wrongdoing is often "guilty until proven innocent." Drawbacks to this kind of voice can be countered by establishing means for evaluating and addressing grievances. This makes it possible for a wider array of actors—not just individuals and parties but also NGOs, civil society organizations, and social movements—to target elected politicians, unelected bureaucrats, and corporate actors alike. Their impact comes through reembedding state action by forcing it to answer to societal principles of organization and damaging the political capital of those who act irresponsibly (Smulovitz and Peruzzotti 2000). Action of this sort can also mobilize traditional accountability mechanisms, such as the courts and regulatory agencies. These factors offer incentives for political actors not to commit wrongdoing and to act in the public interest.

Societal accountability mechanisms alone are not enough, however. Calls for "inclusion" in economic decision making and local "ownership" of policies can be heard on all sides of the debate. But as is clear in Latin America, talk is cheap without institutions: "Paradoxically, the clamor regarding citizen participation does not come with any attempt to include the opinion of citizens in weighty institutional decisions. For example, these opinions were not taken into account at the moment that public enterprises were privatized [in El Salvador]. . . . When the authorities denounce the lack of citizen collaboration, it seems they are trying more to cover up their own inadequacy and lack of will to confront societal problems than to include citizens in the management of public affairs."[26]

Even radical movements incorporated into government face problems of institutional responsiveness. Progressive governments can create spaces and opportunities for participation for popular movements, but only "as long as the movements in some form accept being embedded into state institutions, which weakens their ability to inspire social mobilization" (Zibechi 2005, 15). Becoming an actor in the political arena can mean adopting the "logic of the state" rather than of resistance. This can be good, as continual resistance is tiring and ultimately not as effective as coordination, but it can also lead to co-optation and the disappearance of

26. "La participación ciudadana," *El Salvador Proceso: Informativo Semanal,* año 21, número 911, 19 julio 2000.

critical voices. Staying connected to popular bases is vital, both for legitimacy and for staying attuned to issues of importance to communities. Societal mechanisms are not always effective, and state actors undoubtedly find ways around them. But with the right combination of factors (mobilization, legal action, and media, for example), their use can lead to a more responsive democracy. In both Costa Rica and El Salvador, such mechanisms were instrumental in slowing or halting privatization efforts.

State-Society Synergies

The state continues to play a key role in creating the institutional means for achieving social and economic rights; without political action, accountability is weakened (Crouch 2000; Torres-Rivas 1997). States can (though they do not always) strengthen the capacities of the public by ensuring a free press, supporting public television and radio, creating spaces for commissions and working groups that admit civil society organizations, supporting consumer defense groups, establishing mechanisms by which complaints from consumer organizations or ombudsmen can be heard, and promoting resources for public education. The resources and power of different civil society groups vary, with great advantage afforded to business organizations. When groups are forced to wrestle unaided in the marketplace of ideas, those with greater resources enjoy a tremendous advantage. This analysis suggests that neoliberal policies that advocate for extensive civil society responsibilities for oversight and management, especially in public goods sectors in which private firms provide services, may be misguided. Civil society alone cannot ensure that economic policy is embedded in societal norms. It is not that civil society and social capital are not important; rather, they are weak accountability mechanisms in the absence of institutional means of influencing debate and holding policy makers accountable. Because citizenship claims may contradict market principles, social objectives have to be *politically* secured through the mechanisms discussed previously if states are to achieve the "full protection and promotion" of social and economic rights as set out in UN agreements.

The manner in which accountability is institutionalized (or not) has important implications for "double movements" (Polanyi 1944). Some double movements are themselves legal and constitutional mechanisms that arise in response to a perceived need for greater protection of the public interest. Other double movements comprise protest as a strategy, especially when alternatives prove inadequate. For example, in Costa Rica in 2000, the population attempted to participate in decisions regarding openings to the private sector in electricity and telecommunications, fully expecting to be included in the process based on its experiences with democracy. But the people were thwarted by politicians and thus resorted to street protest and other direct action techniques. In El Salvador shortly after the Peace Accords, social protest declined considerably as expectations rose. But as traditional accountability channels proved inadequate, protests increased. A series of strikes against the privatization of health care in 2002–3 and water in 2006–7 were the most recent and dramatic examples. Also, the ways in which the state incorporates certain subgroups of civil society may fragment double movements along institutional lines. For example, in 2000, unions and environmentalists both offered alternatives to privatization of the Costa Rican electricity and telecommunications firm, yet because of greater influence and channels of interest representation within the Costa Rican state, the unions were able to get their version before the Legislative Assembly. Environmentalists understood their weaker position and adjusted their strategy accordingly: "Unions have the political power to push forward their proposal, but us? Not necessarily. . . . In the long run, the struggle is going to play out not only in the Assembly but in the streets."[27]

In this chapter, I have shown how the implementation of economic and social rights in public goods sectors entails the institutionalization of certain organizing principles. Although states may fail to institute healthy public goods sectors, this is not a given; many states can and have created adequate, capable, and accountable structures, even in the least probable places (Tendler 1997; Muhairwe 2005). Both Costa Rica and El Salvador have built state and community institutions to address the need for public goods, environmental protection, holistic planning, and public accountability. This sets up a counterfactual to neoliberal public goods approaches: the unrealized potential for state- and community-led public provision. In chapter 4, I will discuss the fraught processes of grafting market-oriented blueprints, policies, and principles onto the institutional terrain described here. As we will see, value conflicts underlying these different policy choices, especially when accompanied by a failure to live up to promises for social and economic rights, can trigger public discontent. Rising expectations and inadequate channels of accountability exacerbate this tendency.

27. Gabriel Rivas-Ducca, Friends of the Earth and the Federation for Environmental Conservation, Costa Rica, interview with the author, 28 January 2003.

"OVER OUR DEAD BODIES":
THE EMERGENCE OF PRIVATIZATION POLICIES

The institutional arrangements discussed in chapter 2 did not arise spontaneously from programmatic theories of public goods management but rather emerged from struggles and compromises over ownership, control, and design of essential resources sectors. Likewise, challenges to interventionist states after 1980 did not arise from an amorphous "globalization" but from purposeful alterations in the structure and regulation of global markets through capital mobility, trade liberalization, and flexible production. The current global political economy places limits on how states are able to secure domestic economic stability and development, and this in turn constrains their choices in designing rights-responsive public policy. This does not mean that states are powerless (Hirst and Thompson 1996), only that there are new challenges they must face. An analysis of conflicts that have erupted over marketization in Central America in the postwar and post–Cold War periods highlights real-world interests and power relations at stake in the pursuit of different public goods models and underscores the problematic and contentious nature of public goods privatization as a development strategy.

The Postwar Political Economy of Public Goods in Costa Rica and El Salvador

States in Central America made some progress in expanding public goods infrastructure in the postwar period. The relationship between state activity and the fulfillment of rights to essential goods, however, was not always straightforward. In the case of Costa Rica, there was a strong correlation between nationalization, state-led infrastructure expansion, and social and economic rights based on social compromise. After the end of the civil war in 1948, the government abolished the military, thereby making funds that other countries in the region spent on weapons and internal conflicts available for other uses. The newly elected National Liberation Party (PLN) deepened social reforms initiated by an alliance of the National Republican and Communist Parties (CP) in the 1940s (Yashar 1997). Although there was some continued contention among elites into the 1950s (Bowman 2002), they eventually agreed to accept egalitarian policies and participation to keep the social peace, thus enabling the state to carry out policies with the consent of large sectors of the population. Successive governments, regardless of ideological inclination, reproduced this model by investing in health, education, physical infrastructure, and more recently environmental protection. The Constitution, ratified in 1949, formed the legal basis of a uniquely Costa Rican state, which strongly embraced elements of intervention and social democratic consciousness. Article 74 established the inalienability of social rights, requiring those who govern actively to seek the means to create equitable national policies. Costa Ricans widely construed these guidelines to entail the use of state institutions to fulfill national development goals, create political and economic stability, and foster greater liberty, broadly conceived, in which social rights strengthened political freedoms. The legitimacy of the political system rested on the popular belief that social democracy could provide both order and progress.

Costa Rica had relied heavily on private utility companies during the late nineteenth and early twentieth centuries, as had many other liberal states. In electricity, for example, the state granted broad concessions to foreign investors in order to maintain monetary equilibrium and exchange rate stability, yet this system proved inadequate for the wider population, which experienced low rates of coverage and deficient service. A national debate regarding the future of electricity culminated in the nationalization of hydroelectricity resources and the foundation of a national regulatory body, the National Electricity Service (SNE) in 1928. SNE immediately became embroiled in struggles with the powerful private electricity companies, a conflict that continued into the 1940s. In a pattern very similar to postprivatization struggles in Argentina and elsewhere in Latin America, the SNE discovered that "investors were not interested [in greater capital investments], given the lack of profitability and the inability to recoup their inputs under current tariff structures, and given illegal connections" (Rodríguez Argüello 2000, 85).

Costa Rica finally chose nationalization as the route to ensuring adequate electrical coverage. Just as double movements in Polanyi's time were pragmatic responses to the deficiencies of unregulated markets, "state interventionism . . . can only be explained vis-à-vis the imperative of responding to the multiple demands of society, and one of those, unsatisfied, was the provision of electricity" (Rodríguez Argüello 2000, 134). As discussed in chapter 2, Costa Rica is remarkable for the high level of infrastructural and resource development that followed. "Autonomous institutions" in water, electricity, and telecommunications actively and effectively promoted the extension of services to both urban and rural populations, which in turn contributed to a marked improvement in the quality of life for the average citizen. This "solidary model" reflected an implicit social pact that promoted a relatively egalitarian distribution not only of income but also of goods and services.[1] Public goods policies included even the tiniest and most isolated communities, and as a result, more than 99 percent of Costa Ricans enjoy access to electricity, 97 percent to improved water sources, and 92 percent to proper sanitation (see table 9). Government services operate relatively efficiently, prices are substantially lower than elsewhere in the region,[2] and—important for this discussion—Costa Ricans see an active, interventionist state as central to citizenship.

Although the Salvadoran Constitution of 1950 adopted many of the same principles as the Costa Rican Constitution regarding social and economic rights, outcomes have been radically different, especially in rural areas. The military-oligarchy coalition that controlled, respectively, the political and economic power of the country during the pre–civil war period was little disposed to ensuring that the needs of the population were met. Though this coalition supported import-substitution industrialization (ISI), it was built on an authoritarian rather than a social democratic basis. Powerful groups were interested in securing their own power base but tended to ignore growing injustices until they finally spurred civil war. During the war, the Duarte administration attempted to integrate Christian Democratic principles into public policy, but the U.S. Agency for International Development (USAID) and private sector resistance to state intervention stymied their efforts (Segovia 2002). The war itself sapped

1. This model should not be confused with *solidarismo*, which is more concerned with coordination between labor and management in decision-making processes.

2. The only other country with comparably low electricity rates is Honduras; it is also the only other one that had not privatized electricity distribution.

Table 9 Basic goods indicators in Central America

Country	Electricity in home[a]	Residential electricity prices[b]	Improved water source,[c] 2004 (% households)[a]			Improved sanitation source,[d] 2004 (% households)[a]		
	(% households)	(USD/cents per Kwh)	Total	Urban	Rural	Total	Urban	Rural
Costa Rica	99.1	8.06	97	100	92	92	89	97
El Salvador	79.6	14.34	84	99	70	62	77	39
Guatemala	78.5	11.79	95	99	92	86	90	82
Honduras	71.1	7.76	87	95	81	69	87	54
Nicaragua	72.4	17.13	79	90	63	47	56	34
Panama	Not reported	12.71	90	99	79	73	89	51

[a] Economic Commission for Latin America and the Caribbean (ECLAC 2007).

[b] Organización Latinoamericana de Energía (2007).

[c] Improved sources include household connections, public standpipes, boreholes, protected wells and springs, and rainwater collections. Unimproved sources are unprotected wells and springs, vendor-provided water, bottled water, and tanker truck–provided water.

[d] Improved sanitation includes connection to public sewers, connection to septic systems, pour-flush latrines, simple pit latrines, and ventilated improved pit latrines. Not considered improved are service or bucket latrines (excreta manually removed), public latrines, and open latrines.

resources for investment, pushed public goods from the policy agenda, and destroyed (often literally) the country's physical infrastructure; by 1990, only 54.2 percent of the population had access to electricity,[3] 66 percent had improved water sources, and 73 percent had sewage treatment.[4] Fifteen years after the end of the conflict, the water and electricity sectors showed moderate improvements; 80 percent of the population had access to electricity, and 84 percent had access to improved water sources. Yet only 62 percent received improved sanitation services, a loss of 11 percent since 1990.

It is difficult to evaluate these contradictory changes reliably, as coverage tends to improve in countries emerging from civil war (United Nations Development Programme [UNDP] 2001). The involvement of nongovernmental organizations in water provision, as well as state resources channeled to rural areas, contributed to improvements. The case of electricity in El Salvador highlights the complexity of evaluating progress, as well as the relative contribution of public and private sectors. San Salvador's electricity distribution company CAESS (Electrical Lighting Company of San Salvador), which the government nationalized in 1986, had expanded coverage to 82.2 percent of the urban population by 1990.[5] Yet the company never expanded to rural areas, and in 1990, only 22.6 percent of rural inhabitants were covered. According to an employee of the Lempa River Executive Hydroelectric Commission (CEL), "private firms were not interested in bringing services to these areas because the way the electrical sector is structured, the real business for private companies comes with high levels of consumption."[6] Here, we see the first signs of conflict between market-based management of public goods and the ecological principles discussed in chapter 1: private firms require more rather than less consumption for profitability; a healthy environment requires the opposite.

Because profits from the lucrative urban company were private before 1986, they were not available to finance electricity coverage in the unprofitable (but socially relevant) outlying areas. A state-run rural distribution company, paid for by public revenues, became necessary precisely because private companies were not expanding outside the capital. Principles of equity, rights, and social justice were not part of the calculus of

3. CEL, Boletines de estadísticas eléctricas.
4. ECLAC, BADEINSO, 2002.
5. CEL, Boletines de estadísticas eléctricas.
6. Alirio Romero, secretary-general, STSEL (Industrial Union of Electricity Sector Unions) (public sector), interview with the author, 20 August 2003.

the private firm, which skimmed off the funds that might have made it universally possible to institute these principles. Even in urban areas, private investors, aware that the concession might not be renewed, became less inclined to invest in the sector as the end of the concession period neared. "In the ten years (before nationalization), the company was allowed to deteriorate,"[7] thus harming urban consumers. The Salvadoran government, true to its reputation for protecting private interests even at the cost of social neglect, did not nationalize CAESS's assets until the war led to a near collapse of the electricity system. After only ten years in state hands, the government reprivatized electricity distribution, with mixed results (see chapter 4).

In the water sector as well, the Salvadoran state has not historically acted out of a commitment to social and economic rights but rather to shorter-term political considerations. In 1961, the government created the public water company the National Aqueducts and Sewers Administration (ANDA). This autonomous institution, like those in Costa Rica, was supposed to provide water and sanitation services through a centralized entity across the entire national territory. In practice, the early ANDA did not take responsibility for this more ambitious project and instead focused on larger cities. Just as the private electricity distribution company sought densely populated areas to improve profit margins, state actors used ANDA to serve readily accessible populations with minimal effort, thereby enhancing ability to govern and support for elite rule. The state firm was relatively successful in those places where efforts were channeled, as reflected in table 9: discrepancies between urban and rural water and sewage coverage were greater in El Salvador than in any other country in the region.

Some lessons from the Salvadoran record should be noted: with resources and capacity, both public and private firms have found some success at carrying out the technical task of public goods provision. Yet private firms did not have incentives to invest in unprofitable areas without state intervention. States, meanwhile, were more likely to invest in poor or sparsely populated areas when they had the political incentives to do so, but the privatization of profits debilitated them. Thus, for sectoral success under any Salvadoran scenario, greater institutional capacity and responsiveness to social ends would be necessary. This highlights important path-dependent differences among countries in terms of economic and

7. Santos Cordón García, secretary-general, SIES (Salvadoran Electrical Industry Union), interview with the author, 23 July 2003.

social rights: although the rhetorical acceptance of such rights may be identical, other requirements—such as state capacity and political will, reinforced by accountability—are indispensable to their realization. Without these other factors, rights discourse will be nothing more than words.

If, given the right incentives, state-owned enterprises can play a pivotal role in channeling resources into public goods, as the postwar record suggests, why did international financial institutions and others abandon the idea of state-led development during the 1980s and 1990s? Was it that even if states were once successful at expanding infrastructure, those days were gone? Had the global political economy changed too dramatically for the state to carry out such tasks? In the pages that follow, I argue that a liberal economic order in public goods arose not due to the exigencies of globalization but rather due to the implementation of a political and economic project, backed by identifiable interests, and manifested in concrete institutions. This project tied the hands of the state, making it difficult to improve on once-successful public sector strategies for expanding infrastructure and ensuring access to basic goods. "Globalization" only provided a rhetorical justification for these projects.

Post–Cold War Triumph of Neoliberal Ideology

"Neoliberalism" refers to a set of policy prescriptions, widely disseminated in Latin America under the rubric of the Washington Consensus, in which markets were the preferred mechanism for economic management. It comprised theories, policies, and practices with ideational elements of the classical liberalism of Friedrich Hayek, the monetarism of Milton Friedman, and the public choice theory of James Buchanan. It also shared family resemblances with Robert Nozick's libertarianism. Neoliberal political theory warned of the dangers of state intervention, rent seeking, and interest-group politics. Neoliberal practice translated those theories into "free market" policies, including privatization, trade liberalization, and fiscal austerity. The ideas reflected in these practices, as discussed in chapter 1, included the belief that markets are the most efficient mechanisms for allocating scarce resources, that a "minimal state" and individual property rights constitute the best route to producing just outcomes in economic and social relations, and that "experts" are best equipped to formulate and direct economic policy.

Neoliberal ideas influenced disciplines beyond economics, as could be seen in the kinds of questions asked by social scientists and by the kinds of assumptions upon which some studies were based. The effect was to crowd out other organizing principles of deep relevance to an analysis of reform processes and outcomes, such as those discussed in chapter 1: power, social justice, and sustainability. Some refer to this influence as "economic imperialism," that is, "the application of economic reasoning to areas traditionally considered the prerogative of other fields such as political science, legal theory, history, and sociology."[8] Early work on the "politics of economic adjustment," for example, seemed to accept in varying degrees the assumption that neoliberal reform was necessary because of state failure and focused mainly on how collective action problems arise and are overcome (Haggard and Kaufman 1992; Nelson 1990). Although these studies were useful for understanding the narrow scope of political action that were their focus, I argue that the changing political economy of Latin America over the past few decades can be better understood if we move beyond economistic and interest-group theories to adopt a more critical stance regarding neoliberalism.

Several promising works in this vein emerged in such divergent areas as economic sociology, economic geography, and poststructuralism (Bockmann and Eyal 2002; Brenner and Theodore 2002b; Rose 1999). This work on "neoliberalization" clarified the manner in which neoliberal discourse worked in tandem with the actual exercise of state power and public authority to renegotiate the boundaries between state and market. Peck and Tickell (2002) pinpointed three related but analytically distinct moments that comprised this process of neoliberalization: proto-neoliberalism as a nascent intellectual movement, roll-back neoliberalism as a concrete program of retrenchment, and roll-out neoliberalism as a deeper state-building project. The early intellectual basis for neoliberalism can be found in such institutional environments as the Mont Pélerin Society (founded in Austria by classical economists, including Hayek), the Institute for Economic Affairs (based in London), the Heritage Foundation (based in Washington, D.C.), and the Cato Institute (a libertarian think tank, also in Washington, D.C.). Each of these institutions worked tirelessly to create knowledge that could be used by policy makers to justify greater reliance on markets in sectors that in the postwar period were the domain of the state. U.S. economics departments, most notably the University of Chicago's under Friedman, and early neoliberal projects, such as the Chilean experiment under Augusto Pinochet, also contributed to the embodiment of neoliberal ideas in public policy.

8. "The History of Economic Thought," New School University, Department of Economics, http://homepage.newschool.edu/het/.

These policies did not emerge spontaneously from neoliberal ideas alone, even where the state was a poor provider of public goods. They came about as a result of a conscious effort by these groups, as well as international financial institutions, to promote market-led reform—sometimes through ideas and persuasion and sometimes through pressures and loan conditionalities. Some local elites, moreover, embraced this effort to serve their own ends. The result was that governance in public goods sectors shifted toward markets and away from states, despite doubts, discussed in chapter 1, about the appropriateness of this shift. Roll-back neoliberalism was associated with attempts to destroy and discredit state activities in potential market spheres, while roll-out neoliberalism operated by building and consolidating neoliberal forms of state authority and structures of regulation. The latter strategy served to solidify gains from retrenchment while attempting to resolve contradictions created by the destruction of old compromises, policies, and state forms. This political project was strengthened by "the technocratic embedding of routines of neoliberal governance, the aggressive extension of neoliberal institutions . . . , and the continuing erosion of pockets of political and institutional resistance to neoliberal hegemony" (Peck and Tickell 2002, 384).

Neoliberal actors strived to secure policy-making dominance by arranging institutions in ways that prevented the implementation, discussion, or even consideration of other types of policies. Some examples included the operational independence of central banks and other technocratic strongholds adhering to strict fiscal and macroeconomic discipline; international laws and agreements falling outside of democratic control, such as trade agreements that prevented states from causing "distortions" through intervention or from interfering with investor rights (Wade 2003); and the use of economics programs, international financial institutions, finance ministries, and think tanks to set the terms of economic debate (Dezalay and Garth 2002). These mechanisms depoliticized the policy-making process, that is, framed it as too technical for ignorant elected officials or masses to understand. Thus, "the neoliberal project of institutional creation is no longer oriented simply towards the promotion of market-driven capitalist growth; it is also oriented towards the establishment of new flanking mechanisms and modes of crisis displacement through which to insulate powerful economic actors from the manifold failures of the market, the state, and governance that are persistently generated within a neoliberal political framework" (Brenner and Theodore 2002a, 375). Such neoliberal strategies acted to preempt state intervention, effectively limiting the range of protective "double movements" (Polanyi 1944) available to state actors.

Citizen reaction to these transformations varied according to past experiences with the state. Just as institutional contexts influence the shape of reforms, a lack of accountability and the attendant mistrust of the state also have path-dependent characteristics. In El Salvador, rather than improving state capacity and accountability in public goods sectors, neoliberal policies naturalized assumptions about the state's inability to provide and framed the state out of provision, thus reinforcing the public sector's negative image. The state's inattention to social and economic rights created a feeling of hopelessness regarding public services: "public institutions could respond better [to the needs of the population], but there is nobody holding them accountable; so whether they do their job well or poorly, nobody tells them anything."[9] This served to reduce resistance to early privatization policies, thus facilitating their implementation (though experiences with first-wave privatizations spurred protests of later privatization efforts).

The situation in Costa Rica was different, as the population benefited from an effective public sector and was more resistant to its dismantling. Although elites in both countries seized on the opportunities presented by "inexorable globalization" to benefit from market openings, the social democratic frame and institutional success of public goods in Costa Rica provided a powerful bulwark against such opportunism. Radical challenges to the Costa Rican model were suspect, even to some businesspeople: "In the economy, society, and culture of the country, Costa Rica is highly statist. From the time you are born until you die, you are connected to the state . . . from state schools to state hospitals to state water. . . . When policy decisions are made, you have to take into account these socio-cultural and socio-economic characteristics. If someone thinks they are going to come and privatize everything all the way up to the president, they are lost in space. They do not understand Costa Rican reality, history, or idiosyncrasies."[10] Although they tended to favor competition where possible, the business classes in Costa Rica in general did not support widespread privatization. The next question, then, is why privatization in public goods sectors was even considered in Costa Rica. Costa Rica is a good case

---

9. Silvia de Larios, investigator, PRISMA (Salvadoran Investigative Program on Development and the Environment), interview with the author, 11 August 2003.

10. Álvaro Ramírez, UCCAEP (Union of Costa Rican Private Business Chambers and Associations), interview with the author, 22 January 2003.

with which to test claims that failed states and more efficient private sectors drive privatization policy, as it is a context in which such arguments are "least likely" to be true (Goldstone 2003).

Why Is Privatization Policy So Widespread? The Case of Costa Rica

What drove privatization campaigns in Latin America? Was it that state-owned enterprises (SOEs) "did not function well [and] it was next to impossible to make them function well" (Nellis 2002, 4)? What interfered with these campaigns to privatize? Was it rent-seeking interest groups preventing dispassionate technocrats from implementing sensible policies, as reform-minded classical economists would have us believe? If so, the main concern becomes identifying and overcoming impediments to reform. Scholars studying the "politics of economic adjustment" (Nelson 1990; Haggard and Kaufman 1992) deepened this debate, arguing that, reforms such as privatization would be limited where the state could not secure autonomy from interest groups. This was because potential winners were diffuse and only benefited at indeterminate points in the future, while potential losers were specific, organized actors whose interests would be quickly and clearly harmed. The success of reform thus depended on a strong, autonomous team of (ostensibly neutral) technocrats that could direct the economy without interference from resistant interest groups.

How well does this analysis explain market-oriented reforms? If diffuse beneficiaries were disorganized and powerful rent-seeking losers organized, for example, why were reforms such as privatization so inexorable and far-reaching? This paradox is better understood by attending to the interests behind the construction of a liberal economic order, which organized for and were served by that order. These actors must be examined with the same scrutiny as those who resist if we are to understand reform processes. Pressures from the World Bank, International Monetary Fund (IMF), and Inter-American Development Bank also should not be understated. In addition, opposition to reform becomes less mysterious "once we are rid of the obsession that only sectional, never general, interests can become effective" (Polanyi 1944, 154). With this critique as a starting point, I use the case of Costa Rican electricity reform to show how the interests of elites dovetailed with reformist prescriptions of international financial institutions (IFIs), how this serendipity was exploited in a concerted attack on state-owned enterprises, and how this allowed privatization policies to progress as far as they did (though not without resistance).

The case study methodology I employ is particularly suited to this kind of theory testing (see appendix). Unlike statistical analysis, the question is not, "What do I need to show to be convinced that privatization is based on state failure X percent of the time?" Rather, it is, "Given the strong prior belief that privatization arises because of state failure to provide goods adequately, does a close examination of this least likely case shake that belief?" (Goldstone 2003). This method is also useful for examining some of the most interesting facets of social phenomena, which are often either slow-moving causes or slow-to-appear outcomes (Pierson 2003). The short time frame within which much social science work measures causes and effects does not capture these dynamics. Causal, slow-moving processes may be cumulative (e.g., technological change, price shifts, demography, cultural outlooks), may be structured by threshold effects, and may involve extended causal chains. Causal chains follow the logic of "x triggers a, b, c, which yields y." Pierson's (1994) examination of retrenchment, for example, reveals how the reforms of Prime Minister Margaret Thatcher and President Ronald Reagan triggered other events that facilitated later state cutbacks. This causal sequence may not produce its true effects immediately: "a conservative government's main impact on the welfare state might be felt a decade or more after it left office" (Pierson 1994, 188). Such long-term effects may not be the immediate goal of policy, but they are by-products all the same. Eventually, a threshold may be reached whereupon slow-moving variables create a critical level of pressure on the established institutional settings, precipitating a reevaluation of preferences and expectations and a shift in previously stable arrangements. This may cause a domino effect on other institutions. While a single change alone, like change of regime or party, is not likely to change institutions, a prolonged process of change is likely to create a substantive shift.

I argue that, far from saving Costa Rica from an unsuccessful model of state-led development, market-oriented public goods policies over time undermined the institutional efficacy of this still-promising approach. Neoliberal policies harmed the capacity of the state to carry out important functions, fostered disillusionment by restricting the parameters of debate, and debilitated a functional and relevant alternative to the neoliberal paradigm. Market openings became widespread because the state had more difficulty fulfilling its goals under neoliberal constraints, and because people were repeatedly told that because of crisis, it *could not* continue to do so. This occurred despite evidence that Costa Rica is quite capable at providing essential goods, and market governance is quite out of place in a social democracy. Pressures for institutional transformation arose from a combination of interest-based and ideological projects, facilitated by the exogenous shock of the debt crisis all of which generated tensions and contradictions that precipitated change (Blyth 2002). After a brief presentation of the Costa Rican case, I will summarize this causal argument.

Crisis Narratives and the Emergence of Privatization in Costa Rica

Adherents to the Washington Consensus interpreted the debt crisis in Latin America as mainly the result of overextended states and irresponsible borrowing. With liberalization, privatization, and fiscal austerity, they claimed "principled debtor countries could grow their way out of debt" (Cline 1989, 177); without these measures, the crisis would linger. This narrative of "crisis" gave urgency to the interpretation that drastic reform was required. But this was only one possible interpretation of both the causes and remedies of the crisis. Other versions, while not denying the significance of the debt problem, might emphasize exogenous factors contributing to indebtedness, such as the lending frenzy of the 1970s, global recession, and interest rate hikes by the United States. They might also point out, as have numerous religious organizations, that the principle on many Latin American loans had already been paid, that the usurious rates were unjust, and that loans might be forgiven. Finally, some acknowledgment of the positive role state institutions played in developing public infrastructure may have justified targeted state investments to stimulate growth in essential sectors, as well as caution in the widespread application of privatization policies. However, adherents to the Washington Consensus did not give much credence to these alternatives and instead stressed fiscal austerity, structural adjustment, and public sector reform as urgent solutions to a range of development problems.

Even in this crisis context, however, theory would predict that privatization would be least likely to be advocated in a country where state institutions were most successful, if advocated on efficiency and optimization grounds. Similarly, privatization would be most likely to be encouraged where there were greater incidences of state insufficiency. Yet reformers promoted privatization far and wide. As mentioned previously, Costa Rican institutions provided the most extensive and least expensive public services in Central America, rivaling those of industrialized countries. In addition, gross domestic product (GDP) per head was higher in Costa Rica than in the rest of Central America during most of the twentieth century, a condition partly attributable to its active state sector. Costa Rica was also more consistent in these policies than other countries in the region, backed as they were by "a broader consensus and implemented by a state bureaucracy with a high level of training and competence" (Bulmer-Thomas 1987, 274). Regardless of this history, privatization was on the agenda from the moment Washington Consensus policies made their entry onto the Costa Rican stage in the early 1980s during the Monge Álvarez administration.

At this time, the government implemented a series of IMF structural adjustment programs, which viewed privatization of state institutions as a possible solution to state budget imbalances. Justified by claims of "crisis," Costa Rica's autonomous institutions, especially the highly lucrative Costa Rican Electricity and Telecommunications Institute (ICE), came under attack in various ways. The politically influential Calderón and Figueres families, which boast four presidents between them over the past few decades, were central to these efforts. Elites and their "team" of heavyweight advisors included former finance minister and Central Bank president Francisco de Paula Gutiérrez, who formed the "Tomorrow Is Too Late" panel (discussed later); Dr. Eduardo Lizano Fait, president of the Governmental Commission on the Internal Debt and head of the "Tomorrow Is Too Late" panel; Dr. Oscar Arias Sanchez, former (and recently reelected) president and Nobel Peace Prize winner; José Figueres Ferrer, former president and member of one of Costa Rica's most powerful families; Carlos Vargas Pagán, former president of the Legislative Assembly; and Rodrigo Oreamuno, former vice president. They also included members of the National Association of Economic Advancement (ANFE) and the Costa Rican Coalition for Development Initiatives (CINDE),[11] and were well represented in the editorial pages of *La Nación*.[12]

Even as political parties alternated in power, many individual members of this group remained within ministries, on advisory boards, and in other influential positions, and during the 1990s, "the number and power of political appointees and outside advisers increased significantly" (Sanchez Ancochea 2005). Long after the debt crisis had subsided, these elites and

11. The stated role of CINDE, an organization originally funded by the U.S. Agency for International Development (Clark 2001), was to promote foreign investment in Costa Rica. In the 1990s, CINDE flooded the airwaves with commercials in favor of marketization and privatization. (I would like to thank an anonymous reviewer for drawing my attention to these activities.)

12. Information culled from several interviews conducted by the author and from Segura Ballar (1999). See Wilson (1994) for an interesting discussion of elites in the Costa Rican context.

their intellectual counterparts continued to criticize state-run enterprises in areas that were potentially profitable for the private sector. Although ICE's efficiency indicators were exceptional, prices were low, consumer satisfaction was relatively high, and the company was deemed a powerful motor of national development, these actors reframed it as a burden on the state. In 1996, they formed a committee of "experts" that convened to discuss fiscal policy and the future of Costa Rican institutions. Their conclusions, released under the ominous title "Tomorrow Is Too Late," recommended the immediate sale of Costa Rica's power generation facilities, and a majority of a panel of former presidents set up by the president at the time, Jose Maria Figueres, endorsed them. The only dissenter was former president Rodrigo Carazo—the (in)famous leader who, in 1982, refused conditions demanded by the IMF, thereby forfeiting millions of dollars in loans.[13] Although the committee and the panel were ostensibly established in response to another looming fiscal deficit, they were accused of exaggerating the crisis in order to gain personally by the privatization of ICE. There was a scandal, for example, when a local newspaper reported that President Figueres's family held stock in a private company, Energía Global, which had benefited from earlier openings in the electricity generation market.[14] Ignoring these charges of rent seeking, the team pressed on, arguing repeatedly for the potential benefits of privatization and later (when privatization had become a politically unviable term) of "modernization."

In March 2000, the "Energy Combo" bill (hereafter "Combo"),[15] designed in part to modernize ICE by opening it to private sector competition, was submitted to the Legislative Assembly. Opponents of private sector participation in the electricity sector expressed concern that the Combo would lead to higher costs, inequality of access, environmental destruction, and loss of revenue for the state—as well as eventual privatization—and were fully anticipating lengthy public discussions regarding the future of this important institution. On March 17, thousands of citizens attended

13. Carazo was also the first president of the Council for the Defense of Institutionality (CDI), a nonprofit organization that formed to counter neoliberal attacks on Costa Rican institutions.

14. "The Ex-President Denies Influence Peddling; [José María] Figueres [Olsen] Would Have Benefited His Family Businesses," *La República*, 26 January, 2000. Other members of the pro-privatization coalition alleged to have ties to electricity generation were Oscar Arias Sánchez and Carlos Vargas Pagán.

15. The full name of the bill was Law for the Betterment of Public Electricity and Telecommunications Services, and of State Participation and was called a "combination" bill because it addressed two sectors at once.

the Legislative Assembly session to listen to the debates. Instead of hearing a discussion of the pros and cons of the bill, however, they heard only support from both major parties; legislators passed the bill in one session without opponents having recourse to their usual channels of dialogue and lobbying.[16] The following day, several groups that had been organizing against the Combo returned to the assembly to find the doors locked. Radio Internacional Feminista described the ensuing events thus:

> Outraged to be shut out of the debate once again, the protesters decided to climb the walls to get in. The police then came and used force to get them out. The debates were halted and the deputies went on "vacation." Further frustrated, protesters took to the streets again (and) were met by the police who attacked them [with police batons and tear gas]. . . . On Thursday, March 23rd, 26 students were released from jail . . . more than 100,000 people marched in the streets of San José, and at least 30 rural communities throughout the country mobilized and created barricades in support of the protest.[17]

Public sector employees, students, taxi drivers, teachers' unions, farm-worker associations, and civil society organizations called a general strike that lasted until April 5, when President Rodriguez rescinded the bill.

This dramatic account of events is consistent with more moderate reports that stressed the severity of the political crisis. In a country where political cooperation and calm deliberation were customary, these events were alarming. Costa Rica's political culture rarely deteriorated to the levels of polarization and social conflict characteristic of many other Latin American countries, but in response to the Combo, the ubiquitous calm erupted into conflict. According to President Abel Pacheco (2002–6), "the message was clear: the people do not want privatization";[18] just mentioning it was political suicide. Opinion polls at the time reflected this fact, showing a mere 15.3 percent of Costa Ricans expressing support for opening ICE to competition, 66.9 percent supporting non-market-based internal reforms, and 24.7 percent preferring it to be left as is (UNIMER 2000).

16. Albino Vargas, secretary-general, National Association of Public and Private Employees (ANEP), interview with the author, 20 January 2003.

17. http://www.fire.or.cr/protest.htm. Two of my interviewees were among those against whom the police had used force. They reported surprise and fear at the use of tear gas and police batons, a practice that had been unheard of in the recent history of this relatively peaceful country.

18. "Candidato tico es nieto de panameño," *La Prensa* (Panama), 2 February 2002.

Faced with this grassroots opposition, reformers responded, not by ceasing their efforts to open ICE to the private sector, but by transforming—through discourse and practice—their "crisis" orientation. Costa Rican elites worried publicly about whether the country could afford public enterprises in electricity and telecommunications, while simultaneously implementing policies that indirectly weakened ICE. They sought to create a crisis "to remove the political logjam to reform" (Williamson 1994, 20) that the Combo represented. One prong of this strategy was to expropriate surpluses from public entities while denying them access to credit, using an IMF formula for handling debt (Haglund 2006).[19] Authorities compelled the highly profitable ICE not only to turn over profits but also to generate surpluses by cutting expenditures to balance the federal budget, regardless of internal investment needs. The result of this surplus expropriation was that state firms were not able to invest adequately in their own infrastructure.

The main argument for expropriating surpluses and limiting spending of autonomous institutions rested on the claim that deficits were hurting the economy. But the size of the deficit is not what matters; it is how funds are used, with investment being preferable to consumption. If the rate of return on investments exceeds the cost of borrowing, then deficits can be sustainable.[20] Moreover, deficit spending can actually create positive externalities, such as "crowding in," wherein state expenditure on infrastructure and services improves the profitability of private investment and thus leads to higher capital formation (Heilbroner and Bernstein 1989; Taylor 1993). The history of Costa Rica and Central America in the post–World War II period bears out these claims. Proponents of harsh deficit restrictions not only ignored the history of development in many now-developed countries (Chang 2002) but also discounted the experiences of countries like Costa Rica that used deficit spending effectively to create strong, equitable social support systems. Closely tied to the issue of deficits is debt. Costa Rica's internal debt during the Combo standoff made up a large proportion (67 percent) of its total debt and certainly put a strain on public finance. But the growth in internal debt occurred in tandem with a

19. This crisis orientation was later supplanted by an equally panic-stricken discourse about the "stagnation" that the country was purportedly experiencing and which the Central America Free Trade Agreement, it was claimed by those same elites, would remedy (Vargas Solís 2005).

20. Deepak Nayyar, economist and vice chancellor of the University of Delhi, lecture presented at the Cambridge Advanced Programme on Rethinking Development Economics, Cambridge, UK, July 2004.

reduction in external debt, with total debt actually decreasing after 1990, according to Central Bank statistics. A single-minded focus on the internal debt "generated the impression of a greater fiscal problem than that which existed in reality" (Rodríguez-Clare 1998, x, 100).

The argument is not that debts and deficits can grow indefinitely: extreme budget shortfalls and long-term debt can, of course, harm development. The argument is that they were exaggerated in the Costa Rican context for the purpose of shifting power away from autonomous state institutions. If policy makers were simply following sound economic logic, they would certainly not entertain selling off income-generating assets such as ICE's operations. Costa Rican elites advocated privatizing or restricting investment in precisely those lucrative institutions from which the government received millions in surplus profits to pay off internal debt. The real problem beneath government indebtedness was an insufficient taxation system; privatization would provide a one-time boon but would not address the underlying structural problem (Schipke 2001). Worse, it would deprive the state of income from very profitable state-owned enterprises, thus exacerbating the fiscal situation.

The policy of surplus extraction and spending limitations on public institutions had negative material consequences. The total demand for electricity and telecommunications services grew tremendously after 1970, but investments in these sectors did not keep pace with growth or with their historical trajectory. Before the shift toward fiscal austerity, ICE used financing from development banks, such as the International Bank of Reconstruction and Development, the Central American Bank for Economic Integration, the Inter-American Development Bank (IADB), and the National Bank of Costa Rica. Yet investment in new capacity stagnated under the new policy regime. The annual rates of growth of real investment in ICE were 21.88 percent from 1990 to 1994 and 2.57 percent between 1995 and 1997. Tellingly, the gap between needed and actual investment in the latter period corresponded closely to the net surplus transferred from ICE to the central government (Cordero 2000). In line with the "crisis" discourse, privatization advocates argued that the declining investment was due to the burden that state-owned enterprises placed on already strained government budgets. But ASDEICE president Fabio Chávez argued that this was "totally false": "ICE, being a self-sufficient and lucrative business that charges just enough over cost to be able to reinvest in new projects, should have no problem apart from the state. . . . In fact, it contributes as well. ICE investments create dynamism in the rest of the economy, and this year in taxes, ICE collected 61 billion colones [approx. US$155 million], which were given to the state to use for other things."[21]

The empirical record suggests that the crisis of investment instead rested on a confluence of factors—some incidental, others intentional, some based in interests, some in ideology—that came together to effect the defunding or underfunding of public services in such a way that they appeared to be inefficient and were thus more vulnerable to privatization. Four of these factors will be discussed in detail—changes in the international environment, political interference in autonomous institutions, problematic accounting strategies, and a regressive taxation system.

International Pressures

As discussed earlier, the debt crisis of the 1980s placed great pressure on Costa Rican finances. U.S. interest rate hikes were in large part responsible for the crisis, transforming a debt-based strategy for development, not necessarily harmful in itself, into a catastrophe. The hemorrhaging of resources out of Costa Rica was thus in part due to changes in interest rates that were independent of its model of development. These changes had a direct, adverse impact on sectoral development in electricity, with high rates of interest negatively affecting the sector's financial, and thus productive, capacity. They also opened the policy space to neoliberal policies, with their emphasis on fiscal crisis and confiscation of surpluses.

There were also changes in lending practices of IFIs, such as the IADB and the World Bank. Development loans for potentially commercial projects in energy, transportation, water and sanitation, and telecommunications—once a key source for funding for public infrastructural investment in Costa Rica—began to dry up at the end of the Cold War. Lending increasingly focused on supporting private initiatives, and private firms more and more frequently carried out large projects that governments once executed. The IADB claimed that governments, not lenders, encouraged private investment in public utility sectors. The IADB only "anticipated" this shift by creating the Private Sector Department, which was "to finance private sector participation in infrastructure investments through long-term direct lending, syndicated lending, and guarantees in the LAC [Latin American and Caribbean] Region" (Garcia, Rodriguez, and Rossi 2000, 19). But as one ICE executive explained, the mandate clearly issued from the bank to the state, not vice versa:

21. Association of ICE Employees, interview with the author, 30 January 2003.

ICE has historically had a partner in the IADB. Decades earlier it was the World Bank, but later it was the IADB. The IADB changed its course in terms of the conception of economic models, of the country, and of investment. They said, "We are not going to continue supporting the electricity sector, and even less telecom, if investment is public." . . . They talk a lot about the "Washington Consensus," a model in which the state is reduced to focus only on education, health and housing, while the private sector does everything that is possible for it to do. It is almost religious.[22]

The story is not new. A study on electricity reform in Argentina, Bulgaria, Ghana, India, Indonesia, and South Africa indicated that the need for immediate capital due to retraction of credit for the public power sector from the international financial community drove reforms in all cases (Dubash 2002). International banks increasingly shifted their emphasis from promoting state-led development to privatization and market-led development. What is puzzling is the application of this logic to the Costa Rican situation. Its institutions proved to be responsible borrowers with excellent loan amortization records, as well as efficient providers of public services. More important, Costa Rica used "solidary spending" in creative ways to improve the quality of public goods, as well as the overall health of the economy, the putative goal of development lending.

The IMF was also implicated in challenges to this model of development, with its recipe for appropriating surpluses from autonomous institutions based not on their current availability but rather on an abstract formula that failed to account for the broader development paradigm and deprived institutions of funds otherwise earmarked for investment (Stiglitz 2002). Again, the ICE executive's experience is telling:

A week ago, we had a mission from the IMF here, which comes every year. Apparently ICE is like a whale in a fishbowl: very important, so they visit us a lot. Just outside the meeting they said to me, "Look, what you are doing is good, business-wise; you are doing things right, you are growing, you are investing in very lucrative endeavors, and this allows you to do things that are not lucrative, like installing public phones and rural electricity. But from the macroeconomic point of view, you are causing the government problems." So I think

22. Confidential interview with the author, December 2002.

the problem is one of perception, or the model. In the end, it has been made more or less difficult to obtain financing.

IFIs praised social indicators in Costa Rica while insisting that the country was not doing enough to promote fiscal austerity or divest from the very state-owned enterprises that were largely responsible for high ratings in social development. Over the course of two decades, the IMF continued to recommend stronger central government control over "autonomous" public enterprises and adoption of a "more ambitious" privatization program.[23] Meanwhile, the IADB conditioned its 2004 loan on the sole consideration that Costa Rica reduce its fiscal deficit.[24] Recognition of the positive institutional arrangements that fueled Costa Rica's outstanding social indicators was rare, perhaps because these arrangements contradicted assumptions regarding the superiority of market-led development extolled by the international financial community.

A final external factor that weakened the Costa Rican approach to public services was geopolitical. Since the end of the Cold War, countries worldwide tended to follow policies analogous to the main economic power in their region, and this had major consequences for development (Stallings 1995). U.S. influence over economic policy in Latin America was due partly to the decline of Soviet and European support and increased U.S. foreign direct investment. It also stemmed from the transmission of ideas and "best practices" through an epistemic community of academics, think tanks, and U.S. multinationals, as well as through negotiations with regional financial institutions (Biersteker 1995). Direct pressure from the United States was evident as well: "Costa Rican banks won't lend a cent to any state enterprises, because the U.S. Agency for International Development (USAID) would react by cutting off aid to Costa Rica."[25] Costa Rica's location in the Americas has meant pressure to conform to the U.S. (rather than Asian or European) model of development.

With the advent of the Central America Free Trade Agreement (CAFTA), even stronger pressures prevailed to comply with U.S. demands to open its efficacious autonomous institutions to private sector competition. In early 2004, a delegate who previously declared Costa Rica's public

23. "The IMF Asks for a 'Reorientation' of Economic Policy and More Reforms," *La Nación*, 7 March 2003.

24. "Regional Managers of the IADB Analyze Credit of $350 Million," *La Nación*, 2 February 2004.

25. Daniel Oduber Quirós, former Costa Rican president, interviewed by Reding (1986). Although USAID began reducing its aid to Costa Rica in the 1990s, it continues to influence development policy decisions.

institutions off-limits in trade deals negotiated their partial opening to competition under CAFTA. State actors, in the interest of political self-preservation, could have shied away from privatization if it were to incite social unrest, as in 2000. Why accept CAFTA? One possible explanation is that U.S. trade representative Robert Zoellick warned Costa Rica's negotiators that the country's unique state monopolies were incompatible with the treaty's objectives. If they refused to discuss opening state firms to competition from the United States, they risked being excluded entirely.[26] This threat placed the Costa Rican government in an uncomfortable position—compromise to please the United States or choose the dangerous path of resistance that honored prior commitments to protect public enterprises. Ordinary Costa Ricans reacted negatively to Zoellick's strong-arm tactics, giving ammunition to state actors who might reject such coerced policy responses.[27] Costa Rica's electricity and telecommunications union, meanwhile, vowed to resist CAFTA "in the streets" because of its trade in services provisions.[28]

In sum, what seemed to be inevitable factors of a new globalized environment were actually policy choices by powerful international actors that limited policy space for developing countries. Liberalization of trade and finance, far from protecting these countries from external shocks, actually made them more vulnerable to the vagaries of global markets and to pressures to conform to otherwise alien strategies of economic organization. This raises an interesting counterfactual: what would have happened if Costa Rica were located in a region that did not place such a premium on privatization? It seems likely that government investments in electricity and other developmental areas would not be deemed so problematic.

Internal Politicization

Of course, external forces cannot be held entirely responsible for applying a historically incongruous model to the Costa Rican economy: some government actors and local elites, as mentioned earlier, also advocated these

26. "The United States Suggests a Free Trade Agreement Without Costa Rica, Due to Its Telecommunications Monopoly," *La Nación*, 3 October 2003.

27. Of the 55 percent of Costa Ricans aware of CAFTA, half (51 percent) said that Costa Rica should reject demands by the United States to open public services to private participation, according to an opinion poll released in October 2003 by UNIMER Research International (unpublished).

28. "Union Rejection and Business Support for the [Free Trade] Agreement with the United States," *La Nación*, 26 October 2003.

trends. The economic "team" supported implementing IMF-inspired policies for balancing the fiscal account and the enforcement of IMF-imposed debt caps, even when the country had no loan agreement with the IMF.[29] A fundamentally restrictive view of fiscal policy was at the heart of their approach. Rather than focusing on how to increase the income of the central government and Central Bank to close funding gaps, differing social demands were pitted against one another with a tone of resignation: "The Costa Rican state is a unitary entity, with rich and poor elements within it. If we want more education and we don't have a way to finance it, and we want ICE to invest more, eventually the state bears a cost. The decision here is what to do. More education or more to ICE. . . . We could leave ICE to do what it wants and cut the central government in half. This implies cutting education, social assistance, etc."[30] Although this appeared to be simple economic reasoning, ignoring the income side of the fiscal account and leaving social programs to battle one another for funding unveiled a deeper bias against state-owned enterprises. The accounting mischief behind these calculations will be discussed later, but a quick comparison with El Salvador will help to illustrate this bias.

Despite being an "autonomous" state institution, GESAL (a Salvadoran geothermal generation facility) had experienced problems with political interference: not only would the state transfer money from the institution to the central government, but also, as one employee put it, "mid-level functionaries think they are my bosses."[31] This changed when Enel Green Power, a private Italian firm, obtained a stake in the company. Thereafter, political actors could no longer make demands regarding how the institution did business (except in routine instances of regulation), and expropriation of funds had to be approved by shareholders. In both countries, the transfer of surplus income from autonomous state institutions to the central government was legal. But in El Salvador, reformers saw this as inefficient and responded with privatization, the result of which was to deprive the state of its "petty cash drawer."[32] This led to greater autonomy, efficiency, and profits for the institution but also to the elimination of transfers for other state budgetary purposes.

---

29. Representative of the Central Bank of Costa Rica, confidential interview with the author, 27 January 2003.

30. Carlos Vargas Pagán, assessor of the Pacheco Administration, interview with the author, 29 January 2003.

31. José Antonio Rodríguez, general manager, GESAL (Geotérmica Salvadoreña), interview with the author, 22 July 2003.

32. Ibid.

The attitude in Costa Rica toward virtually identical political interference in the affairs of the state-owned electricity firm was quite different. As an ICE engineer put it, "ICE, is thrown into the same 'public sector' bag, and if there are limits on public spending and the central government cannot balance its own budget, ICE's spending and investment is limited. This creates a lot of inefficiency."[33] Instead of productive investments in capacity, state firms in Costa Rica were forced to purchase nonproductive government bonds from the Central Bank at interest rates of up to fifteen points below those of state banks. Because of their high profitability, ICE and other state institutions provided millions of dollars to the government through their bond purchases. This, in part, helped to "resolve" the external debt crisis of the 1980s by increasing internal debt. Paradoxically, neoliberals used this internal debt, a large proportion of which the state owed to ICE and other autonomous institutions, as a reason for preventing ICE from obtaining external loans: "The problem (with ICE obtaining its own external financing) is that ICE is very big, and its decisions regarding external financing are part of the public sector debt of Costa Ricá. . . . Costa Rica has a high level of debt that limits its ability to do other things."[34] In short, the ever-indebted government compelled ICE to generate surpluses and buy government bonds at submarket rates and then prevented it from seeking loans to invest in its own infrastructure *because* the government owed too much to ICE and other autonomous institutions.

These comparisons illustrate a double standard at the heart of the neoliberal model: for the state-owned enterprise in Costa Rica, reformers considered surplus extraction "responsible fiscal management"; for the private firm in El Salvador, reformers considered it "political interference." If ICE were privatized, as neoliberals had advocated for many years, such revenues would have been strictly off-limits to the government and would likely have been directed to profits rather than invested in public works or passed on to customers, as occurred in utility sectors elsewhere (Fischer, Gutierrez, and Serra 2003; Wolfram 1998). These nearly identical situations—one in which reformers sought to protect private electricity firms and the other in which reformers saw public electricity firms as fair game for intervention—belied the contention that market-friendly policies simply offered technical solutions to difficult economic problems. Market-friendly policies did not depoliticize public goods sectors. Rather, they

33. Engineer, CENPE (Centro Nacional de Planificación Eléctrica, ICE), interview with the author, 12 December 2002.

34. Representative of the Central Bank of Costa Rica, confidential interview with the author, 27 January 2003.

redefined how surpluses and benefits were distributed and whose interests were served. This obviously had political consequences: in El Salvador, economic organization based on market principles reproduced the distribution of privilege and precluded redistributive policy, while in Costa Rica, economic organization undermined state policies designed to orient the economy and channel resources based on broader, more socially minded principles.

Costa Rican elites also worked with international actors to solidify market-oriented policies. The most powerful example is the negotiation of CAFTA, which by law opens public institutions like ICE to competition and increased contracting with the private sector. Why would these actors want to create legally binding openings to the private sector, when so many Costa Ricans had expressed grave doubts about them in 2000? The electricity sector in Costa Rica had long been the site of struggle between those who saw it as a strategic sector for state-led development and a pillar of social citizenship, and those who saw it as a favorable terrain on which to develop private businesses. During its long history, ICE had been a revenue-generating public monopoly that also funded other social goals. According to former President Carazo, ICE was "a terrific business, one that provides great profits for the Costa Rican community."[35] Yet despite—or perhaps because of—this great success, private actors had long sought to reap its benefits for themselves.

A series of corruption scandals that erupted in 2004 illustrate how certain actors were able to benefit from openings to the private sector and cast doubt upon claims that simple efficiency considerations, not special interests, drove marketization. The scandals implicated actors at the highest levels of government, including former president Miguel Angel Rodriguez Echeverría and former ICE director José Antonio Lobo, who were charged with accepting millions of dollars from the French company Alcatel for assisting Alcatel in securing a contract with ICE. Former President Rafael Angel Calderón Fournier, meanwhile, was accused of illegally obtaining hundreds of thousands of dollars from a loan made to the Costa Rican Social Security Institute by the Finnish government to purchase medical equipment. Finally, former president Jose Figueres Jr. purportedly received a US$900,000 bribe from Alcatel. Although some of these transactions brought equipment and supplies to Costa Rica that could not have been obtained locally, critics charged that a greater emphasis on contracting with the private sector rather than on strengthening internal

35. Interview with the author, 21 January 2003.

capacity was creating unnecessary opportunities for corruption.[36] Although strong measures were taken against those involved in these scandals, opponents of public-private partnerships worried about Costa Rica's capacity to monitor even more such contracts.

These opponents also complained of another type of political meddling contributing to ICE's marketization, namely, the so-called 4–3 law. This rule permitted the losing party in elections to appoint three of the seven members on ICE's board of directors, while the acting government could appoint four members, including one presidential delegate. The two majority parties were afforded great control over major decisions of ICE, while workers, technicians, and civil servants had less. A special "mixed commission" of labor, student, religious, women's, and environmental groups convened shortly after the antiprivatization protests in 2000 to discuss ways to modernize the institution without openings toward the private sector. These groups all mentioned lack of autonomy as a key factor debilitating the institution and the politicization of the board of directors as an obstacle to alternatives to marketization. The process of political appointments, they argued, resulted in political considerations overriding engineering, technical, scientific, and environmental matters, as people with little understanding of the sector made key decisions (Special Mixed Commission on ICE 2000). This, they believed, led to inattention to sector goals and unnecessary moves toward market openings.

The irony, of course, is that both those who promoted privatization and those who opposed it were using technical arguments regarding the reduction of "political interference" in public goods sectors to support their positions. The former based their argument on the primacy of economic expertise and a lack of sound state-led options, while the latter based theirs on the importance of scientific expertise, social accountability, and the earnest exploration of still-viable alternatives.[37]

Accounting Mischief

Another impetus for marketization stemmed from how government actors calculated risk. The appropriation of ICE's surplus was justified on the grounds that the state assumes a risk in guaranteeing the solvency of state

---

36. Iván Molina Jiménez, "Corrupción inherente," *Semanario Universidad,* 4–10 November, 2004; Raúl Marín Zamora, "Hijo de la Segunda República," *La Nación,* 9 November 2004.

37. These conflicting discourses are discussed at greater length by Sojo (2004).

institutions. But this argument appeared disingenuous given that ICE had not experienced a current account deficit in recent memory:

> Interviewee: When ICE or any public enterprise invests, the Costa Rican state commits to covering this if for some reason it is not repaid.
> Interviewer: But this has not happened in 20 years.
> Interviewee: No, it hasn't yet, but if you look at most Latin American countries, states and taxpayers have had to cover institutional deficits.[38]

If autonomous institutions are mostly running surpluses, as was ICE, the transfer of funds is virtually unidirectional. Table 10 shows a consistent pattern of surpluses for such institutions in Costa Rica (highlighted), ranging from 0.3 to 1.1 percent of GDP annually.

Spending limitations were based not only on dubious arguments regarding the riskiness of SOEs but also on macroeconomic accounting that treated investment as a cost, thereby overestimating the deficit: "When ICE lays out a credit, it is identified as a deficit. That is the issue. I have a balanced loan, with current and capital income; my financial records say that I have billions in net utility. But this is considered a deficit because everything that does not come from current income is counted against me. So even though as a business I am financially successful and healthy, and any bank would want to lend to me, I am stuck."[39]

Heterodox economists critique the basic IMF "financial programming" framework that monetizes fiscal deficits, thus creating a fusion of fiscal and monetary policy that severely limits policy options (Taylor 1993). It is not that accounting per se is problematic; without reliable economic indicators, economic policy can easily become subject to political whim or will (Toye 2003). But to prioritize certain accounting mechanisms and variables over alternative indicators is equally misguided, especially when they threaten to debilitate state functioning: "The ingenious policy of debilitating ICE is to limit its capacity for action from a financial point of view. If it were the independent institution of the Costa Rican state that it should be, it would have the capacity to assume debt, plan projects into the future, and address demand; nevertheless, when it is added into the great state

38. Representative of the Central Bank of Costa Rica, confidential interview with the author, 27 January 2003.

39. Financial executive, Costa Rican Electricity and Telecommunications Institute (ICE), confidential interview with the author, 18 December 2002.

Table 10 Public sector financial balance, Costa Rica, millions of colones[a]

	1995	1996	1997	1998	1999	2000	2001	2002
Global public sector	−63,076	−100,070	−74,802	−72,413	−141,613	−184,903	−157,345	−326,446
% of GDP	−3.0	−4.1	−2.5	−2.0	−3.1	−3.8	−2.9	−5.4
Central Bank of Costa Rica	−30,530	−38,901	−39,849	−42,403	−71,226	−87,679	−63,579	−86,645
% of GDP	−1.4	−1.6	−1.3	−1.2	−1.6	−1.8	−1.2	−1.4
Nonfinancial public sector	−32,546	−61,169	−34,953	−30,010	−70,387	−97,224	−93,766	−239,801
% of GDP	−1.5	−2.5	−1.2	−0.8	−1.6	−2.0	−1.7	−3.9
Central government	−72,748	−99,364	−87,983	−89,232	−99,851	−146,568	−156,708	−259,312
% of GDP	−3.5	−4.0	−2.9	−2.5	−2.2	−3.0	−2.9	−4.3
Autonomous institutions	23,127	18,273	26,904	40,798	29,791	38,708	29,801	19,327
% of GDP	1.1	0.7	0.9	1.1	0.7	0.8	0.6	0.3
Public businesses	17,075	19,923	26,126	18,424	−327	10,636	33,142	183
% of GDP	0.8	0.8	0.9	0.5	0.0	0.2	0.6	0.0

SOURCE: Budget Authority of the Treasury Ministry and the Central Bank of Costa Rica.

[a] 385 colones = US$1.

package, problems begin. Why does the IMF, when it measures the country's indebtedness, include investment debt? I can't explain, but they do. Obviously, this puts the country in an unfavorable position."[40]

A rare moment of IMF backpedaling on the topic of expenditures for infrastructure underscores the gravity of the charges leveled by critics. The IMF admitted that their programs "may have hurt some countries' ability to invest in roads, ports, utilities and other public works."[41] Despite these rhetorical changes, institutions under neoliberalism are increasingly ruled by political technologies such as accountancy, budgets, and audit rather than social indicators or an ethic of service (Rose 1999). Neoliberal analyses of ICE routinely downplayed or ignored its essential role in the economy: the significance of investment that bolstered national competitiveness, its role in energy independence, its effect on employment and social equality, and its tax contribution. Quantification and costing are rightfully part of public policy, but how they are used varies because of *politics*, as do the social and political costs and benefits of these accountancy choices.

Taxation

Fiscal deficits, when they occur, can be addressed by either reducing state expenditures, raising taxes, or both. Although broad-based tax reform was part of the Washington Consensus agenda, neoliberal policy reform focused more intently on reducing state expenditures. This was certainly true in Costa Rica, where state spending was restricted with the implementation of structural adjustment policies in the 1980s, but agreement on tributary reform and the resolution of fiscal imbalances through taxation remained unrealized through the end of the 1990s. Despite exceptionally progressive social policy, tax evasion was high and rates were low and somewhat regressive. Considering the potential for reforms to bring in large sums to resolve fiscal imbalances that weakened institutions such as ICE, why were reforms delayed? After all, "independent of ideology, nobody likes a crisis" (Cornick et al. 2004, 24). One reason was that the Libertarian Movement (a political party) worked hard to impede reform. It argued in part that taxing worldwide profits and corporations would drive

---

40. Rodrigo Alberto Carazo, Jr., PAC deputy, interview with the author, 29 January 2003.
41. Managing Director Anne Krueger quoted in "IMF Says Loan Policies May Hurt Nations' Road, Utility Spending," *Bloomberg*, 24 April 2004.

out foreign investment.[42] Indeed, some argued that progressive taxation is at odds with the neoliberal model:

> The lack of sufficient discussion regarding taxation and the fiscal basis of this model of development has meant that the issue is resolved by cutbacks, always with short-term thinking: cutting back here today, impeding investment. Why? Because the model of the last 20 years determined that we were going to initiate offers external to the country, and in order to make us attractive to investors, the winners would not have to pay taxes. . . . We went from having approximately a 16% rate to not quite 13%. That is unsustainable. How can we eliminate pressures on institutions like ICE? By raising taxes.[43]

Global financial liberalization meant that investment from abroad was contingent in part on the taxation system: lower tax rates were more attractive. It is apparent that investors value other things besides avoiding taxes, such as stability in law and market structures and high-quality human resources. Costa Rica has much to offer in this area: with high levels of human development, a relatively satisfactory productive infrastructure, and a long history of democratic stability, the pressures for a "race to the bottom" in taxes should be surmountable. But in reality, the state did not collect taxes from many multinationals, which greatly weakened Costa Rica's tax base.[44] For example, Intel, a U.S. multinational giant with important investments in Costa Rica, does not pay taxes. Although Intel has provided many other benefits to the economy, including a contribution of 5 percent of GDP, it does not bode well for national accounts when even highly competitive corporations are not obligated to contribute to state revenues.[45]

Even if tax reform were successful, the battle for funding social projects would not end. As with most economic policy over the past several decades, there were conflicting views regarding the desired goals of tax

42. In 2006, the Libertarian Movement and the Popular Block stalled reform by complaining to the Constitutional Court that the process of reform was unconstitutional. "Fiscal Plan Loses Battle in the Sala IV," *La Nación*, 22 March 2006.

43. Carlos Sojo, director, Latin American Social Sciences Faculty (FLACSO), Costa Rica, interview with the author, 30 January 2003.

44. "U.S. Investors Will Not Pay Taxes Here," *La Nación*, 18 January 2003.

45. "Intel Contributes 17.000 Million to the State Treasury," *La Nación*, 7 October 2006. In this article, two major figures in the drive for marketization, Oscar Arias and Alberto Trejos, argue that Intel is doing enough by creating employment, despite paying no taxes on its profits.

reform. The IMF view was that any new income should be spent on infla-tion targeting and exchange rate flexibilization, not social expenditures.[46] The Central Bank soon thereafter announced that it would take up to 70 percent of the income drawn from new taxes for recapitalization to address inflation.[47] It is unclear how these visions for earmarking tax income will be reconciled. Greater freedom to reinvest profits of firms like ICE could strengthen state capacity in public goods sectors. Yet inflation targeting and exchange rate flexibilization are likely to hinder such investments and undermine the fiscal basis of the Costa Rican model. Moreover, the lower-ing or removal of tariffs as called for by CAFTA is likely to reduce state income even further. These difficult issues clearly are not simply technical matters: how they are resolved will determine the future of social democ-racy in Costa Rica.

Summary

Neoliberal policy in Costa Rica threatened to create a self-fulfilling proph-ecy of state failure. The ability of public firms to continue providing effec-tive services was undermined by precisely those policies that neoliberals claimed were designed to save the country from collapse. Political actors with concrete interests made *choices* at each step in the causal chain "x triggers a, b, c, which yields y"; it was not inevitable. Crisis orientation (x1) spurred on by pressure from IFIs, the United States, and private investors (x2) and neoliberal ideology on the part of international and domestic elites (x3) led to structural adjustment policies (a), shrinking of credit on interna-tional markets (b), and surplus expropriation that deprived state institu-tions of funding (c), which over time debilitated institutions and paved the way for increasing efforts at privatization (y).[48] Privatization is not on the agenda simply because of failed state interventions; rather, it is due to the "multiple conjunctural causation" of history, ideology, and politics. I illustrate the spatial and political dimensions of this process in figure 2.

The causal pattern described previously was not deterministic; there were several branching points along the chain open to contestation and where alternatives may have emerged. As I argue elsewhere in the book,

46. "The IMF Believes Resolving Fiscal Problems Should Be a Priority for the Country," *La Nación*, 23 January 2006.
47. "Mayoría de recursos de plan fiscal para capitalizar Central," *La Nación*, 24 February 2006.
48. MacLeod (2004) shows how similar policies reduced state autonomy in Mexico.

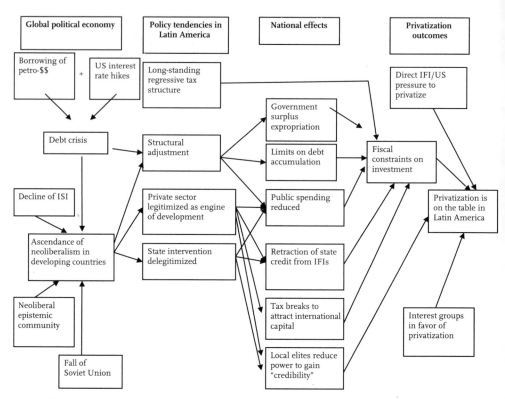

Fig. 2 The neoliberal shift and its effects

tax reform and state- or community-led institutional reform were two historical alternatives that neoliberal policy priorities partially suppressed.
This argument about the presence of privatization is in some ways applicable to the Salvadoran situation, but there were divergences at certain "critical junctures." The strength of Costa Rican institutions, for instance, led
to a slower "adjustment," more resistance to government surplus expropriation and privatization (both within and outside the state), less and slower
contracting, and creative new forms of finance within the public utility
sector. The state continued to operate, albeit imperfectly, as an instrument
of interest representation, sovereignty, and dialogue—which is why privatization has, as of this writing, stayed on the table rather than become
policy. Those who give no agency to developing countries are wrong in the
sense that elites and popular sectors can and do alter the manner in which
economic policy making occurs, and radical transformations may face
strenuous opposition:

Interviewer: Do you think eventually there will be openings in ICE? More, I mean.

Interviewee: Over our dead bodies.[49]

Yet those who give determinative agency to local actors underplay the significant structural constraints that not only actually prevent resistance but also make resistance appear to be an impossible strategy. As one respondent from El Salvador explained:

A lot of times you will hear, "Why don't people do anything?" Well, maybe it is because the time of war is past, and they can see that the hoped-for outcomes were not achieved. . . . Since the people lived the repression with their own flesh and blood, they've been left [with a feeling of hopelessness]. On a national level, the same could be said: El Salvador is repressive, and instead of protesting or seeing what could be done, people leave the country. One form of protest is exit, so with the high levels of migration that we have, this analysis makes sense. They are migrating faster today than during the war.[50]

Without representative institutions that empower rather than repress or co-opt citizens, the links between agency and structure and between demands and accountability are weak for the less powerful (Katznelson 2003).

Privatization emerged not simply because states failed to provide public goods—in some cases, they did not fail at all—but because, in many cases, those who supported liberalizing reform were themselves part of powerful distributional coalitions that stood to gain through collusive ties and rent-seeking behaviors (Schamis 1999). Even in Costa Rica, where the state is capable of providing essential goods and markets governance in these sectors is uncommon, market-friendly policies made headway. This analysis underscores the contentious nature of public goods privatization as a development strategy. As we will see in the coming chapters, even deeper institutional and political clashes followed from institutional transformations that shielded markets against political democracy, made effective state action difficult, and prevented the incorporation of public-minded values into policy.

49. Fabio Chávez, president, ASDEICE, interview with the author, 30 January 2003.

50. Silvia de Larios, investigator, PRISMA (Salvadoran Investigative Program on Development and the Environment), interview with the author, 11 August 2003.

4

THE INSTITUTIONALIZATION OF
MARKET-LED PUBLIC GOODS PROVISION

> World Bank and Inter-American Development Bank . . . loans come
> with conditionalities of privatization, opening the economy, and
> deregulating the State. . . . It is a very powerful concept, very coherent,
> but it did not work here, and does not work because our society does
> not operate this way.
>
> —SALVADOR ARIAS, economist and Legislative
> Assembly deputy, El Salvador

Why and how privatization and other market-oriented policies emerged,
as discussed in chapter 3, raises questions about the effect of these policies.
If they were not simply sensible solutions to terrible crises proposed by
neutral technocrats, then what kinds of solutions were they? The empirical
record reveals that the indiscriminant transfer of marketization policies,
far from providing a general remedy to public goods failures, created new
fiscal, technical, and legal barriers for countries to overcome, while, in
many cases, doing little to increase state capacity to meet development
objectives. Positive outcomes were far more contingent on preexisting
political and institutional context than the discourse would have us believe.
More deeply, the increasing institutionalization of market-oriented values
in public goods sectors undermined institutional forms oriented toward
meeting human rights obligations, as outlined in chapter 2. I examine the
institutionalization of neoliberal norms below, and their effects on public
services, regulation, and state finances. In order to test the argument "that
governments perform less well than the private sector" (World Bank 1995,
1), I examine closely the case of El Salvador, where such arguments are
most likely to be true due to its abysmal record in providing public goods.
Comparisons to Costa Rica illustrate similar patterns in institutional shifts
but not convergence. The implication of these similarities is not that history does not matter—it clearly does—but that neoliberal policies introduce comparable difficulties for nonmarket public goods alternatives,
which must be addressed regardless of context.

Neoliberalism: Another "Great Transformation"?

The ascendancy of neoliberal ideas in public policy represented a paradigm shift from the "development economics" approach, which argued that the unique needs of developing countries require distinct economic and social policies, to one in which "sound" economic principles were universal and would allow any economy—developing or developed—to flourish. An International Monetary Fund (IMF) promotional video with the ironic title "Ruritania: Solving Real Problems" reflected the latter outlook.[1] In the video, we are introduced to an imaginary country, Ruritania, which has no history, culture, or politics, but for which IMF policies provide a solution to its "real" macroeconomic problems. This ahistorical application of cookie-cutter liberalization policies led in the 1980s and 1990s to a very real neglect of state institutions and capacities that were indispensable for the success of economic development. Moreover, it ignored important path-dependent, contextual needs of countries at different levels of development. Although greater attention—at least rhetorically—has been given to state capacity and institution building in recent years, the damage done by this neglect of developing country variation was significant.

The economic, political, and social transformations that accompanied the shift to neoliberalism (Burawoy 2001) were perhaps as important as the "Great Transformation" toward market society analyzed by Polanyi (1944). Whereas the change in Polanyi's time operated largely at the national level, however, some of the most important contemporary shifts in economic processes occurred globally. These changing state forms wrought by globalization altered social relations and policy patterns (Jayasuriya 2001), with clear effects on the provision of public goods in developing countries:

- *Economic transformation.* Peaks and declines in industrial production led investors to move beyond traditional profit-making strategies. Latin American countries expended extraordinary efforts to attract private investment, such as assurances regarding rates of return, indexing to the dollar, legal protections against expropriation, market (rather than state) regulation, and legal protections for investments. States pulled back from public goods sectors and reduced taxes on foreign investment. Public goods privatization under these conditions

1. California: Four Media Company, 1999.

was appealing as a source of "accumulation by dispossession" (Harvey 2003); privatization continued apace.

- *Social transformation.* Lower tax revenue and lax labor standards that accompanied new models of production led to reduced state funding for social protection and weakened labor movements. Meanwhile, an ideology of retrenchment depoliticized civil society. Policy makers discounted redistribution that affected "competitiveness" and increasingly saw socially oriented reform as nostalgic or quaint (Torres-Rivas 1996). At the same time, "rights" discourse spread globally, with greater acknowledgment of the responsibility of states to ensure economic and social rights. Struggles over development and the role of the state grew with the rise of transnational social movements, such as those represented at the World Social Forum, and elite alliances, such as the World Economic Forum, dubbed by Gill (2000) a "consciousness-raising forum for the leaders of the world's biggest transnational corporations and for government leaders" (7).

- *Political transformation.* Proponents of a liberal economic order tried to neutralize potential resistance with their own "preemptive movements." While attempting to ameliorate the most egregious effects of markets, they simultaneously instituted rules that placed limits on state capacity to intervene in the economy or implement measures to protect the natural environment and vulnerable members of society. Examples of such preemptive policy included regulatory frameworks, such as TRIMS (Trade-Related Investment Measures), TRIPS (Trade-Related Intellectual Property Rights), and GATS (General Agreement on Trade in Services). These agreements discouraged governments from regulating capital, prohibited countries from favoring national firms, and imposed a market orientation that prioritized investor rights over the rights of society (Wade 1998, 2003). Struggles between capital and opposing interests, as well as the possibility for bargains, compromises, and embedding, were pushed from national agendas. Global governance structures, especially the international financial institutions (IFIs), grew in importance, linked tightly (IMF and WTO) or loosely (World Bank) to Washington Consensus policy prescriptions. The coercive strategies of these organizations tended to enforce liberal market relations by restricting state "interference" to protect "investor rights." Though these institutions rhetorically adopted human rights language, in practice they tended to favor market mechanisms despite their ambiguous effects on economic and social rights. There was also a shift away from horizontal accountability mechanisms toward executive decision making. Institutions such as independent central banks emphasized procedural aspects of economic management over substantive outcomes for the whole population, with macroeconomic stability paramount.

- *Ideological transformation.* Accompanying these changes was an ideological shift, discussed in chapter 3, where advocates presented neoliberal policies as "sensible" (Williamson 2004) and in the interests of all (Gramsci 1971). Hegemonic discourses prioritized "credibility" (i.e., following neoliberal policies in order to be recognized as legitimate; Hay 2004b), while counterhegemonic, anticorporate globalization movements continually challenged these strategies (Silver and Arrighi 2003). The ideological shift varied by country, though ideas put forth in global development circles trickled down to shape developing country policy.

It was in this global context that national-level policies and struggles operated. Even though more and more people in the world were living under regimes in which they could exercise collective control over government (Dahl 1999), many of the postwar bargains began to unravel after 1980. All systems (liberal, developmental, ISI, etc.) relied on specific institutional forms to attain desired outcomes. As those forms shifted, so did their capacity to maintain achievements (Jayasuriya 2001). The concerted effort among neoliberals globally to retrench state-led economic policy (Yergin and Stanislaw 1998) slowly dismantled projects associated with Roosevelt's New Deal for the United States and Truman's Fair Deal for developing countries, leaving an even more frayed safety net and a weakened capacity of the state to fulfill protective and regulative functions. State forms changed because "the institutional buffers that shielded state-society alliances from the international liberal order [were] eroded" (Ó Riain 2000, 200). The impact of the global economic crisis that began in 2007 can be understood, in part, as a slow, cumulative outcome of these dramatic shifts in public policy.

The new institutional arrangements disembedded economic policy from social, political, and ecological principles and reembedded them in market-friendly state forms, shifting market values to the center. Policies such as full cost recovery, privatization, investment protection, and sanctity of contract emerged in the name of "correct" (i.e., market) pricing, efficiency, competition, profit, individualistic consumerism, and capital accumulation. Those policies, in turn, preempted or displaced principles of social and economic citizenship and justice, collective goods, and the preservation of land and labor as such. As the Inter-American Development Bank (IADB) framed the issue, "there is one area [of public utilities policy] in which no compromise should be made and that is, in meeting the objective of long-term service sustainability by ensuring that financial flows rise to a level compatible with full cost recovery, while guaranteeing economic efficiency as a general goal of service provision."[2] Political issues regarding ownership and control, as well as the social goods criteria that were behind nationalization in the first place, are left out of the calculus of "service sustainability."

Do these market values promote sustainable public goods, as the IADB quote suggests? Beyond the obvious omission of ecological values as criteria, these policies also produce institutional conflicts and political instability. When neoliberalism is institutionalized, it creates contradictory mandates that states must navigate in their attempts to ensure public goods under the strict fiscal and macroeconomic conditions a neoliberal regime imposes. Greater technocratic decision making alienates citizens and marginalizes the perhaps less technically informed but no less important public perspectives. Finally, policies presented as *fait accompli* can cause resentments and conflicts that last for years (Nancarrow and Syme 2001). While these policy strategies weaken mechanisms of state provision, the "disciplinary" apparatus of the state is strengthened simultaneously to prevent protective double movements. This may promote calm for a time, but, as evidenced by the sometimes violent antiprivatization protests across Latin America, only for a time.

Privatization in El Salvador, with Some Comparisons to Costa Rica

Nations like El Salvador and Costa Rica were obliged to navigate their relations with multinational corporations and international institutions in this context of neoliberalization. How countries weathered and absorbed these transformations depended on previous history and institutions, as comparative-historical analysts would expect (Stark 1998). El Salvador is a good case with which to test theoretical claims that marketization will improve conditions of public services where states prove inadequate to the task, as it is a context in which such arguments are "most likely" to be true (Goldstone 2003). The evidence shows, however, that even (or maybe especially)

2. Inter-American Development Bank, "Public Utilities Policy," July 1996. GN-1869-3, http://www.iadb.org/sds/ifm/publication/publication_492_79_e.htm. A similar statement can be found in Kessides (2004).

here the results have ranged from mediocre to dreadful, with many "unintended" consequences. I will briefly introduce the actors that favored privatization in El Salvador and then present arguments they used in support of markets as a response to inadequate public goods. The evidence presented casts doubt on the validity of these arguments by demonstrating the contradictory institutional effects of marketization and privatization in provision, regulation, and finance. Some comparisons with Costa Rica illustrate the pervasiveness of these effects.

In El Salvador, reforms promoting fiscal austerity, privatization, retrenchment of public goods, and openings to international investment flows became the reigning orthodoxy among elites in the mid-1980s (Segovia 2002). Salvadoran president Alfredo Cristiani (1989–95) and his right-wing National Republican Alliance (ARENA) Party were at the forefront of these efforts to construct a new economic system. Other key proponents were the business community, led by the National Association of Private Business (ANEP); the neoliberal think tank Salvadoran Foundation for Economic and Social Development (FUSADES); ARENA appointees in government ministries and autonomous public institutions, such as the National Aqueducts and Sewers Administration (ANDA) and the Lempa River Executive Hydroelectric Commission (CEL); multinational corporations interested in buying assets in the electricity and water sectors; and an array of international entities, such as the World Bank, the IADB, and the U.S. Agency for International Development (USAID). All of these groups enthusiastically followed the line of the once-heralded Washington Consensus regarding privatization and marketization, putting forth a number of arguments about why this approach would be superior to all others for utilities, regulation, and financing of public goods in El Salvador.

Neoliberalism in Utility Sectors

From a purely economic standpoint, the objectives of privatization were to raise government revenues by selling state-owned enterprises (SOEs) and by reducing expenditures on subsidies, capital investment, and lending; to improve macroeconomic balance through greater foreign direct investment (FDI); to harness private funds for infrastructure investments and research and development; to expose enterprises to competition in order to reduce costs and improve efficiency; and to improve transparency in the relations between the public and private sectors. Given these objectives, privatization should have had the greatest impact on, respectively, the fiscal health of the government, capital formation, efficiency and rationality of enterprises, and patronage and corruption. Privatization could also generate increased tariffs or licensing fees that produce income for the state. All of these justifications were used in favor of privatization in El Salvador (ANEP 2001). Selling SOEs, neoliberals argued, would generate alternative sources of finance, alleviate claims on already meager resources, allow debt to be paid, and free the state to focus on tasks that truly pertained to it with greater efficiency (FUSADES 1992). Because of El Salvador's history of a devastating civil war, a lack of investment in infrastructure over decades, and the consequent gap between spending requirements and capital constraints, this analysis was compelling. From exploded transmission lines to long-term neglect of the infrastructure of a nation at war with itself, the need for capital formation was indeed urgent.

Yet the conditions under which governments can take advantage of these benefits are only met with difficulty in most developing countries, and privatization processes create contradictions that frustrate outcomes. For example, though privatization was supposed to relieve fiscal pressures on the state, restructuring of the electricity sector designed to make the sector attractive for private investors, "required El Salvador to take on debts equivalent to 5.1% of the GDP between 1991–1997" (Lara Lopez 2006, 14). This number rose to 6.4 percent of GDP "if we take into account the financing of other projects that included the privatization of energy" (Lara Lopez 2006, 15). In 1996, the IADB authorized loans to develop and improve the sector but stipulated that rate increases be put into effect. This caused conflicts in the Legislative Assembly due to both the costs of these loans to the already strapped government and the costs of rate increases for poor consumers.[3] Yet increases went through, and the loans were approved. This generous state investment in electricity infrastructure before privatization benefited the firms that bought assets thereafter rather than users or citizens who repaid the loans.[4]

Competition in bidding for contracts and acquisitions could, if carried out properly, reduce costs and increase income for the state. Unfortunately, these processes are not always carried out with transparency, with competition, or with full information. The history of bidding in El Salvador was no exception. The bank privatization process was extensively criticized for lacking transparency and for manipulation by elites to their own advantage, which resulted in a concentration of ownership of the powerful

---

3. "Privatización, incrementos tarifarios en la energía eléctrica y endeudamiento externo," *El Salvador Proceso: Informativo Semanal*, número 722, 21 August 1996.

4. "Privatización de las sociedades distribuidoras de energía eléctrica," *El Salvador Proceso: Informativo Semanal*, número 753, 16 April 1997.

financial sector in the hands of a few elite families (Albiac 1998). This also occurred with telecommunications privatization, which evidenced irregularities and political jockeying involving the ARENA Party as well as the Supreme Court.[5] The bidding process in electricity distribution seemed less controversial on the surface, though once privatization was carried out, a private monopoly prevailed. Moreover, the AES Corporation, the firm that won more than 80 percent of the distribution market in El Salvador, was simultaneously embroiled in a bidding collusion controversy in Brazil that cost the government an estimated US$1.2 billion.[6]

Maximizing government revenues at the time of sale also, paradoxically, interfered with other possible cost reductions and regulations, as the state generally sweetened deals to attract high bids and to "ensure investor confidence." This resulted in contracts with promises regarding high profit rates, few reciprocity requirements, loose operational rules, and other perks. ANEP argued this was the best way to secure foreign investment—on investors' terms (ANEP 2001). The U.S. Embassy and Chamber of Commerce agreed, bragging that the Salvadoran "Foreign Investment Promotion and Guarantee Law" provided attractive incentives for investment, such as the following:

1. Unrestricted remittance of net profits, capital gains, and funds from liquidations to country of investor origin
2. Unlimited remittance of royalties and fees for the use of foreign patents, trademarks, technical assistance, and other similar services, subject to taxation
3. Fifty percent allowable remittances in services
4. One hundred percent ownership by foreigners allowed[7]

The terms of agreement at the sale or contract signing were the main determinant of investment rates and technology transfer. But under these conditions, there was little room to require investors to spend profits on research and development, to invest in needed projects, or to fulfill any other kinds of "reciprocity" (Amsden 2001). Indeed, since "El Salvador's investment legislation does not require investors to . . . transfer technology, incorporate set levels of local content, or fulfill other performance

5. "Polémica licitación en ANTEL (I)." *El Salvador Proceso: Informativo Semanal*, número 710, mayo 22 1996.

6. "Secret Deal That Kept Brazil in the Dark: Electricity Privatisation in Which Enron Had a Role Turned out to Be a Disaster for the Government," *Financial Times*, 21 May 2003.

7. U.S. Embassy and U.S. Chamber of Commerce document, "The Practical Guide to Doing Business in El Salvador."

criteria,"[8] the promise of infrastructure expansion in privatized sectors remained unfulfilled.

Despite some income from the sale of SOEs in El Salvador, government revenues actually decreased after privatization, and the fiscal deficit increased (Lara Lopez 2006). This was due in part to continued investments in privatized sectors by the Salvadoran state, estimated to be US$213.8 million between 1999 and 2003.[9] Both right and left criticized the state-owned CEL for continuing to construct electricity generation plants: ARENA finance minister Juan José Daboub questioned why CEL was working in areas where the private sector should be given precedence, while the opposition FMLN Party wanted to know why CEL had to build plants when the private sector was supposedly taking on that responsibility.[10] Similarly, expenditures by the Social Investment Fund for Local Development (FISDL), a public entity, increased rural electricity coverage from 45 percent to 55 percent from 1999 to 2003. According to the private electricity distribution companies CAESS (Electrical Lighting Company of San Salvador) and DELSUR (Electrical Distribution of the South), expanding rural electrification was not profitable because of infrastructure costs and low consumption levels. But they agreed to carry out the work if FISDL was paying.[11]

Sadly, even these public investments did not dramatically improve coverage overall. According to household survey data, 77.7 percent of homes had electricity before privatization; coverage rose to 81.5 percent the year in which companies were privatized but dropped again in 2003 to 79 percent (Lara Lopez 2006). Relying on public investment, moreover, did not stop private companies from raising rates. Electricity privatization was supposed to bring cost reductions for consumers and boost private sector competitiveness. Not only did this not happen (Segovia 2002) but the government reduced subsidies for poor households and approved rate hikes of more than 80 percent for residential customers within months of privatization. As figure 3 shows, electricity rates skyrocketed for residential customers of the largest distribution company, CAESS, after privatization in 1998.

In neighboring Guatemala, electricity rates were half those in El Salvador in 2000, while in Costa Rica, they were close to a third. The regulatory

8. U.S. Embassy, "Investment Climate," Embassy document, July 1998.
9. According to Central Bank figures (Lara Lopez 2006).
10. "Economía y Hacienda discrepan por crédito a CEL," *La Prensa Gráfica,* 29 January 2004.
11. "El 45% de la población rural no tiene energía eléctrica," *La Prensa Gráfica,* 1 October 2003.

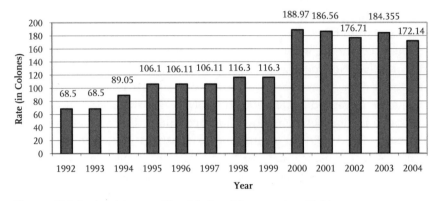

Fig. 3   El Salvador: Mean residential electricity rates (154 Kwh), 1992–2004
SOURCE: Centro para la Defensa del Consumidor (Center for Consumer Defense), El Salvador.
NOTE: The exchange rate is fixed at 8.75 colones to the dollar.

agency (SIGET) approved rate hikes set by the distribution companies themselves, even though the Electricity Division of the Economy Ministry rejected these changes, which "hit consumers hard."[12] Distributors, it seemed, transferred not only costs but also high profit margins on to consumers. It was unclear why the regulatory agency allowed the changes, but it gave consumers no explanation. This situation caused some consternation: "SIGET freed itself of responsibility, saying it is just acting based on technical considerations: 'managing the market and energy service with the interests of end users in mind would be a political act,' they say. But in fact, opting for the market to the detriment of justice is a political and ethical decision."[13]

Residential customers were not the only ones to complain; so did the Departmental Mayors' Council (CDA). In 2003, CDA president Ramón Ernesto Palma argued that the prices that municipalities paid for monthly electrical services were becoming unsustainable because of the almost systematic increases established by distributors. In Tecapán, for example, rates increased by 60 percent in two months. In Berlín, where the country's primary geothermal plant is located, as well as in other municipalities, mayors had to take out loans to keep up with payments. They felt it was particularly unjust that they were charged so much because they "are

12. Jorge Rovira, *Noticiero Hechos*, Channel 12, 14 May 2001.
13. "Doble confusión para el consumidor," *El Salvador Proceso: Informativo Semanal*, año 21, número 952, 23 May 2001.

the ones that run permanent electrification projects in the communities, which helps out the distributors."[14] The mayors called for a clarification of the methodologies that distributors used to set rates, reinforcing the call from the public. There also were negative downstream effects of rising electricity prices for poor community water providers, which relied on energy for pumps and equipment. Exclusion remained a problem, with a large percentage of the population lacking affordable access to electricity, despite promises of increased private sector investments (United Nations Development Programme [UNDP] 2001).

Although CAESS claimed to have reduced losses and improved efficiency, the average consumer did not see much of a change in service quality. Rather than reduced prices and higher quality, Salvadorans faced an increasing number of system failures after privatization (see table 11).[15] A barrage of complaints from consumers claimed they were charged for energy they never used, and an audit by SIGET concluded that electricity distribution companies charged more than US$1 million more than they should have (Lara Lopez 2006).[16] These experiences raised doubts about

Table 11   El Salvador: Number of system failures in electricity distribution, 1999–2002

Year	CAESS	DELSUR	CLESA	EEO	DEUSEM	Total
1999[a]	4,722	3,752	3,315	2,890	1,994	16,673
2000[b]	4,652	1,536	6,048	5,423	1,308	18,967
2001	4,739	3,511	8,500	6,348	2,040	25,138
2002	5,655	11,310	8,670	7,345	1,519	34,499
Total	19,768	20,109	26,533	22,006	6,861	95,277

SOURCE: Centro para la Defensa del Consumidor (Center for Consumer Defense), El Salvador; based on data from the General Electricity and Telecommunications Superintendent (SIGET).

NOTE: CAESS = Compañía de Alumbrado Eléctrico de San Salvador; CLESA = Compañía de Luz Eléctrica de Santa Ana; DELSUR = Electrical Distribution of the South; DEUSEM = Distribuidora Eléctrica de Usulutan ; EEO = Empresa Eléctrica de Oriente.
[a] Data for DEUSEM correspond to the July to December period only.
[b] Data for DELSUR correspond to the second half of 2000, and for EEO up to September only.

14. "Comunas denuncian alzas en cobros," *La Prensa Gráfica*, 27 April 2003.
15. Compañía de Alumbrado Eléctrico de San Salvador (CAESS), Compañía del Luz Eléctrico de Santa Ana (CLESA), Empresa Eléctrica de Oriente (EEO), and DEUSEM are all subsidiaries of AES. DELSUR is owned by the U.S. company Pennsylvania Power and Light.
16. "DPC monitorea servicios eléctricos y telefónicos," *La Prensa Gráfica*, 24 September 2003.

the wisdom of continuing to privatize basic services, considering the inability of Salvadoran regulatory institutions to prevent these negative outcomes.[17]

Users were not the only ones that were adversely affected by privatization. Other negative consequences arose because investors could legally expatriate profits, thus upsetting the balance of payments and reducing in-country productive capital. The district attorney investigated AES shortly after it consolidated its hold on the Salvadoran market for tapping sectoral assets to balance its books internationally, thus nearly bankrupting the distribution company for the first time in one hundred years.[18] This sort of divestment can devastate a small country like El Salvador, but it is not by definition illegal. This does not mean that no illegal activity happens in the private sector, however. The Enron scandal and the California energy crisis of 2000–2001 were examples of how a key sector was made vulnerable through the acts of questionable legality carried out by private businesspeople in pursuit of profit. Several interviewees pointed to the irony that El Salvador was pressured to go down the same path. If the regulatory bodies of the United States could not control such behavior, they asked, how could El Salvador be expected to do so?

A favorite answer of businesspeople and neoliberal economists alike was competition. Private firms in competitive environments would be forced to improve their operations because corruption was inefficient; market forces would thus discourage it. Yet competition was elusive in the privatized electricity sector, for many of the same reasons that it failed to prevent the crisis in California. At best, electricity market structures were oligopolies (minimal competition among a few firms), and even without corruption, such arrangements gave firms great leeway in artificially inflating prices. In key sectors such as electricity and water, even cases that started off competitive often resulted in oligopolies or monopolies because of barriers to entry and industry consolidation. This was the situation with electricity distribution in El Salvador, in which nearly the whole industry was eventually consolidated under the umbrella of AES Corporation.

The argument that privatization was less corrupt because of competition becomes implausible under these conditions. Big firms also had an advantage in winning initial contracts, as they were more able to absorb

---

17. "Privatización: impacto en las tarifas y subsidios," *El Salvador Proceso: Informativo Semanal*, año 21, número 908, 28 June 2000.

18. Leonel Gómez, former CAESS manager and government advisor on electricity issues, interview with the author, 25 August 2003.

start-up costs or take a loss under low initial bids only to raise prices or renegotiate later, as in the notorious case of Aguas Argentinas (Rodríguez 2006). They also had better access to funding and possessed proposal-writing and bidding expertise that gave them an advantage over smaller firms. And if all else failed, they could acquire the competition. Small markets like those found in Central America were especially vulnerable to oligopoly, as they could not realistically sustain more than a few firms, especially in electricity and water sectors. El Salvador was well known for its concentration of wealth and power in just a few hands, which had direct consequences for any attempts to build competition into what were effectively oligopolistic and monopolistic markets (Paniagua Serrano 2002).

In cases where the outright sale of SOEs was too controversial, proponents of marketization, such as FUSADES, unreservedly promoted contracting to solve state budget problems (Beyer 1999). The assumption was that private sector project management was inherently superior to public sector management and that monitoring and supervising contracts was less expensive than public works carried out by the state. Using technical assessment criteria, ministers should, it was argued, be able to establish the terms of contracts, with clearly delineated expectations and costs, which in turn would allow the government to prioritize different tasks. The treasury inspector's office would be able to use contracts to ensure that government money was not poorly spent. To achieve these goals, they argued, it would be necessary to strengthen the treasury and the ministries, as well as create an evaluative mechanism that prioritized projects and determined their economic viability and social benefit. The institution building necessary to achieve these tasks was framed as creating the conditions for proper market functioning, rather than expanding the rules and reach of the executive branch, though the latter is, in effect, what these reforms achieved.

Reformers also advanced contracting as a way to improve the performance of public employees. To make headway in flexibilizing the public workforce and professionalizing the public sector in general, reformers suggested new and novel contracting schemes for certain well-defined tasks, which would allow competition among functionaries based on the achievement of such tasks (FUSADES 1999). Greater flexibility for managers would allow them to reward personnel based on accomplishments and cost-benefit analyses (i.e., how cheaply they were able to do their work). The Salvadoran business elite argued from a realist perspective, maintaining that globalization was a fact that workers must learn to accept, and that the only way workers could augment and sustain their salaries was to improve productivity to ensure industries' competitiveness (ANEP 2001). Public sector labor should be more flexible, with a middle ground between the rigid protection of jobs and the unlimited capacity to fire. "Barriers to entry" should be reduced to create competition for jobs, especially between the old and entrenched versus the young, hungry, and spry.

Although "flexibilization" certainly occurred in the formal Salvadoran workforce since privatization, productivity gains were less clear. Electricity union leaders, including those that had resigned themselves to the irreversibility of privatization, insisted that increases in labor productivity, if any, were due less to workers motivated by competition and more to the continuation of established output levels but at lower staffing, training, and remuneration rates.[19] This labor strategy is related to higher turnover and a less-skilled labor force, as well as various negative and sometimes dangerous consequences. In April 2003, workers from the Electrical Industry Union of El Salvador (SIES) traveled to the U.S. offices of Pennsylvania Power and Light (PPL) Global to denounce systematic violations of its collective bargaining contract with DELSUR, one of PPL's subsidiaries. In particular, they were concerned about the number of injuries and deaths that had resulted from inadequate health and safety regulations employed by subcontractors.[20] When they returned to El Salvador, DELSUR greeted the delegates with accusations that they were putting workers' jobs at risk for their personal benefit. Despite interventions by the Ministry of Labor, the dispute lingered, with SIES denouncing administrators for "inhumane treatment, repression, and anti-union discrimination."[21]

Elsewhere on the labor front, there were two employee deaths at the distribution company CAESS in August 2003, while this field research was under way. A high-level manager denied that the company was at

19. Santos Cordón García, secretary-general, SIES (Sindicato de la Industria Eléctrica Salvadoreña) (distribution), interview with the author, 23 July 2003; Jose Neftaly Yanes, SIES, interview with the author, 27 August 2003.

20. AFL-CIO and UNITE! 2003, "Central America: Labor Rights and Child Labor Reports Pursuant to the Trade Act of 2002, Section 2102(C)(8)–(9)," American Federation of Labor and Congress of Industrial Organizations and the Union of Needletrades, Industrial and Textiles Employees, Report to Congress, 5 June 2003.

21. SEIS, "Un Laudo Arbitral, ganado a sudor y lágrimas . . . para la historia sindical," http://www.misindicato.org/?art=1002 (accessed 5 March 2009); Union Network International, http://www.union-network.org/uniamericas.nsf/0/53BE0E8134D23E9BC12571780 0729DDA?OpenDocument (accessed 24 May 2009).

fault, insisting that it had given all the training and equipment required to ensure worker safety and that the workers simply had not used the equipment provided.[22] Two other interviewees, a union representative and an industry expert, countered that although the specifics of these particular cases were unclear, the safety procedures the CAESS manager referred to were not the norm. To save money, inexperienced contractors were much more frequently employed in jobs seasoned workers formerly held, and a devaluation of the labor force had led to a reduction in the quality of work performed.[23]

Contracting, it turns out, is riddled with complications beyond safety concerns, ranging from corruption and monitoring difficulties to transaction costs and lost efficiency. The most outrageous and expensive corruption case to occur in the region in decades was prosecuted in El Salvador and involved contracts with the water company ANDA. The attorney general and the treasury inspector filed several charges against former ANDA president Carlos Perla, ex-ANDA employee Mario Orellana, and twenty others for illicit association and business dealings, corruption, accepting bribes, illegal contracts, violations in the bidding processes, and other unsavory acts.[24] Millions of dollars flowed through real estate, friends' credit cards, and foreign bank accounts. In one instance, the new ANDA administration asked the Dispute Resolution Chamber of the Supreme Court of Justice to declare illegal a rehabilitation project for eighty-five wells that stemmed from a contract signed by Perla on the grounds that it was "damaging to the public interest."[25] Drillmasters, the contracted firm, filed a counterclaim against ANDA that the work cessation order violated their contract, caused damage and losses to the company, and was thus illegal. Drillmasters eventually lost the case, indicating that even in El Salvador, justice sometimes prevails.

Although the ANDA corruption story seemed to bolster neoliberals' case that state managers cannot be trusted, it actually undermined the argument that private firms should be granted public sector contracts whenever possible. Where regulatory capacity is weak and large sums of

22. Representative, AES/CAESS (Electric Lighting Company of San Salvador), confidential interview with the author, 20 August 2003.

23. Leonel Gómez, former CAESS manager and government advisor on electricity issues, interview with the author, 27 August 2003; José Neftaly Yanes, SIES, interview with the author, 27 August 2003.

24. "Contraloría ordena juicios por fraude in 2 proyectos ANDA," *La Prensa Gráfica*, 21 October 2003.

25. "Estudian nueva querella en obra dada por Perla," *Diario de Hoy*, 1 May 2004.

money change hands between private and public actors, monitoring difficulties, information deficits, and temptation converge to the detriment of
the public good. But what are the prospects for contracting in a country
like Costa Rica, which has a relatively strong justice system, fair courts,
effective regulatory institutions, and public accountability? The evidence is
not promising. In 1990, the government opened the Costa Rican electricity generation market to the private sector in response to an acute need
brought on by a drought-related energy shortage. This potentially beneficial usage of the private sector, however, was carried out in a way that
undermined state institutions and established a regime of privilege in
which a few private firms enjoyed guaranteed success. Rather than having
prices set locally using market mechanisms, contracts allowed private
companies to peg generation rates to the U.S. consumer price index. This
resulted in rates nearly three times higher than the costs of energy from
the plants of the Costa Rican Electricity and Telecommunications Institute
(ICE). The contracts obligated the publicly owned ICE to purchase all the
energy produced by the suppliers, even when ICE's own cheaper production was sufficient. This amounted to private firms operating with a guaranteed profit, while ICE purchased unneeded energy at a premium, paid
for by consumers.

The comptroller general and the attorney general of the republic both
ruled that these contracts violated the law and called for their renegotiation. However, powerful disincentives obtained. The U.S. State Department, for example, through the Overseas Private Investment Corporation
(OPIC), expressed its strong disapproval. As an environmental leader complained, "OPIC intervened, directly threatening the Costa Rican government with reprisals. . . . This case is pathetic because both the attorney
general and the comptroller demanded a renegotiation [of the public-
private contracts] due to their damage to the national interest."[26] The Association of Costa Rica Energy Producers disagreed, stating, "The State or an
entity of the State cannot abandon its contracts."[27] That the contracts were
ruled to be harmful to the national interest by legitimate public interest
institutions was deemed less important than the "sanctity of contract"
revered by market fundamentalists. The fear of legal reprisals and other
penalties resulted in a disregard for the comptroller's or the attorney general's rulings, which violated market principles. Here, we clearly see a

26. Gabriel Rivas-Ducca, Friends of the Earth Costa Rica/FECON (Federation for Environmental Conservation), interview with the author, 28 January 2003.
27. Ing. Mario Alvarado Mora, executive director, ACOPE (Costa Rican Association of
Energy Producers), interview with the author, 20 January 2003.

clash between the court's attempts to protect the public from injurious contracts and the U.S. government's and local elites' views that private contracts must be respected regardless of their cost. In this case, Costa Rican state institutions lost the battle for legitimacy.

These legal complications were compounded by the fact that international rating agencies such as Fitch New York and Standard and Poor's constantly monitored countries like El Salvador and Costa Rica for behavior that could constitute a violation of investor rights. Considering the shifting global political economy, these countries were eager to avoid spoiling investment ratings. ARENA's president Saca of El Salvador said that he understood that investors "should not be given negative messages" and that contracts, once signed, would stand.[28] This limit on exit capabilities weakened the legal and financial position of the state vis-à-vis contractors and allowed firms to force the state to pay added costs to exit from a deal, costs that taxpayers and consumers shouldered. Once multiyear contracts were in place, only severe mismanagement or highly damaging results would lead a state agency to consider terminating or refusing to renew them.

In the unfortunate case of Nejapa Power (a subsidiary of El Paso Energy International), the Salvadoran General Electricity and Telecommunications superintendent Ernesto Lima Mena maintained that the contract between the Nejapa Power and CEL was so disadvantageous to the state-owned enterprise that if it were honored to the end, the state would lose US$24 million (215 million colones) each year for the entire fifteen-year contract period.[29] In a twist eerily like the private generation contracts in Costa Rica, the contract obligated CEL to pay for the entire energy capacity of the plant, hot flows or cold reserves. This created conditions that were "inexplicably advantageous" to the private firm: no matter what they produced, they enjoyed a guaranteed profit. In the end, the Salvadoran government was forced to pay US$95 million to extricate itself from the contract.

In another highly criticized contracting episode, Duke Energy (one of the companies implicated in the market manipulation that led to the California energy crisis) bought three electricity generation plants in 1999 for the fire-sale price of US$125 million.[30] The IADB recommended this privatization because it deemed the state "inefficient," even though the publicly

28. *La Prensa Gráfica*, 12 August 2003.

29. "Nueva Polémica en Torno a CEL," *El Salvador Proceso: Informativo Semanal*, año 21, número 925, 1 November 2000.

30. "Duke Energy to Buy a Controlling Stake in Salvadoran Plants," *Wall Street Journal*, 2 August 1999.

owned plants were all profitable before privatization, and the state officials that ran them had their own successful private businesses.[31] Duke invested US$70 million to add capacity to the Acajutla plant, but the other two plants were not functioning for over a year, and CEL continued to pay for their cold capacity.[32] Workers at Duke plants faced firings, "flexibilization," decreased benefits, and contracting out despite promises to respect previous collectively bargained contracts.[33] Furthermore, these plants, as well as Nejapa Power, produced expensive thermal energy, which led electricity costs to skyrocket, as well as increased Salvadoran dependence on foreign oil and the percentage of dirty energy that served the sector. Even in generation—the electricity subsector with the best prospects for competition—competition did not materialize to reduce costs or prevent harmful outcomes.

Caution with regard to markets did not mean that private sector participation in El Salvador was a complete failure. Private firms were more autonomous than state-owned enterprises under neoliberalism because of protections for private investors that state firms did not enjoy. Private actors were also much freer to make decisions regarding the operation of firms, and companies on average were profitable (CEPAL 2003). Yet the information deficits, transaction costs, and unintended consequences of seemingly simple contracts were severe. The complexity of public goods, where defining product quality and laying out all contingencies in the contract is impossible, exacerbated the lack of exit possibilities. Only in the process could the buyer (the state) learn exactly what was valuable, rendering detailed clauses regarding expectations impractical (Sclar 2000).

The Salvadoran economic elite ignored or seriously underestimated these deficits and costs, as well as the sheer number of contracts that would have to be overseen under the neoliberal vision. The public sector would have to bear the cost of establishing and maintaining a stable, ongoing, competitive market for public contracts, as well as the cost of being both participants and guarantors of that market. The Salvadoran Treasury Department barely had enough resources and capacity to carry out its functions *without* having to supervise hundreds of new private contracts, as the Carlos Perla case demonstrated. Moreover, the goods involved in electricity and water works projects tended to be complex, and evaluations and cost-benefit analyses of projects would have to be carried out by a heretofore

31. Industrial Union of Electrical Workers (STSEL) workers, meeting with the author, 20 July 2002.

32. "Nueva polémica en torno a CEL," *El Salvador Proceso: Informativo Semanal*, año 21, número 925, 1 November 2000.

33. Alirio Romero, secretary-general, (STSEL) Sindicato de Industria de los Trabajadores del Sector Electrico, interview with the author, 20 August 2003.

nonexistent office with enough personnel, expertise, and independence to evaluate the economic and social benefits of such highly technical contracts. For these evaluations, they would undoubtedly be forced to rely on information from private contractors, opening up the process to further corruption and misinformation, and rendering their benefits dubious.

Information asymmetry and sectoral complexity led governments, in some cases, to hire outside "experts" to evaluate potential contracts. This was generally not cheap; in 2002, the Salvadoran government allowed the Autonomous Executive Port Commission (CEPA) to hire two advisors for sixty calendar days to supervise public bidding for the port concession at Acajutla. The pay was US$234,000, or more than US$2,000 per day per person, including weekends. This amounted to more than the cost of a school lunch program that fed 635,000 children for three months (UNDP 2002b). Despite the questionable payoff of such expenditures in a country so poor, CEPA's president openly defended them because, as he argued, "the work is complex."[34] By June 2005, no concessions had been granted, though the original advisors had been replaced by a new, less expensive set, who conceded that the advice given by the previous experts "was not the most suitable for Acajutla."[35] "This is the kind of thing," one port worker in La Libertad told me, "that makes you want to take up arms again."

Neoliberal Regulation

Everyone from ANEP to the UNDP agreed that in privatized industries there should be laws to ensure competition and strong, autonomous, transparent regulation and supervision in essential goods sectors. The vast majority of my respondents, from all ends of the political spectrum in Costa Rica and El Salvador, said that regulation was a necessary part of water and electricity management and that with greater privatization there must be greater regulation than what existed at the time (see table 12).

Yet these respondents differed in their understanding of what that regulation should entail. There are substantial differences between regulating competition, the environment, labor rights, contract quality, and compliance. Each of these types of regulation requires a different legal framework, distinct sets of norms and priorities, and, in some cases, a different

34. "CEPA Contracts Two Advisors $265,437," *La Prensa Gráfica*, 23 July 2002.
35. "6 Foreign Advisors Analyze Bidding," *La Prensa Gráfica*, 25 June 2005.

Table 12 "With privatization there should be [greater/equal/less] regulation"

Respondents answering	Costa Rica				El Salvador			
	Greater	Equal	Less	d/k, n/a, depends	Greater	Equal	Less	d/k, n/a, depends
Electrical generation	93.8	3.1	0	3.1	63.3	16.7	0	20.0
Transmission	93.8	3.1	0	3.1	70.0	13.3	0	16.7
Distribution	93.8	3.1	0	3.1	—	—	—	—
Water provision	87.5	3.1	0	9.4	76.7	3.3	0	20.0

SOURCE: Interviews with the author.

NOTE: Total n = 62. d/k = don't know; n/a = not applicable.

institutional entity (e.g., local communities, state agencies, self-regulation). Self-regulation, for example, creates a set of norms and behaviors very different from social norms (Cerny 1999). Neoliberal regulatory schemes tend to focus on increasing state capacity for monitoring competition. According to Michael Camdessus, former managing director of the IMF, an adequate regulatory framework "ensures equal access to markets and thus promotes equality of economic opportunity; . . . encourages competition, eliminates unnecessary business costs and, thus, promotes efficiency and growth."[36] Because most benefits from privatization are supposed to result from competition, this emphasis is understandable. Without competition, the benefits of privatization are questionable at best. Yet it is not easy to regulate competition in sectors that lend themselves to natural monopoly, such as water and electricity. Moreover, successful regulation of private firms requires much more than securing competition, especially when it comes to incorporating ecological principles. Decisions of regulators can affect emissions, plant siting (particularly important for hydroelectricity and thermal plants, as well as transmission lines), and types of generation that are encouraged (dirty or clean energy). Weak environmental regulations, or regulations oriented only toward market efficiency, thwart optimal outcomes from the perspective of the health and well-being of society and the environment.

Salvadoran business saw things differently, arguing that the state's role in environmental protection should be to harmonize conflicting laws, to approve norms and standards of protection "according to the national reality," and to design market incentives for cleaner technologies and instruments for remunerating "environmental services." The state would take no protective action, and there would be few penalties for violations in this vision (ANEP 2001). Unfortunately, this market-based approach had a dubious track record. Under the structural adjustment policies of the 1990s, environmental imbalances worsened, especially in management and quality of hydroresources, access to potable water, and lowered water quality (Rubio 1997). No amount of competition on its own would ensure universal service, consumer protection, and education regarding conservation and long-term protection of resources. These outcomes require strong, independent regulatory institutions, still a distant dream in El Salvador, despite the promise of the General Electricity and Telecommunications Superintendent (SIGET) discussed in chapter 2. Privatization

36. "Toward a Second Generation of Structural Reform in Latin America," address given at the National Banks Convention, Buenos Aires, Argentina, 21 May 1997.

without a broader vision of economic development and sustainability is thus no panacea.

Regulatory reformers in Costa Rica were more concerned about "deregulation" than building a regulatory apparatus from scratch, as in El Salvador. The prevalent feeling among reformers in the 1980s was animosity toward regulation, based on the perceived need to replace state-owned enterprises in the economy with private firms, and the view that the long-standing regulatory agency, the National Electricity Service (SNE), interfered with this process. In electricity, reformers argued that technological advances obviated the need for monopoly structures and that regulatory change was necessary to ensure competition while leaving prices to the market. The goal was to create "modern," capable, independent, and strong regulatory agencies, "above all in order to guarantee equal treatment and similar rules of the game for private businesses (principally multinationals), who were already forcefully present and strongly promoted by development banks" (Rodríguez Argüello 2000, 201).

Deregulation started in earnest in 1996, when reformers transformed SNE into the Public Services Regulatory Authority (ARESEP). One rollback accompanying this legislation was the elimination of the regulatory agency's right to grant concessions to service providers. The elimination of this jurisdiction weakened the possibility of sanctioning firms at the moment of granting concessions, leaving Costa Rican regulators with only the ability to revoke concessions already granted, a much more difficult process. Following the advice of the IADB, reformers advanced an economic and technical concept of regulation, with a rather restrictive focus regarding rates and quality control. The kinds of capacity building in human capital that took place at this time were mainly training personnel regarding concessions of public works to the private sector. Though not all actors in this process were neoliberals, the neoliberal element was certainly present: "We cannot keep fixing prices one by one, but rather must implement the models that we already have, based on consultations with the IADB. . . . We have yet to create quality discipline, which does not exist in regulated firms, and the main circumstance that makes this difficult is that the majority of regulated firms are public" (Rodríguez Argüello 2000, 290).

This discourse of state failure and the impossibility of state-led reform permeated the reform process. Reformers reframed the impressive indicators that Costa Rica had already accomplished in public goods sectors as dependent for their maintenance on private sector participation, even though the private sector played no role in their achievement. Claims about the "inefficiency" of public firms abounded, despite the lack of evidence that Costa Rican SOEs were indeed less efficient than private firms. Such discourse was systematically examined and critiqued by Ricardo Segura Ballar, an ICE engineer who documented what he called the "ideological terrorism" of privatization supporters: "Either Costa Rica privatizes services, sells businesses, cuts personnel costs, and reduces wages, or it will (find itself) on the brink of collapse" (Segura Ballar 1999, 27).[37] Regulatory reform was designed to address this "inevitable" move toward the private sector. The focus on competition and eliminating the regulator's role in granting concessions created some ambiguity that eventually contributed to the contracting debacle discussed earlier.

Because reformers had difficulty "rolling back" (i.e., privatizing) firms directly in Costa Rica, they instead rolled out "flanking mechanisms" (Brenner and Theodore 2002a) of focused, competition-oriented regulation. There was some degree of retrenchment, but the degree to which neoliberal strategies permeated reform was limited because of Costa Rica's inherited social democratic institutional landscape: "In contrast to other countries, Costa Rica had put forth its regulatory framework before reforming service provision markets (privatization, promoting competition, etc.). The countries whose situation is the opposite face pressures from service providers to establish less demanding regulations than those that we were able to establish under our system" (Rodríguez Argüello 2000, 209). ARESEP remains strong and is still more than adequate relative to agencies in El Salvador and other countries in the region. But in both countries, regulations were designed (or redesigned) with markets in mind.

Neoliberalism and State Finance

Finance is the final area of development discussed in chapter 2 in which states attempted to institutionalize mechanisms for ensuring the adequate provision of public goods. I will now briefly review some of the evidence regarding the effects of neoliberal policies on financing for development in public goods sectors. I already discussed in chapter 3 the macroeconomic limitations that forced public firms in Costa Rica to limit expenditures on investment, not because companies were managed irresponsibly but because the central government was expropriating their surpluses and

---

37. Segura Ballar is referring to the rhetoric used by privatization supporters in an article in the newspaper La República, "The Country Privatizes or Collapses."

refusing to allow them to obtain financing. There were also strings attached to government loans, such as the Water and Sanitation Sector Modernization Project, in which the World Bank stipulated that Costa Rica conduct privatization feasibility studies and contract out services to the private sector in order for the loan to be approved.[38] The urgency of these loans increased when government officials put the brakes on sectoral development through financial strangulation. Although the water sector functioned with an operative surplus (income was greater than expenditures on administration, operations, maintenance, and depreciation), the water company, AyA (Institute of Aqueducts and Sewage Systems), was not allowed to use its financial leverage to obtain outside funding because of internal credit limitations, which the Central Bank set at 6 percent of net worth. Although its management was well within the range of "prudent," AyA—like ICE—faced debilitating limitations. Coupled with a drastic decline in development aid, investments fell substantially, which greatly weakened the sector and made it virtually mandatory to attract funds from outside the state to mend the disrepair.

In El Salvador, as well, the mantra was contracts and privatization rather than increasing state revenues or launching state-led reform. It was true that the fiscal health of the Salvadoran government was not particularly strong. However, the questions should have been: What were the sources of this dire situation? And was privatization a valid solution? Many authors blame the austerity policies of recent decades for achieving "stability" in terms of fiscal control, at the cost of "dismantling fiscal policy itself" (Rubio 1997, 22). Following neoliberal fundamentals, the government virtually abandoned its role in securing resources, redistribution, and economic stimulus. Pressing social demands and a regressive, ineffective tributary system exacerbated a serious fiscal imbalance between state income and spending (Moreno 2000; UNDP 2001).

The roll-back in state support for public sector water provision in El Salvador created a number of challenges for the water provider, ANDA. The government prioritization of debt payments and a retraction of credit from the IADB for the public sector directly impeded public works (Artiga 1999).[39] The ARENA government further cut ANDA's investment budget steadily after 2002 (González and Salgado 2005), causing consistent

38. World Bank. 2004. "Costa Rica—Water and Sanitation Sector Modernization Project," http://www.wds.worldbank.org/servlet/WDS_IBank_Servlet?pcont = details&eid = 00 0104615_20040311165040 (accessed 26 August 2006).

39. Beatrice Carrillo—Procuraduría, (Attorney General) water privatization seminar in San Salvador, August 2003.

rationing and water scarcity in ANDA's network and a 12 percent fall in water provision over the decade from 1994 to 2004.[40] With a dilapidated infrastructure, overexploitation of water resources due to uncoordinated planning, and lack of technical and human capacity, these systems were not strengthened but rather "abandoned to their own devices, left to die."[41] No coherent, national reforms were formally introduced or implemented through the 1990s, although piecemeal privatizations had occurred in municipalities across the country.

There was a great deal of evidence that reformers exaggerated the fiscal benefits of privatization and contracting. As we saw in the contracting debacles earlier, the Salvadoran state lost much more than it gained from its Duke and Nejapa contracts, and the privatization of these profitable entities actually reduced state income. As Hachette (1996) argued, privatization for primarily fiscal reasons was "actually a trap," as the benefits of divestiture were short term, while the costs could decrease long-term public sector net worth. A significant stream of revenue can be lost when states sell companies in profitable sectors, thereby reducing autonomy from capital and straining financial capacity. Private firms investing in developing countries, especially in the water sector, often renegotiated contracts several times over the course of a project to obtain better conditions (Gausch 2004).[42] In addition, taxation of private firms was not guaranteed, especially in an economic environment in which states commonly offered tax waivers to attract foreign investment and lacked the capacity to prevent or prosecute tax evasion. Along with the imperative of rescuing troubled firms in key sectors, these waves of privatization amounted to classic examples of "socializing costs" and "privatizing benefits."

The "Most Likely" Case of El Salvador: An Appraisal

El Salvador provides a good context for testing theoretical claims that privatization improves public services where states have failed because it is a case in which such arguments are "most likely" to be true. But gains from the liberal transformation were mixed. Public monopolies in electricity that were supposed to improve with unbundling and private competition were transformed instead into private monopolies.[43] Service

40. "Recortan $16 millones a ANDA en 2006," *La Prensa Gráfica*, 27 December 2005.

41. Julio Menjívar Chacón, ANDAR (Asociación Nacional para la Defensa, Desarrollo, y Distribución de Agua), interview with the author, 17 July 2003.

42. From a sample of 1,000 infrastructure concessions in Latin America from 1985 to 2000, almost 75 percent in the water sector were renegotiated—on average only 1.6 years after signing—compared with 10 percent in electricity.

43. At the time of this writing, 85 percent of distribution in the country was in the hands of a single U.S. multinational, AES Corporation.

improvements were questionable at best, while externalities that were already serious continued or worsened, due in part to the incentive of profit-oriented firms to externalize costs. Privatization not only led to a loss of income of profitable companies but also opened up tempting opportunities for corruption. In the water sector, the tremendous presence of non-govermental organizations arose from state neglect, which worsened under the priorities of neoliberal structural adjustment programs that led the state to abandon further sectoral policies (CESPAD 1991). In addition, reforms generally weakened rather than strengthened state capacities, as in Central and Eastern Europe, where the countries that most closely followed neoliberal precepts (especially mass privatizations) suffered poorer growth, lower state capacity, and weaker property rights (King 2002).

Private investors were supposed to save the public from the inadequacies of state provision; instead, the arrival of neoliberalism reinforced official neglect of social and economic rights by shifting responsibility to the private sector, by taking the spotlight off state actors, and by allowing state capacity building to fall by the wayside. Reforms, especially privatization, allowed elites to regroup under insecure postwar conditions and to colonize new spaces of power, thereby reproducing the inequalities at the base of Salvadoran social conflict. Although the structure of the economy changed, the level of economic injustice did not. If anything, it intensified with the concentration of wealth in five, rather than the notorious "14 families" (Albiac 1998; Paniagua Serrano 2002).

Institutional Isomorphism in Public Goods Sectors

It is instructive to compare how the same policy prescriptions of privatization and marketization affected the public goods sectors in our two cases. As table 13 indicates, financial cutbacks, legal restrictions on state action, and deregulation undermined state efforts to protect the population against damaging private contracts and weakened the capacity of both countries' public sectors.

Although important path-dependent outcomes were evident in Costa Rica's ability largely to resist privatization, the neoliberal push had a noticeable impact on both countries' public goods systems. I will discuss the implications of this in the conclusion.

Neoliberal Transformation of Public Goods

The utilities, regulatory structures, and financing mechanisms that states and communities created in the postwar period to link economic activities

Table 13   Neoliberal effects on water and electricity: Costa Rica and El Salvador

	Costa Rica	El Salvador
Public utilities and cooperatives	Electricity and Telecommunications Institute (ICE) • Financial capacity weakened by spending and debt limitations • Damaging contracts • Weakened institutional autonomy The Institute of Aqueducts and Sewage Systems (AyA) • Financial capacity weakened by spending and debt limitations • Weakened institutional autonomy	The Lempa River Hydroelectric Executive Commission (CEL) • Damaging contracts (Nejapa, Duke) • Lost income from privatizing profitable companies Geotérmica Salvadoreña (GESAL) • Less "political interference" but continued state investment in sector The National Administration of Aqueducts and Sewage Systems (ANDA) • Damaging contracts • Little focus on capacity building
Regulatory agencies	The Public Services Regulatory Authority (ARESEP) • Deregulation • Focus shifted to regulating competition (though agency remains strong)	• Regulatory reform in the water sector not part of conditionality, though regulation is supported • SIGET balance still leans toward private sector • Planning shunned
Public or semipublic finance	• Government only able to secure funding through traditional sources (development banks, USAID) if privatization or contracting is stipulated • Forced to find alternative mechanisms (trusts and other fiduciary mechanisms)	• Social Investment Fund for Local Development (FISDL) pays for projects that the private sector will not cover, even in their coverage area • Government only able to secure funding through traditional sources if privatization or contracting is stipulated
Externalities	• Increased use of thermal energy sources	• Rate hikes in electricity, no real service improvements • Continued low coverage in water • Increased use of thermal energy sources • Outsourcing → reduced technical and human capacity within the state, greater injury rate • Expensive "advisors" paid by government

with desired socioeconomic outcomes were quite different from neoliberal models (see table 14). During the transition, public utilities faced retrenchment, commodification (market promotion), unbundling, and "decentralization," causing fragmentation and disarticulation with social goals.[44] Meanwhile, trade instruments, such as CAFTA, effectively banned governments from favoring state providers (Wade 2003), and IFIs granted loans mainly for projects involving the private sector. Efforts to ensure full cost recovery squeezed poor consumers, while the elimination of cross-subsidies placed severe constraints on the solidary development that worked so well in Costa Rica. Companies achieved cost savings at the expense of workers, who were often downsized or "flexibilized." Regulatory strategies shifted from coordination among state agencies to institutional insularity. Under this regime, active, holistic state planning and development goals were subordinated to the magic of competition and market-based incentives for achieving regulatory goals. Countries were reluctant to place strict regulations on powerful multinationals in the competition for foreign direct investment.

In fiscal policy, the role of ministries in budget allocation was reduced and greater restraint was required to meet tight macroeconomic targets. A reluctance to raise taxes on business exacerbated the fiscal situation. Discretionary instruments geared to meet social ends were eliminated in favor of rule-based macroeconomic management and taxation geared toward limited state spending. SOEs were financially hamstrung by central government expropriations of profits, while privatized firms were protected from these same interventions. Reformers framed states as the problem, rather than policies that financially weakened SOEs: "Budgets, productivity and accountability [were seen by IFIs as] conceptually separate issues. The possibility that greater resources [could], by themselves, improve productivity and accountability, [was] not seriously considered."[45] Reforms were taken as technical rather than social and political issues.

---

44. Decentralized development can be positive, and decentralized mechanisms have been used effectively to ensure that public goods are provided broadly, that profits remain within communities, and that control remains local. But in sensitive sectors, such as water and energy, holistic planning, integrated management, economies of scale, and broad-based funding mechanisms require some degree of centralized administration. Moreover, when decentralization becomes a euphemism for privatization, as many critics argue in El Salvador, the control over decisions and resources that characterizes community-led development is lost.

45. Tim Kessler, "Review of the 2004 World Development Report 'Making Services Work for Poor People,'" *Network IDEAS*, http://www.networkideas.org/themes/human/oct2003/hd08_Tim_Kessler.htm (accessed 5 July 2008).

Table 14   Neoliberal institutionalization of public goods: Sectoral effects

	Target of reform	Institutional characteristics
Neoliberal reform of utility sectors	Electricity, water, and sewage firms	• Profitable subsectors unbundled and privatized; unprofitable sectors remain state responsibility • Restrictions on public investment • From permanent workers to contract employment • Full cost recovery → higher tariffs • Fragmentation in planning
Regulatory agencies	Bodies charged with market regulation, environmental protection, and state planning objectives	• Pricing policy responds to market forces, not ability to pay • Discursive emphasis on competition, though monopolies rarely prevented in practice • Monitoring quality, environment, and reciprocity rely on contracts, self-policing, markets for pollution, etc. • Emphasis on investor protection and sanctity of contract
Public or semipublic finance	Public utilities	• Internal profit transferred to central government • Subsidies reduced or eliminated
	IFIs, banks	• Loans for infrastructure provided only to private firms
	Central government	• Tax-based transfers for investment or consumer subsidies limited
	Other	• Creates barriers to public creative financial instruments

Political questions were excluded from economic governance, and procedural (rather than substantive) objectives were prioritized.

Despite the explicit goal of reducing the role of the state and freeing it for other tasks, liberalization in Central America and beyond did not reduce state involvement but rather created a different kind of governance (Vogel 1996), with stronger property rights, hardened budget constraints, and centralized decision making, especially regarding macroeconomic and trade issues. New governance structures required new and different state capacities, some of which placed greater burdens on the state than running SOEs themselves (MacLeod 2005, 56). Revenue streams lost through the privatization of profitable firms and reduced funding for public works, not surprisingly, weakened state-led development. In some cases, market-based reforms actually dismantled state capacity by retrenching and outsourcing sectoral responsibilities that were once part of state functioning. This neoliberal version of "creative destruction" (Brenner and Theodore 2002a) was costly in terms of lost state productive capacity, as well as reduced technical and human capacity of state employees. Institutions take time, resources, and effort to build; once they are dismantled, functioning can be impaired (Burawoy 2001). Although employees and equipment can move elsewhere, capacity itself is not readily fungible. Reduced institutional variation resulting from marketization thus limited the resources and capacities available for responding to public goods challenges (Lanzara 1998).

Reforms also weakened state autonomy and altered state-society ties. Central government control over financial decisions left state-owned "autonomous" institutions with little independence. State responsiveness to social needs was seen as a distortion of the market. Once privatization occurred, state actors found themselves with less control over resources and the means of production of public goods, as well as fewer policy options for addressing negative externalities. Private firms were oriented, by law, toward securing profits for stockholders rather than ensuring the satisfaction of economic and social rights (profits were privatized). Deregulation, meanwhile, allowed private firms greater leeway in determining how to cut costs and organize production to maximize profits (costs were socialized). Regulatory activities focused more on fostering competition than meeting any particular planning goals or holistic objectives, such as river basin management. Information deficiencies complicated the role of the regulator, especially in countries with limited bureaucratic capacity and in which powerful multinational firms operated. Strapped regulators were forced to rely on information provided by firms or self-monitoring to judge whether private sector decisions were in the public interest. Thus, the ties between economy and society, moderated by the state, shifted to favor the private sector.

Subordinated Logics and Disembedded Public Goods

As discussed in chapter 1, the neoclassical approach permitted states to intervene in public goods sectors only when markets, the preferred allocative mechanism, failed to produce optimal outcomes. Neoliberalism further reduced the space for state initiatives while expanding opportunities for market actors by devising private sector mechanisms and competitive schemes for everything from "environmental debt" to electricity marketing. Private property rights and pricing remained the preferred means for overcoming free-rider problems, with enlightened self-interest obviating the need for collective action to overcome prisoners' dilemmas. Efforts to satisfy market logic by ensuring that private firms could operate profitably entailed pricing where goods were once free, higher prices where they were once cheap, and "full cost recovery" where they were once subsidized. In other words, neoliberal restructuring shifted goods from nonexcludable to excludable categories. Inequality in access to goods, generally considered a problem, came to be seen as a solution (see table 15).

These cases illustrate the disembedding of public goods from substantive connections to society and their reembedding in market priorities (Polanyi 1957). This reembedding was accompanied by mechanisms that locked in reforms, effectively eliminating the possibility that alternatives would even be considered, much less chosen. The effect of organizing public goods according to market principles was the marginalization of

Table 15 Neoliberal reorganization of public goods: Sectoral effects

| | | Excludability | |
		Yes	No
Rivalry	Yes	Marketized or commodified common-pool resources: full cost-recovery utility management, private property rights for common-pool resources	Fewer traditionally managed common-pool resources
	No	Pay-to-use versions of formerly public goods: private security, private schools, toll roads, lighthouse fees at harbors	Shrinking "pure" public goods sectors

other ideals: social, political, and environmental (see figure 1). But as privatization experiences around the world have shown, markets are hazardous mechanisms by which to allocate essential resources. For one, structural discrimination is virtually inevitable when access is granted to those with better market positions. Women are often hardest hit by fees and shortfalls in social goods, as in general they are ultimately responsible for family welfare and must compensate with their own resources and labor (Aslanbeigui, Pressman, and Summerfield 1994). This has also adversely affected ethnic minorities, whose communal resources have slowly been privatized, as on the Atlantic Coast of Nicaragua (Pitsch and Ritzenthaler 2000). Targeting to address inequality in privatized sectors has direct costs in personnel training, capacity building, and monitoring, as well as indirect transaction costs, yet states receive no monetary return on these inputs. In some cases, it creates "a vicious cycle whereby cuts in benefit entitlements leads to demands for lower taxes . . . which in turn leads to pressure to cut entitlements still further and so on" (Tsakalotos 2004, 422). In already polarized countries such as El Salvador, this approach naturalized inequality and legitimized the status quo. In social democratic countries such as in Costa Rica, it undermined the bedrock of that system: solidarity.

The shift to exclusionary economic regimes not only undermined social solidarity and exacerbated existing inequalities but also threatened the health of populations. For example, in places where water was subjected to full cost recovery, people were forced either to pay a large proportion of their income for water or to seek other sources that were unfit for human consumption. In South Africa, thousands of people were cut off from potable water supplies because they could not pay tariff increases that amounted to up to 50 percent of their income. Residents began retrieving water from nearby rivers that were severely polluted, and weeks later, South Africa plunged into the worst cholera outbreak in modern history.[46] Market realities also undermined environment and labor protections: private firms resisted such protections, as compliance could be costly. Further, capitalist competition reduced incentives by forcing cost cuts that did not improve the bottom line. Regulation of sensitive sectors placed burdens on the state that were sometimes greater than public ownership itself, especially where firms set rates and artificially restricted supply under oligopoly conditions. For less-developed countries and small local governments, where power relations and regulation favored the private sector, the problem was even more acute.

46. See Jon Jeter, "South Africa's Driest Season," *Mother Jones*, November–December 2002.

The commodification of public goods thus pitted different interests against one another. This is true of most economic policy that, while not always zero sum, by definition distributes rewards and sacrifices in politically determined ways. For essential goods, the conflict can be quite significant. An example is the tourist industry in Costa Rica, which relies on the protection and preservation of land, water, and biodiversity to attract "buyers" (i.e., visitors) seeking an authentic natural experience. Agricultural, urban, and profit-making interests, however, rely on exploiting land and water for other ends. This can and has led to usage conflicts. Beyond this "public" problem, however, there is a deeper issue of the commodification of land itself: even "green" tourism does not protect land and water in ways that answer to their own reproductive needs. It answers tourism's needs by building hotels in ecologically sensitive areas and redirecting water to toilets and swimming pools and away from the ecosystem. Attempts to commodify water rights and access highlight these conflicts, as well as the conflict between commodification and preservation, and underscore the importance of state intervention in moderating or preventing these conflicts.

Proponents of contracting, privatization, and deregulation may admit that reform can be complicated and requires a strong and capable state, but they fail to mention why, then, marketization policies should be implemented at all. If the state can be strengthened and reorganized to supervise difficult market arrangements, then why should it be hopelessly and forever incompetent at carrying out the provision of key public services? Incentives can be built into state operations, and internal reorganization and external coordination before and even without privatization are not only possible but, in many cases, highly successful. The case for privatization is unconvincing unless the private sector possesses skills, innovation, expertise, or technology that public providers do not and cannot possess and unless those contributions can be effectively utilized in the receiving context. The devastating reality is that places most in need of the outcomes reformers promise seem least likely to benefit because of contextual deficits. Privatization, contracting, and concessions require a degree of state capacity and commitment to social and environmental values that are not prevalent in countries like El Salvador but which must be built. Yet if privatization is most likely to work in the places where it is least needed, then the whole approach deserves greater scrutiny.

5

POWER, RESISTANCE, AND NEOLIBERALISM AS INSTITUTED PROCESS

> Liberal democracy has seemed to emphasize the "liberal" more than the "democracy." Continuing like this will put the very idea of democracy into question, and threaten its survival.
>
> —EDELBERTO TORRES-RIVAS, Guatemalan sociologist

> A good sign of a vibrant democracy is the fact that privatization has continued its march.
>
> —U.S. EMBASSY IN SAN SALVADOR, "Country Commercial Guide: Fiscal Year 1999"

So far, I have discussed neoliberalization in terms of three related processes: the creation and dissemination of new norms and ideas (chapter 3), retrenchment (chapter 4), and market-oriented state building (also chapter 4). This chapter reviews the power relations and struggles over values at the root of this neoliberal economic and political project. Specifically, it examines how marketization processes eliminated or weakened accountability mechanisms in ways that placed the quality and sustainability of policy at risk.

The empirical data illustrate this disembedding of public accountability and explain why, despite a dismal track record, neoliberal models of public goods management continued to be pursued. It was not because "there is no alternative," as Prime Minister Margaret Thatcher argued. Rather, it is because their advocates—for example, multinational corporations seeking access to scarce resources, international financial institutions, and some local elites—had greater control over policy processes, access to media, resources to carry out legitimating research, and leverage to forestall alternatives. Although this power imbalance created some apathy among popular sectors in Costa Rica and El Salvador, the real story is that resistance took hold. These "double movements" varied in accordance with how local values and aspirations were embedded in (and disembedded from) institutions, customs, and protections. This chapter outlines the contours of this struggle over accountability and voice in public goods sectors.

Public Accountability and Shifting Power Relations Under Neoliberal Reform

Accountability mechanisms are the backbone and lifeblood of democracy, helping to ensure that the *demos* structures and feeds the whole. The realization of social and economic rights in public goods sectors depends on the health of these mechanisms.[1] Yet as the opening quotes illustrate, the discourse of "democracy" can be used in multiple and contradictory ways. Classical liberals and libertarians alike frame free markets as virtually synonymous with freedom, and their establishment and protection—along with periodic elections in which ruling parties rotate in power—are presented as central to democratization. The policies and practices of international financial institutions of the past several decades reflected a similar faith in markets and a desire to reduce the role of the state in the economy as supporting democratization. They believed that a free-market economy "would compel governments to be more accountable, less corrupt and hence more efficient developmentally, for they would be judged on their performance and thrown out if they did not deliver public goods effectively" (Leftwich 1993, 609). A deeper understanding of democracy that transcends voting and economic growth, however, would also give importance to limiting capital and markets for social purposes, such as promoting equality, sustainability, and social justice.

The "three-dimensional" analysis of power introduced in chapter 1 (Lukes 1974, 2004b) can help to deepen our understanding of shifts in accountability and in social relations that resulted from the institutional and social embedding of this faith in markets. I will discuss several factors related to power: the creation of rules, laws, and incentives that favored market actors and protected investors from legal challenges; the adoption by political parties of neoliberal discourses and practices to promote "credibility" for investors and to satisfy international financial institutions; the use of technical arguments and centralized decision making by unaccountable experts to exclude the public and some elected officials; the use of fear and a discourse of crisis to sway nonbelievers; and the dominance of promarket advocates in the "marketplace of ideas."

These strategies of power altered both formal and informal mechanisms of accountability. Effects were detectable at multiple levels: in conflicts and decisions observable in the political sphere (one-dimensional view of power); in favoring some issues over others or in excluding issues

---

1. See chapter 2 for a summary of accountability mechanisms at stake in this analysis.

entirely from the public agenda (two-dimensional view); and in naturalizing organizational and ideological principles so that policies, behaviors, and even desires that may not reflect true societal interests were accepted as normal or even inevitable (three-dimensional view).

Legal and Organizational Strategies

Reformers designed the "roll-back," "roll-out," and "self-limiting" strategies discussed in chapter 4 to support market-oriented activity and to remove restrictions on market actors, the benefits of which, they argued, would "trickle down" to the rest of society. In practice, these changes focused economic policy narrowly on macroeconomic stability through fiscal austerity, creating incentives such as tax breaks and rent-free land in exchange for investment, and instituting norms that protected investors from legal challenges. Structural adjustment policies, trade instruments like the Central America Free Trade Agreement (CAFTA), and deregulation all reduced the threat that legislators or regulators could pose to the market model. In the process, state policy was "decoupled" from democratic accountability, to the benefit of transnational capital (Cerny 1999).

Much has already been written about the lack of accountability of structural adjustment and fiscal austerity policies (Veltmeyer, Petras, and Vieux 1997; SAPRIN 2001; Woods 2003). Technocratic, expert-driven policy was the norm under these programs. They not only included little or no public input but also tied the hands of those who would use government budgets to meet citizen claims to employment or public services (Hansen-Kuhn 1993; Rubio 1997). Despite greater calls for "ownership" by institutions such as the World Bank, an examination of their more recent Poverty Reduction Strategy Papers (PRSPs) found that "the most important element of the PRSPs . . . are the mandatory policy matrices (which) detail the now standardized Bank-Fund assortment of policy 'reform' including liberalization, privatization, fiscal and administrative reform, and assets management."[2] International financial institution (IFI) conditionalities such as these took some of the most important decisions regarding fiscal and monetary policy out of state, much less democratic, control (Cerny

2. Jubilee South, Focus on the Global South, AWEPON, Centro de Estudios Internacionales, and World Council of Churches, "The World Bank and the PRSP: Flawed Thinking and Failing Experiences." See also African Forum and Network on Debt and Development (AFRODAD), "Africa's Experience with the PRSP: Content and Process: A Synthesis Report of 10 African Countries," Harare: AFRODAD PRSP Technical Paper, 2003, www.focusweb .org/publications/2001/THE-WORLD-BANK-AND-THE-PRSP.ht ml (accessed 6 July 2008).

1999). Despite the talk, no institutionalized means existed for holding IFIs accountable for outcomes arising from their policy prescriptions.[3]

Trade agreements, such as CAFTA and NAFTA (the North American Free Trade Agreement), epitomized the roll-back of state protections and the roll-out of market-supporting mechanisms. They removed fundamental decisions regarding public ownership, investor controls, dispute resolution, and environmental and labor protections from the hands of national courts and elected representatives and placed them into the insulated framework of "free trade." The lessons of NAFTA were ominous. The 1968 takeover by the Costa Rican Electricity and Telecommunications Institute (ICE) of the ineffectual Electric Bond and Share Company would almost certainly, under CAFTA, be construed as an attempt to limit competition and threaten the profits of private investors. Moreover, U.S. trade representative Robert Zoellick informed Costa Rica's negotiators early on that the country's unique state monopolies were incompatible with the objectives of CAFTA. The threat of exclusion from the agreement placed the Costa Rican government in an uncomfortable position—compromise to meet its terms or honor commitments to protect public enterprises.[4] In the end, the negotiators—appointed by the executive and not directly accountable to the population—allowed provisions to be included in CAFTA that mandated openings of state-owned enterprises such as ICE to private sector competition. Short of renegotiation or stopping the implementation of CAFTA, there will be little chance to prevent the precise private sector openings proposed and resisted in 2000.[5] By transforming policies opposed by mass movements into law, CAFTA stifled the national conversation regarding managing public goods by simply removing it from debate.

Public monopolies have already been threatened under NAFTA, as the United Parcel Service's (UPS) case against the postal services in Canada illustrates.[6] UPS based its claim of unfair competition on the argument that Canada Post's vast public mail service infrastructure illegally subsidizes its parcel and courier services—those areas with which UPS competes. Since most public services, including electricity, health care, and

---

3. Tim Kessler, "Review of the 2004 World Development Report 'Making Services Work for Poor People,'" *Network IDEAS,* http://www.networkideas.org/themes/human/oct2003/hd08_Tim_Kessler.htm (accessed 5 July 2008).

4. "The United States Suggests a Free Trade Agreement Without Costa Rica, Due to Its Telecommunications Monopoly," *La Nación,* 3 October 2003.

5. See chapter 3 for an account of the public protests of 2000.

6. For more information on the effect of investor agreements, see *Trade Secrets: The Hidden Costs of Free Trade,* a film by Jeremy Blasi and Casey Peek (2002).

education, have both a public and a commercial component, they too can be challenged under these rules. As corporations become increasingly skilled in the use of trade agreements to improve their own market positions, the threat of campaigns to take over the most profitable dimensions of public enterprises increases, especially in countries such as Costa Rica with well-established and effective public infrastructure.

CAFTA's chapter on investment, which was modeled after NAFTA's infamous Chapter 11, presents an even more serious threat. It grants foreign investors the right to external arbitration in disputes between investors and governments, transcending even the legal and procedural provisions for citizens or corporations under domestic law. Democratic decision making was completely sidestepped with the advent of this mechanism, which not only permitted companies to win taxpayer money by suing states for lost profits but also removed arbitration proceedings from national courts' jurisdiction to a private, unaccountable tribunal with almost no provisions for civil society participation. As Oxfam America contended, "These special tribunals lack the transparency generally afforded by normal judicial proceedings and are empowered to order governments to directly compensate investors for regulations that hurt them, regardless of the public good that the regulations might serve."[7]

If the people of Central America doubt that this mechanism could be used to undermine regulations regarding safety, health, public interest, or the environment, they need only take a closer look at the history of NAFTA. A range of attacks on government activity and public policy occurred at all levels of government—federal, state, and local (Public Citizen 2005). One sobering example was the successful challenge by the California firm Metalclad to the denial of a permit for a toxic waste facility by a Mexican municipality. Though the local community strongly opposed the permit, Metalclad was awarded $15.6 million in taxpayer money. Even the Canadian government was not immune. After banning the cancer-causing gasoline additive MMT, a corporate challenge led to the ban's reversal and a $13 million award (again, of taxpayer money) to its producer, the Ethyl Corporation.

A recent case of comparable dimensions that would almost certainly be tried under CAFTA is the Harken Costa Rica Holdings case.[8] A drilling

7. Stephanie Weinberg, policy advisor, Oxfam America, "On the Implementation of the Dominican Republic-Central America Free Trade Agreement," written testimony before the U.S. House Committee on Ways and Means, 21 April 2005, 7.

8. National Resources Defense Council and Friends of the Earth, "The Threat to the Environment from the Central America Free Trade Agreement (CAFTA): The Case of Harken Costa Rica Holdings and Offshore oil," press release, 29 June 2004.

concession granted to Harken was found to conflict with the country's environmental law. Harken attempted to retaliate by bringing a suit for US$57 billion in damages, more than three times the Costa Rican gross domestic product (GDP), to an international arbitrator. But the government refused and instead resolved to fight the case in Costa Rica. Harkin withdrew its case and agreed to national arbitration, but those talks failed, and the dispute remains unresolved. Under CAFTA, Harken would have had the right to sidestep the national courts altogether and have its claims heard before an international tribunal, regardless of the wishes of the Costa Rican government or people.

Unfortunately, corporate assaults on national decision making are costly. Six NAFTA cases filed against the United States, Canada, and Mexico have already garnered US$69 million for foreign investors, and the U.S. government alone has spent millions in legal fees fighting investors' claims (Public Citizen 2009). Nineteen cases were still under review as of 2009 and are likely to result in more taxpayer money going to reimburse investors for acts "tantamount to expropriation." The small nations of Central America will have great difficulty fighting corporate challenges and risk bearing staggering costs if they do. There are also political costs of contentious agreements such as CAFTA. Already, massive protests and even deaths in clashes over CAFTA had occurred in Guatemala, Nicaragua, El Salvador, and Honduras. Meanwhile, Costa Rica's public sector unions, backed by student, rural, and citizen groups, vowed to resist CAFTA because of its threat to public institutions.[9] CAFTA is the main source of increasingly consequential levels of polarization in the region.

Perhaps CAFTA's most profound effect on public policy making was in changing the "policy space" within which economic decisions were made. For any economic policy to be effective, "developing countries must have the ability, freedom, and flexibility to make strategic choices in finance, trade, and investment policies, where they can decide on the rate and scope of liberalization and combine this appropriately with the defence of local firms and farms" (Khor 2001, 37). Many saw the inclusion of nontrade issues, such as investment, competition policy, and government procurement in NAFTA and CAFTA, as an attempt to enforce a liberalizing discipline by limiting decision-making power in precisely those areas where discretionary policy might lead countries down an alternative

9. "Union Rejection and Business Support for the [Free Trade] Agreement with the United States," La Nación, 26 October 2003; "Presagian días difíciles en Costa Rica por TLC," La Prensa (Panamá), 13 March 2006.

path, away from privatization and liberalization. The ratification of CAFTA expanded rather than narrowed which claims could be compensated under NAFTA by including "the assumption of risk," "expectation of gain or profit," intellectual property rights, and a new category of government contracts, such as those for natural resource concessions. These provisions challenged states' prerogatives to decide how to manage resources or provide for basic human rights, and neither citizens nor their elected officials had any meaningful way to contest outcomes. In effect, CAFTA enshrined the rights of investors into law while marginalizing the rights of citizenship and inclusion, so crucial to democracy.

Even without trade agreements, market-friendly policy encroached upon state institutions of horizontal accountability. Judicial and oversight bodies, such as comptrollers, attorneys general, and human rights ombudsmen, were increasingly marginalized when their decisions clashed with market principles (Haglund 2006). "The sanctity of contract" as an inviolable right, for example, meant that several judgments against damaging electricity generation contracts were ignored in both El Salvador and Costa Rica.[10] Critics vilified the Costa Rican Constitutional Court in the press for its rulings against privatization, which they deemed too "political" (as if privatization were not political). Attacks on such institutions undermined checks and balances and strengthened executive power. The dissolution of El Salvador's monetary board and the resulting dominance of the Central Reserve Bank in fiscal and monetary policy making had a similar effect (Albiac 1998).

Executive concessions of unprecedented resources and privileges to the business community further challenged horizontal accountability mechanisms. In 1998, for example, the Salvadoran government signed a contract with France Telecom that mandated automatic rate hikes, undermining a key regulatory function of approving rates. Despite public outcry, the regulatory agency would not amend the contract because "it is signed and all we can do is put up with it until it is renegotiated" at the end of the five-year concession.[11] The Legislative Assembly purportedly could not get involved either, "because it is a private contract and they have no authority." In the same year, electricity companies presented rate hikes as if they were inviolable, even though privatization was supposed to lower costs for consumers. Even the deputies that approved the law permitting privatization were surprised at the increases. SIGET, the regulator, did not explain

10. See chapter 3 for an account of these rulings.
11. "CTE Contract Unlikely to Be Amended," *Financial Times*, 7 May 2001.

the hikes, thereby implicitly sanctioning them. As one editor commented, "Presenting the rate increases as a *fait accompli* does not help instill confidence in a government that says it values citizen participation. President Calderón Sol came to the rescue of SIGET, saying that this was a technical decision that should be seen as necessary and unquestionable."[12]

This was not the first time that conflict arose in El Salvador due to decrees that stifled debate. In 1990, Executive Decree 483 was passed, limiting budgetary control within autonomous state institutions. As in Costa Rica, this measure was designed to force fiscal austerity and spending limitations to balance the general budget, with negative consequences for expenditures on investment and employee wages and benefits. According to one public sector union, it was unfair "for 20 years of struggle to be wiped away with one stroke of the pen, especially since this change will benefit the few at the expense of the many."[13] They promised massive protests, yet the government did not back down.

The business community's influence in some instances was even more direct. The main business organization, the National Association of Private Business (ANEP), greatly influenced government policy, and its former president, Antonio Saca, won the national presidency under the ARENA banner in 2004. ANEP took a daring approach to influencing public policy, by publishing an annual list of "things to do" for the government. One ANEP report boasted that, in less than one year, "around half of the short-term proposals of ENADE 2000 [were] implemented" (ANEP 2001). The business community also intentionally disrupted efforts to embed economic policy in socially minded objectives. The Salvadoran Chamber of Trade and Industry, ANEP, and the National Broadcasters Council, for example, actively opposed the 1992 Consumer Protection Law, which had been negotiated during the peace agreements to protect users of products and services against negative business practices. Elites argued that the law gave too much power to the government for defining monopolies, setting prices, and imposing sanctions, as well as violated freedom of expression, free association, and free markets. They proposed corporate self-regulation and internal codes of conduct as solutions preferable to a binding law.[14] At the request of these groups, President Cristiani

12. Editorial, "Jugarretas de la privatización," *El Salvador Proceso: Informativo Semanal*, número 796, 25 February 1998.

13. "Tensiones laborales en el sector público," *El Salvador Proceso: Informativo Semanal*, número 430, 30 May 1990, 11.

14. "La Ley de Protección al Consumidor," *El Salvador Proceso: Informativo Semanal*, número 520, 24 June 1992.

reformed the law, thus upholding free-market ideals at the expense of rec-onciling conflicts inherent to the economic model.[15]

ANEP was also slow to join, reluctant to participate in, and quick to abandon the Foro de Concertación, an important body that emerged from the Peace Accords to negotiate over economic and social issues, leading to its eventual disintegration.[16] As one commentator noted, "The weakness of civil society leads one to suspect that without international pressure, such mechanisms [as the Foro] will not survive" (Tandermann 1995, 60). Instead of focusing on inclusive, deliberative mechanisms such as the Foro, however, international pressure consisted mainly of advocating greater economic liberalization. ANEP later called for tripartite negotia-tions in the Consejo Superior del Trabajo (a scaled-back version of the Foro that included government unions only and focused specifically on jobs), thereby seeking their own, easier-to-manage kind of negotiating body (ANEP 2002). But even here, not everyone was invited: "Optimism [regarding economic inclusion] is reserved for those groups whose links with the current government assure them a privileged place in society. In the case of business, represented by ANEP, this forum has allowed them to whisper their desires for the country into the ear of [the president]: thus they avoid the harm caused by the direction that the national economy is taking."[17] In a country attempting to consolidate its democracy but lacking an institutional culture of inclusion, the continued exclusion permitted by the market-friendly model does not bode well for political sustainability.

As these cases indicate, market-oriented reforms are accompanied by control strategies "from above" that allow limited participation and negoti-ation in their design or implementation (Przeworski 1991). Reformers have an incentive to institute reforms before the electorate or their repre-sentatives can scuttle them, "introduced by decree or rammed through legislatures" (184). Both Costa Rica and El Salvador have seen this kind of fast-track policy process, the former during electricity marketization (dis-cussed at length in chapter 3) and the latter with the passage of CAFTA.[18]

---

15. "Reformas presidenciales a la Ley de Protección al Consumidor," *El Salvador Proceso: Informativo Semanal*, número 523, 15 July 1992.

16. "El poco alentador escenario de la concertación," *El Salvador Proceso: Informativo Semanal*, número 586, 3 November 1993; "Los avatares del foro de concertación," *El Salvador Proceso: Informativo Semanal*, número 540, 25 November 1992.

17. "Sobre la confianza hacia la empresa privada," *El Salvador Proceso: Informativo Sema-nal*, año 21, número 912, 26 July 2000.

18. For a description of this midnight session that allowed CAFTA to pass with little public debate in El Salvador, see Raúl Moreno, "'Madrugón' en la 'democracia salvadoreña': La ratificación del TLC entre Centroamérica y Estados Unidos," *Rebelión*, 4 January 2005.

With increased contracts between public utility companies and private interests, there are even greater levels of secrecy and exclusion. Even in Costa Rica, where accountability is much greater than in other Central American countries, citizens have raised concerns about being excluded from decisions as important as water rights and development. In the case of Sardinal, mentioned in the introduction, a resident fearing the sustainability ramifications of a public-private water partnership complained, "Nobody consulted us [about the project]; they just pushed us aside."[19] In this and numerous other cases throughout Latin America, the rapid implementation of privatization policy and use of authoritarian "decrees of necessity and urgency" led to cronyism, favoritism toward big business, and corruption (Manzetti 1999, 10).

IFI conditionalities, binding agreements, and new mechanisms for promoting markets provided like-minded politicians and technocrats with a means for overriding public opinion and created opportunities for abandoning previous state-society bargains. Salvadoran elites, as well as reformers in Costa Rica, frequently used this strategy (Haglund 2006). Mainstream political parties also adopted neoliberal discourse and practice to foster positive relations with IFIs and "credibility" (Hay 2004b). Even more progressive politicians who wanted to implement programs that contradicted neoliberal orthodoxy had a difficult time: "People still believe that the [Salvadoran] FMLN, via the Legislative Assembly, can protect their interests. But neoliberalism has weakened the state to the point where the FMLN has a hard time using state institutions to carry out its proposals."[20] As the evidence indicates, the balance of power among state institutions and between state and societal groups shifted away from public accountability because of these institutional and policy transformations. These realities, especially as they pertain to weaker public goods sectors, will pose challenges for any new government, left or right, attempting to wield state power for social ends.

Discursive and Didactic Strategies

The adoption of neoliberal institutional arrangements that marginalized public input and decreased state autonomy were accompanied by discursive strategies for stifling those viewpoints that managed to penetrate barriers to the public sphere. "Experts" framed neoliberal economic policies

19. "Vecinos de Sardinal dispuestos a frenar construcción de acueducto" (quotation from resident Ángela Gallo), *La Nación*, 23 May 2008.
20. Raúl Moreno, economist, Center for Consumer Defense, interview with the author, 16 July 2003.

as politically neutral common sense and economic development as a teleo-logical process that followed naturally from "correct" policies. This style of rule, associated with "advanced liberalism" (Rose 1993), depoliticized and professionalized social issues by promising that rational, technical calcula-tions could adjudicate among contesting and opposed interests. Economic advisors from IFIs and donor governments, as well as similarly trained economists, used technocratic strategies to exclude issues from the politi-cal process that did not conform to market principles.[21] Both the economic "team" in Costa Rica (see chapter 3) and Foundation for Economic and Social Development (FUSADES) and ANEP in El Salvador (see chapter 4) used technocratic discourse liberally. Many elites in these countries, much like their counterparts elsewhere, were educated in U.S. universities and embraced the neoliberal model (Albiac 1998). Research institutes, such as FUSADES, expended great resources writing documents, disseminating neoclassical ideas, and holding talks with consultants from USAID and other external organizations. They presented state failure as a given and privatization as a necessity. Hegemonic (neoliberal) analyses and solutions to problems in public goods sectors became the only plausible ones.

Many groups offered alternatives to the neoliberal vision but with only sporadic success in affecting policy.[22] In 1994, Salvadoran labor unions put forth a proposal for the modernization and depoliticization of public entities that provided a less drastic alternative to privatization, but the rul-ing ARENA Party disregarded the proposal. As one commentator com-plained, ARENA "was unwilling even to discuss privatization—a key economic policy—in an honest way, and instead shunned the forum, rev-eled in labor fragmentation, and ran television ads to convince the public of the panacea that privatization would be; public debate is in shambles."[23] This has been the fate of citizen working groups and commissions in both El Salvador and Costa Rica, which were branded illegitimate because they had no "technical" expertise. In Costa Rica, however, the exclusion of these groups in decision-making processes has been much more difficult under neoliberal rule because of their long history of successful incorporation.

Even in Costa Rica, however, the discursive terrain is shifting. To cir-cumvent public resistance to market-friendly policies, elites have devel-oped new discourses of fear and crisis, even more sophisticated than their

21. Agenda control is an example of Lukes's (1974) "second dimension" of power, while a broad acceptance of technocratic logic as "common sense" and the concomitant overlooking of alternatives, is more akin to Lukes's "third-dimension" of power.

22. See, for example, Arriola Palomares (1993) and Goitia (1994).

23. "Rechazo sindical a la privatización," *El Salvador Proceso: Informativo Semanal,* nú-mero 632, 19 octubre 1994.

attacks on ICE, described in chapter 3. John Williamson, father of the Washington Consensus, argued that it can be propitious in situations of resistance to "think of deliberately provoking a crisis to remove the political logjam to reform" or at least to conjure up a "pseudo-crisis that could serve the same positive function" (Williamson 1994, 20). Even perceived crises can be instrumental to reform (Grindle and Thomas 1991). Crises engage higher-level policy makers, open policy spaces to more far-reaching changes, and create pressure to take immediate action. The stakes are higher for decision makers but so is their autonomy.

The rhetorical assault on ICE and its supporters by an economist at the Costa Rican Coalition for Development Initiatives illustrates the use of this discourse to depoliticize privatization policies and discredit opponents. The critique framed pro-privatization groups as neutral and benevolent, "seeking to transfer rents from pressure groups that benefit from ICE's monopoly to citizens as a whole," thus producing "greater efficiency and lower rates . . . resulting in greater local and international competitiveness" (Jiménez 2000, 304–5). It framed opponents, meanwhile, as selfish rent seekers, vainly protecting their interests against the inevitable winds of change, to the detriment of the country. Citizens who opposed privatization were uninformed subjects to be educated and enlightened by exposing "the hidden reasons behind [the position of rent-seeking] interest groups; in that way, those who oppose the change in model will find their position weakened" (313). The media were urged to reveal the dire consequences if ICE were not privatized: "high prices, low quality, fewer job opportunities, and poor resource allocation" (316). The critique did not mention the interests of those who would gain from selling the profitable ICE or the efficiency, low cost, and high quality of current services. It also did not discuss the costs of transferring productive assets to private companies or the difficulties of regulating a sensitive hydroelectric sector. Expert panels and the popular media during this period reflected this one-sided discourse.

Urgent crisis discourses were complemented by a politics of fear, especially during the conflict over CAFTA. A memorandum leaked to the University of Costa Rica's weekly newspaper in September 2007 revealed a deliberate campaign, proposed by Planning Minister and Second Vice-President Kevin Casas and Deputy Fernando Sánchez, to frighten the population and local officials who opposed CAFTA.[24] The letter was addressed

---

24. "El 'Sí' juega la carta del miedo," *Seminario Universidad*, 6 September 2008. The authors of the memo were not rogue elements but Oxford-trained Ph.D.s and key figures in the Arias administration.

to the president of the Republic, Oscar Arias Sanchez, and recommended, among other strategies, saturating the media with messages of the dreadful consequences that could befall the country if the agreement was not ratified (e.g., lost employment, the weakening of democracy, and the rise of a radical left supported by Fidel Castro, Hugo Chávez, and Daniel Ortega); threatening mayors who expressed anti-CAFTA sentiments with severance of government funding; and circumventing rules set by the Supreme Elections Tribunal that restricted the use of public resources to advocate on behalf of CAFTA in factories and other workplaces. Although Arias and Casas both denied that these strategies were actually implemented, the campaign of fear was already evident at banana plantations and maquila factories, in mayors' offices, and in the media.[25] There was also evidence of vote buying in some workplaces.[26]

The government of George W. Bush carried out its own scare campaign on the eve of the October 2007 referendum. Given the history of U.S. interference in other Central American elections, intervention in Costa Rica was not without precedent. In 2006, for example, U.S. ambassador to Nicaragua Paul Trivelli and U.S. Commerce Secretary Carlos Gutierrez warned that a victory by the leftist Sandinistas could "scare off foreign investors and jeopardize Nicaragua's participation in the CAFTA free-trade accord with the United States."[27] On the eve of the 2004 Salvadoran elections, the Bush administration informed Salvadoran voters that voting for the opposition FMLN would mean remittances from Salvadorans living in the United States might be threatened. Although these claims were false—the U.S. executive branch has no power to stop remittances—the elite-run press printed the story on the front page on election day.[28] In a country in which at least 20 percent of GDP consisted of remittances, these threats were real and palpable for a large segment of the population, and they likely contributed to the defeat of the FMLN.[29]

25. I participated in the referendum as an election observer and witnessed several violations of the legally required media blackout up to and including the day of the election. See also "Leaked Memo Sparks Scandal," *Tico Times*, 9 September 2008.

26. "Denuncian compra de votos por TLC," *La Prensa Gráfica*, 22 September 2007.

27. "OAS to U.S.: Don't Meddle in Nicaraguan Election," *Democracy Now!* 24 October 2006.

28. I also observed the Salvadoran elections of 2004. Several people asked me, in my capacity as a U.S. citizen, whether the U.S. executive branch had this power, as it was nearly impossible for them to get accurate information.

29. The official numbers put the remittances rate at 18.2 percent of GDP in 2006. This includes only officially recorded remittances. The true size of remittances, including unrecorded flows through formal and informal channels, is believed to be larger. "Migration and Remittances Factbook," compiled by Dilip Ratha and Zhimei Xu, Migration and Remittances Team, Development Prospects Group, World Bank.

The intervention was somewhat unusual for Costa Rica, however, and underscored the importance of the treaty for U.S. and Costa Rican elites alike. Two days before the referendum, the Bush administration told voters that if they chose "No" to CAFTA, the Caribbean Basin Initiative (CBI, a system of trade preferences already in place for the region) would not be renewed and that the United States would never renegotiate CAFTA.[30] The press picked this up immediately and in effect "provided a day-long free commercial for the Yes side."[31] The press did not mention that several other trade agreements, such as those with Peru and Colombia, had been renegotiated. Nor did they make much of a letter contradicting this claim of inflexibility regarding both CAFTA and the CBI, signed by lead congressional Democrat Nancy Pelosi. The effect was chilling, with support for the "No" side slipping from a double-digit lead to a statistical dead heat in the days before the election. The "No" campaign had little opportunity and few resources to disseminate counterinformation through their usual channels of community-based organizers, while the "Yes" side used their substantial resources on a massive media blitz. On October 7, the "No" campaign was defeated by a razor-thin margin.

Examples of the language of urgency, fear, and inevitability could be found throughout policy documents in El Salvador as well. Propaganda campaigns by promarket groups actively tried to "educate" civil society regarding what to think. But competition in this marketplace of ideas was no level playing field. The Salvadoran private sector, FUSADES, IFIs, and the ARENA Party all banded together to carry out feasibility and promotional studies regarding privatization. Social organizations, such as unions and consumer advocates, meanwhile, did not have comparable resources to carry out studies and, in some cases, were unable even to obtain valid information on the condition of state-owned enterprises and the feasibility of state-centered alternatives. Thus, the main policy emphasis in public goods sectors was privatization (Lungo and Oporto 1995). Without institutionalized means for information creation, dissemination, and legitimization, opponents had little recourse beyond public protest.

Media, which could aid in information dissemination and investigation, are elite-owned in El Salvador (Paniagua Serrano 2002). When electricity

30. "Casa Blanca confirma que no renegociará TLC," *La Nación*, 7 October 2007.

31. "Costa Rica's CAFTA 'Si' Vote Called into Question." Quote from Tom Ricker, codirector of the Quixote Center, a nongovernmental organization with international elections observers present at the referendum. *Upside Down World*, 12 October 2007.

prices rose dramatically in 2001, the main newspapers (*La Prensa Gráfica* and *Diario de Hoy*) "simply relied on expert opinion, following their discourse and using their jargon."[32] These newspapers barely covered the rate increase but "spilled a great deal of ink" on a story about Bible reading in public schools, thus failing to provide the public with the necessary information to understand the issue. The media were also used extensively and unabashedly to criticize and discredit the opposition FMLN, linking them during election campaigns to the same bogeymen as in Costa Rica: Castro, Chávez, and Ortega, as well as most recently to the Colombian FARC guerillas.[33] The Human Rights Defense Attorney (PDDH), who took an active stance against certain neoliberal policies because of what she considered their negative impact on social and economic rights, was a target as well. And in 2005, a local news channel fired the popular journalist Mauricio Funes, whose guests were often critical of government economic policies. His own incisive broadcast editorials had already been cancelled in 2003 for "harsh criticisms . . . of the government's management of the consequences of the January earthquake."[34] Although Funes went on to start his own program on a different channel (and more recently win the presidency in 2009), other critical journalists faced similar obstacles.[35]

The media in Costa Rica were not immune to these criticisms, but a greater variety of sources existed to present alternative viewpoints. *Seminario Universidad*, in particular, provided a consistent and critical voice to balance the promarket messages of the mainstream press. Yet *Seminario* was only published weekly, and distribution of other alternative media was limited. The most widely read newspaper, *La Nación*, was clearly in favor of liberalization. Forty-two percent of all editorials in the month before the CAFTA referendum explicitly endorsed the "Yes" position while criticizing the "No" camp, echoing the crisis discourse from the Combo: "If we reject CAFTA, the consequences will be catastrophic."[36] Meanwhile, none (0 percent) of the editorials presented the "No" position in a positive light,

32. Xiomara Peraza, Department of Communication and Letters, University of Central America, "La prensa escrita y las alzas tarifarias," *El Salvador Proceso: Informativo Semanal*, año 22, número 963, 15 August 2001.

33. "FARC-FMLN contactos de siete años según correos," *La Prensa Gráfica*, 11 June 2008.

34. Explanation by journalist Kristin Neubauer, "Oleada de reacciones en favor de Mauricio Funes," *Reporteros sin Fronteras*, 21 February 2005, http://www.rsf.org/article.php3?id_article = 12613 (accessed 20 June 2008).

35. "Despido masivo de periodistas en El Salvador," *El Nuevo Diario* (Nicaragua), 22 February 2005.

36. Editorial, "Alucinación política," *La Nación*, 5 October 2007.

though the paper did publish letters to the editor and opinion pieces that were critical of CAFTA (at a ratio of one letter arguing "No to CAFTA" for every three "Yes" arguments).[37] The majority of pieces framed opponents of CAFTA as uninformed about the complexity of the issues, if not downright ignorant. Worse, they presented mutual conflicts between opposing sides as if the anti-CAFTA side was alone in perpetrating conflict:

> [CAFTA opponents] perpetrated acts of physical aggression . . . not preceded by threats or offensive words. Rather, they took place in discussions or at counter-demonstrations. . . . The aggression was a product of intolerance, pure and simple, of the rejection of different points of view. . . . These aggressive acts are not isolated. They are the consequence of a campaign that, over three years . . . presented CAFTA, ideologically, as an invasion or an act of vandalism, with sectors that would benefit as accomplices . . . this violence represents a rejection of democratic institutionalism.[38]

Even Eugenio Trejos, rector of the Costa Rican Technology Institute (ITCR) and president of the National Support Front in the Fight against CAFTA was accused of behaving violently. To this he replied, "They have confused vehemence with violence."[39]

Effect on Horizontal and Vertical Accountability and Power Relations

As the previous discussion demonstrates, organizational and discursive strategies accompanying the advent of neoliberalism in Central America upset the balance of power among government branches and agencies and weakened certain channels of accountability between citizens and the state. Structural adjustment, CAFTA, and greater foreign investment gave more relative power to executive and extranational forces regarding economic policy. Concurrently, campaigns critiquing oversight bodies seen as "activist" (i.e., not operating according to market principles) led to a

37. Data culled from an archive search at http://nacion.com/ARCHIVO/ (accessed 25 June 2008).

38. Editorial, "Intolerancia y violencia," *La Nación*, 18 September 2007. Witness testimony places blame for scattered violent altercations on both sides, as well as on overzealous police.

39. "El 'Sí' juega la carta del miedo," *Seminario Universidad*, 6 September 2008.

slow shift within these bodies away from decisions that challenged market orthodoxy. Policies were devised based on the assumption that "special interest groups" should not receive entitlements and that free markets would better adjudicate between competing interests. These shifts strengthened the power of business and investor groups to secure their own interests, as in the traditional pluralist, or "one-dimensional," view of power (Dahl 1961; Polsby 1980).

From a two-dimensional perspective (Bachrach and Baratz 1962), power was evident not only in how issues were decided but also in the ways powerful actors "created or reinforced barriers to the public airing of policy conflicts" (949). Not only were social objectives such as cross-subsidies or job creation in public goods sectors overruled at the policy stage by market-oriented goals, but also the prioritization of market values shifted wider economic discourses so that these social concerns were no longer considered valid objects of policy, and were thus excluded from policy-making discussions. Inflation targeting and technocratic arguments regarding "sound" (market-friendly) economic strategies left policy agendas in the hands of a few "experts" (mainly economists) and out of the reach of citizens and their representative bodies. This served to suffocate or marginalize demands or maim them in the implementation process. It also weakened informal accountability mechanisms, such as social movements, plebiscites, independent consumer defense groups, and other citizen groups, by discrediting and stifling proposed alternatives.

Which values dominated in a particular context was also a function of power; this was where the "third dimension" came into play (Lukes 1974). Market discourses were dominant not because of their inherent superiority but because of promotional campaigns designed to declare their irrefutable merits, discredit opponents, and persuade or manipulate reluctant actors to acquiesce or come to accept the new policies as inevitable, through fear and crisis if need be. Over time, market principles and their concomitant social arrangements came to be accepted by many as self-evident universals, or what Bourdieu (1977) called *doxa*. Neoliberalization could be understood as an attempt to effect changes to this *doxa*, so that the "world as given" would be seen as naturally organized according to market principles. The result was the primacy of discourses and practices that furthered the interests of powerful market actors while making them appear to be common sense. The more public understandings could be shaped to favor a market orientation, the less need for legitimization. Rather than resolve conflicts between interest groups, these strategies insulated certain groups against others and depoliticized economic policy (Schamis 2002). Table 16 summarizes the argument thus far regarding accountability mechanisms under neoliberalism.

But power is not absolute. Although privatization and marketization policies were accompanied by strategies to reframe subjects as consumers and citizenship as mainly voting, in places where the state promised social and economic rights, these restrictions amounted to breaking the social contract: "The fact that entitlements have been to some extent guaranteed by the state means that they have been won in previous struggles and negotiations, become embedded in the social pact between states and citizens, and woven into the moral economy. Entitlements are more than interests or demands that might go unmet in the political process. They are experienced as rights and their potential loss as injustice" (Udayagiri and Walton 2002, 336). Neoliberal policy makers placed great importance on the "rules of the game" for market actors but undermined, intentionally or not, realistic ways of producing broader trust and political harmony. The electorate learned quickly to distrust voting when politicians promised one thing and did another and lost confidence in the state's ability to uphold protections or to ensure that the rules of the game were just (UNDP 2001). Decrees and legislative hardball showed parties, unions, and other representative bodies that technocrats viewed their role in policy making as insignificant. Negotiating over fait accompli bred anger and distrust. The neoliberal model presented few constructive, institutionalized mechanisms for overcoming these types of polarization. But it did not achieve complete hegemony in Central America and in fact provoked strong reactions—double movements—outside and in opposition to the state, as we will see next.

Liberalization, Authoritarianism, and Democracy

Many transitions have been characterized by friction between democratization and liberalization (Bresser, Maravall, and Przeworski 1993), but it was particularly problematic in cases of "democracy from below" like in El Salvador (Wood 2000). Path-dependent legacies—such as extreme inequality in wealth and life opportunities, the substantial mobilization entailed by democratization from below, raised expectations of mobilized groups, and a state trained in the science of repression and containment of unrest rather than the delivery of basic goods and services—could

Table 16   Shifting accountability mechanisms under neoliberalism

	Relevant actors	Shifting accountability mechanisms
Horizontal accountability (balance of power)	Executive branch	• Greater executive decision making authority • Increased use of "fast track" strategies that limit discussion
	Legislative branch	• Teams of "expert" advisors make key economic decisions • Independence of central banks
	Judicial branch	• Judicial review bypassed or ignored when market principles are at stake
	Oversight agencies	• Enforcement and investigative power weakened vis-à-vis private firms
Vertical accountability *Electoral*	Political parties with legislative representation	• Parties forced to answer to the "imperatives" of the global economy (→ progressive platforms are muted)
	Citizens	• Focus on periodic elections to the exclusion of other accountability mechanisms
Societal	Civil society associations, nongovernmental organizations, social movements	• Use of technical discourse to stifle alternatives and disparage opponents
	Ombudsmen	• Creation of fear and an atmosphere of crisis to silence opposition and rush through policies
	Consumer protection agencies	
	Media	

SOURCE: Table adapted from Smulovitz and Peruzzotti (2000).

undermine both democracy and development. Liberalization did nothing to address these legacies and in fact allowed for a realignment of elite power to thwart more radical reforms that might have helped states meet higher citizen expectations and provide for, rather than repress, claimants of economic and social rights. For people who fought hard for social justice, "liberal policies [fell] far short of and may be seen as obstacles to the types of economic reforms they expect[ed]" (Wood 2000, 211).

The Peace Accords were supposed to have remedied the dominance of allied economic and political elites that led to civil war in El Salvador. But substantive and discursive exclusion continued and was met with growing resistance by unions, activists, and concerned citizens. Unfortunately, Salvadoran elites interpreted this resistance as threatening to the country. As President Saca complained, "Civil society groups have assumed a 'representativeness' that they do not deserve. They go out in the streets in protest, threatening stability and scaring away investment, but they themselves have not been elected by anyone and have no right to speak in their name" (ANEP 2002). This attitude endangered spaces for vertical accountability and directly contradicted efforts to bring civil society (rather than simply elected officials) into policy-making arenas. Here, neoliberalism and neoconservatism converged while simultaneously creating a contradiction: one was antistate while the other was authoritarian. The government response to social resistance was punitive: "ARENA reacted by employing security forces rather than the bodies that were designed for post-war conflict resolution (such as the Foro de Concertación)."[40] It also responded through public companies by firing workers who spoke out against liberalization:

> In 2001, CEL [the Lempa River Executive Hydroelectric Commission] launched a campaign to weaken the union [STSEL]. On September 24, CEL fired a union leader, Mario Roberto Carranza Hernandez. . . . In total, 23 members including five executive members were fired as part of the campaign. . . . In addition, CEL pressured workers to disaffiliate from STSEL, resulting in the withdrawal of 48 members. . . . The attack on STSEL accelerated with the firing of its General Secretary, Alirio Romero, and the General Secretary of

---

40. "Problemas laborales en el sector público," *El Salvador Proceso: Informativo Semanal*, número 620, 20 July 1994.

the CEL section, Sará Isabel Quintanilla, on October 18, 2002, in clear violation of collective bargaining agreements.[41]

In an even more ominous development, the government passed an anti-terrorism bill in 2002, which the police subsequently used to charge protesters with terrorism. On July 2, 2007, they arrested seventeen people, charging them with "Aggravated Damages, Acts of Terrorism and Injuring a Police Officer" for attending a protest against the privatization of water in Suchitoto.[42] The arrests seemed designed to discourage social protest and intimidate protesters, as the charges were later dropped. Even international solidarity came under fire, with the Salvadoran government attempting to deport or refusing entry to non-Salvadoran progressives and solidarity activists.[43]

We might expect some authoritarian behavior in a country with a long history of violence and repression. But what about in Costa Rica? As discussed in chapter 3, the protests of 2000 against the marketization of ICE were marred by police violence, including the unprecedented use of tear gas and batons.[44] They were followed by the passage of the Law Prohibiting Blockades, the most punitive of its kind to date. Since then, protests against CAFTA have tested this policy and led to increasing confrontation. Daniel Camacho, director of the Central American Human Rights Commission, called the government's stance against protests "rigid" and "provocative." "It makes one wonder," he said, "whether there is some political reason for this provocation."[45] In his view, government domination by a closed neoliberal group narrowed their focus exclusively to commercial

41. Report of the American Federation of Labor and Congress of Industrial Organizations (AFL-CIO) and Union of Needletrades, Industrial and Textile Employees (UNITE) for the "Central America: Labor Rights and Child Labor Reports" Pursuant to the Trade Act of 2002, Section 2102(C)(8)–(9), 5 June 2003.

42. "Cámara avala aplicar ley terrorismo en caso Suchitoto," *La Prensa Gráfica*, 20 July 2007.

43. "Ecuadorian Advisor to the Salvadoran Social Security Institute Physician and Worker Union (SIMETRISSS) and Long-time El Salvador Resident Expelled for Supposed Involvement in 'Political Activities,'" *Centro de Intercambio y Solidaridad (CIS) Action Alert*, 3 May 2005; "Personal ONG estadounidense es investigado por Migración," *La Prensa Gráfica*, 10 May 2005. During the course of this fieldwork, I also became aware of at least three such cases that were not reported in the media.

44. UCR "Students Against the Combo," confidential interviews with the author, 14 and 28 January 2003.

45. "Males estructurales causan las protestas," *Seminario Universidad*, 2 September 2004, http://semanario.ucr.ac.cr/ediciones2004/M9Setiembre_2004/1588_SET02/pais.html (accessed 9 September 2004).

openings, causing them to ignore social needs in favor of meeting macro-economic targets and promoting free trade. Juany Guzman, professor and former director of the School of Political Science at the University of Costa Rica, agreed. He worried that the government "has not correctly read this juncture and believes that the protests [against CAFTA] are the work of a group of agitators that is using the people." In her estimation, "there is a lot of support for this movement," yet the government chose to ignore its popular basis and attempted to suppress the movement.

As shown historically in Costa Rica, when the space for dialogue on government policy is open to organized and resistant sectors of civil society, there is "a much-reduced space for technocratic initiative" (Portes 1997, 244). The puzzle is why traditional avenues of representation were not open to people in 2000 and again during the negotiation of CAFTA, forcing them to take to the streets.[46] The answer lies in the nature of neo-liberal policy strategies: as long as technocrats think they know best, they will resist critique; "technocracy hurls itself against democracy and breeds the inclination to proceed against popular resistance: to suppress *glasnost* in order to continue with *perestroika*" (Przeworski 1991, 187). It is usually citizens with little formalized structure for input and participation that resort to protest to be heard. But there are avenues for being heard in Costa Rica. This is where the contradictions of neoliberalism meet inherited democratic legacies and democratization processes. As neoliberalism shrinks policy spaces, citizens try to pry them back open, within institutions or on the streets. If that fails, they may lose faith in their leaders and political system and turn instead to pursuing their own selfish interests at the expense of the greater good or even at the expense of democracy itself. Even the highly acclaimed democracy of Costa Rica has, in recent years, evidenced increased apathy and a decline in system support (Seligson 2002), as well as greater political conflict. The precise manner in which citizens responded and were included or repressed depended on inherited political legacies; but respond they did. Spaces of inclusion remain under contestation.

Counterhegemonic Movements

Polanyi's (1944) account of the double movement, in which states intervene with social protections to soften the blow of liberalization, must be

---

46. "Sindicatos preparan protesta regional contra tratado comercial," *La Nación*, 28 January 2004. "Marcha pacífica llaga hasta Asamblea Legislativa," *La Nación*, 26 August 2004.

reevaluated in light of such cases as El Salvador. States may not act in defense of citizens because they are incapable of, uncommitted to, or prohibited from doing so; sometimes all three obstacles are in operation. As in the Russia described by Burawoy (2001), the Salvadoran state "hooked itself into the global economy and became enmeshed in the organization of transnational flows of natural resources, finance, and information" (281), while simultaneously detaching itself from the concerns of the local population. If the problem is state incompetence or unresponsiveness to human needs, simply imposing market "solutions" is shortsighted at best. Although one should not take the comparison too far, this lack of commitment undermined protective social policy during the market transition in Costa Rica as well. As these and numerous other cases show, the substantive neglect and discursive exclusion of citizens during reform processes necessitated new types of double movements—everything from demands for inclusion in public debates to riots and revolts—not simply in response to the harms threatened by a self-regulating market (Polanyi 1944), but in response to threats to democratic participation itself.

A closer look at some of the counterhegemonic movements confronting neoliberal public goods policies in Costa Rica and in El Salvador reveals serious citizen-driven concerns propelling double movements. This creates a quandary for those who believe organized, selfish interests scuttled otherwise beneficial reforms. If privatization was "generally positive" as claimed,[47] then why were so many people fervently opposed to it? Resistance was not confined to public sector unions and civil servants, the actors whose interests were most clearly challenged by privatization. It was those groups that supposedly benefited—housewives, consumers, youth—that filled the streets in large antiprivatization protests in Costa Rica and El Salvador and indeed throughout Latin America. Although workers clearly had an interest in opposing privatization, unions represented less than 20 percent of workers in Costa Rica and less than 5 percent in El Salvador (Anner 2008). They also had low confidence marks from the population at large, so it is doubtful that they should be credited with (or accused of) spurring massive mobilizations.[48]

An organizer of the 2000 protests in Costa Rica provided a different answer regarding who took a stand against privatization:

47. John Williamson, "Discussion of *After the Washington Consensus*," talk given at the Ford Foundation's "Leading Edge Roundtable," New York City, 15 January 2004.

48. A 2002 poll by UNIMER Research International reported that only 36 percent of the Costa Rican population had confidence in unions. Information from http://www.nacion.com/ln_ee/encuestas/unimer/10-2002/Parte4.htm (accessed 7 July 2008).

All the popular organizations: cooperatives, farmers, municipalities, students, environmentalists . . . housewives; all kinds of people. Because behind this [issue] was a subtext regarding the Costa Rican state . . . the people very quickly realized that everything it had been able to accomplish was at stake in the ICE controversy. . . . They were not only hitting the streets to defend ICE, but to defend the Costa Rican model. . . . I think people were very worried because they saw their quality of life go down [after neoliberal reforms] and they understood, broadly speaking, that what was at stake were two very different ways of doing things.[49]

Resistance was pervasive among people who supposedly benefited from privatization precisely because of "the lethal injury" visited by neoliberalism on "the institutions in which [their] social existence is embodied" (Polanyi 1944, 157).

Participatory, socially minded, and environmentally friendly alternatives to the neoliberal model for managing public goods are not difficult to find (Balanyá et al. 2005),[50] although they may be politically difficult to implement (Lemos and Farias de Oliveira 2004; Abers and Keck 2006). Although there is no one clear model that emerges from a review of potential alternatives, this should not concern us; institutional diversity is integral to effective public policy (Ostrom 2005). The key to arriving at appropriate policies for diverse contexts is not "best practices" per se but the existence of spaces for actors with divergent values to discuss possible pathways and to decide which are appropriate for the local environmental, social, and political conditions. Inclusive mechanisms bring to light a variety of contrasting ideas and opinions, thus widening the range of possibilities and decreasing the chances that one group's interests will be prioritized over others. It also helps communities arrive at "legitimate" institutional and political arrangements not based on relations of power but through public discourse (Shapiro 2006). Reformers can thus avoid making the mistake of past reformers who "regarded themselves as far smarter and far-seeing than they really were and, at the same time, regarded their subjects as far more stupid and incompetent than they really were" (Scott 1998, 348). In the

49. María Flores Estrada, Women Against the Combo, and journalist for *Semenario Universitario*, interview with the author, 30 January 2003.

50. See also Public Citizen's "Alternatives to Water Privatization," http://www.citizen.org/cmep/Water/alts; and Public Services International "Municipal Services: Organisations, Companies and Alternatives," http://www.psiru.org/reports/2008-11-munic.doc.

following two sections, I discuss attempts in Costa Rica and El Salvador to present and promote alternatives to neoliberal management for public goods. These popular double movements against increasing marketization came about in response to government complicity in neoliberal transformations that did not always serve to protect the public interest.

Struggles Against "Ideological Extremism" in Costa Rica

The Costa Rican model of social democracy as described in chapter 3 and throughout the book can be seen as a workable alternative to neoliberalism. The dire predictions of its imminent collapse by reformers did not materialize, and its unique social values have survived numerous attacks. Part of the success of the Costa Rican model was that the government abolished the military at the end of the civil war in 1949. Funds that other countries poured into weapons and internal repression were thus available for other uses, and the relative peace enabled government infrastructure projects to proceed without much friction (a few hydroelectric projects excepted). This reality indicates the real benefits for economic and social rights (not to mention civil rights) of demilitarization. The other aspect of the Costa Rican model that was unique in Latin America was the postwar commitment by successive administrations, regardless of ideological bents, to progressive social policy in essential areas for development, such as health, environmental protection, and resource management (e.g., electricity and water), in the name of social democracy.

The government also opened spaces for interest representation, negotiation among differing viewpoints and interests, and direct citizen input into social and economic policy. Costa Ricans expected their wishes to be heeded, and when they were not, they demanded inclusion.[51] Participation took the form of frequent televised public debates on issues of the day, "mixed commissions" to discuss particular policies, citizen ballot initiatives, and an open-door policy at the Legislative Assembly. Beginning in the mid-1980s, demands for greater inclusion by marginalized social actors resulted in an increase in the use of participatory mechanisms: "days of *concertación*" from August 1986 to October 1987 to help deal with the costs of structural adjustment; a "national dialogue" in 1990 that led

51. In recent years, this has been less true, as disillusionment with political leaders and electoral democracy has led to greater cynicism and voter apathy.

to the creation of a tripartite Superior Work Council; a *concertación* mechanism for sustainable development, created in 1993, that included civil societies and governments of both Costa Rica and Holland; an attempt at incorporating the latter mechanism into a national system for sustainable development; and, in 1994, a (largely unsuccessful) national dialogue on fiscal policy (Cortés Ramos 1999).[52]

It is difficult to say exactly when disillusionment with democratic inclusion began in Costa Rica, but it is clear that the so-called Figueres-Calderón Pact in the late 1990s marked a serious crisis of legitimacy for political parties. In 1995, President José María Figueres convened a forum ostensibly to gather public input regarding the fiscal deficit, but despite the pretense of taking into account participant views, it was in fact "designed to achieve rapid approval for government proposals, without the political will to listen to alternatives" (Rojas Bolaños, 2000, 17). After failing to reach an agreement, the government's finance minister announced that the administration's original proposal would be preserved with few modifications. From then on, the Figueres government abandoned even a pretense of *concertación* in favor of political deal brokering with the main opposition party, led by ex-president Rafael Angel Calderón Fournier. The dramatic rise in abstentionism in the elections of 1998 resulted from public rejection of this elite power play (Cortés Ramos 2001).

Costa Ricans, however, were not ready to give up on democracy and, specifically, were not ready to abandon the promise of dialogue, negotiation, and compromise: "The word *concertación* is a prestigious one. It evokes harmony, a musical concert, an understanding among interested parties capable of opening a road to a better future. It is a word not yet spent, not discredited, that indicates one of the few reasonable paths to avoiding moral and economic shipwreck for the country. We will stop this sly and haughty co-government, for whom nobody voted in the past election, from eating it away from inside."[53] Sentiments like this likely motivated incoming president Miguel Angel Rodríguez to initiate a renewed *concertación* process (Rojas Bolaños 2000). The resulting Concertación Commission eschewed both elite and corporatist bargaining in favor of a space for a wide variety of social actors to participate on almost all policy questions. The commission was able to come to consensus on an impressive 150 issues, although the government did not secure approval on the thorny question of opening state monopolies to market competition.

52. See chapter 2, footnote 21, for notes regarding the full meaning of *concertación*.
53. Miguel Picado G., Asociacion Justicia y Paz, http://www.jp.or.cr/pulso/1998/marmig.html (accessed 1 May 2009).

"Reform" of state monopolies became the key polarizing issue over the next several years. If national dialogue was needed to create social harmony in any area of public policy, this was it: "The issue [of public sector reform] reflected the absolute lack of legitimacy of 'technocratic solutions'" and the need for compromise.[54] After the protests against electricity and telecommunications privatization in 2000, the government called for a special Mixed Commission to resolve disagreements underlying the conflict. Initial analysis of this citizens' commission was promising: it created transparency regarding market openings and the actors behind them; unveiled the underlying structural causes of the debilitation of ICE; and "demonstrated that Costa Rican citizens can not only protest, but also make proposals."[55] Participants developed a "Contingency Plan for the Strengthening of ICE" that called for removal of restrictions on public investment, reversal of laws allowing private contracts in the electricity sector, and a halt to further privatization.[56] The process contributed to a national conversation about state institutions but ultimately failed to stop the drive toward privatization. This led to impatience among citizens that only intensified with the signing of CAFTA, which, by executive fiat, opened public institutions to marketization processes. Suddenly, the same policies that had been declared unacceptable by the Mixed Commission were set to be enshrined in international treaty law.

This did not sit well with the population: divisions over CAFTA almost cost the once-wildly popular, pro-CAFTA candidate Oscar Arias the presidency, despite polls indicating a comfortable victory. Opponents were concerned not only about public institutions like ICE but also about the likely consequences of greater marketization in the water sector. Despite assurances by CAFTA proponents that its Chapter 17 would strengthen environmental protection, they feared that other chapters—in particular Chapter 10 (on investment), Chapter 11 (on services and market access), and Chapter 15 (on intellectual property)—would contradict or undermine Chapter 17 and actually weaken environmental protections.[57] Worse yet, Costa Rican law would be subverted by these chapters, and passing future environmental protection measures would be virtually impossible.[58] Besides,

54. Carlos Sojo, director, Latin American Social Sciences Faculty (FLACSO), Costa Rica, interview with the author, 30 January 2003.

55. William Vargas, Catholic Church representative, ICE Mixed Commission, *Se Mueve*, 19 November 2000.

56. Representación Social, Comisión Especial Mixta del ICE, "Plan de Contingencia para el Fortalecimiento del ICE," 11 September 2000.

57. José María Villalta, lawyer, specialist in environmental rights, Foro Ambiental "No al TLC": "No hay ambiente para el TLC," 29 July 2006.

58. Working group on water, Foro Ambiental "No al TLC": "No hay ambiente para el TLC," 29 July 2006.

the protections in Chapter 17 were limited to pollutants, control of chemical and toxic wastes, and protection and conservation of the flora and fauna in wildlife areas. It left out the majority of social movement concerns, including regulation of the administration, exploitation, and use of, as well as access to, natural resources; planning and prevention of overexploitation; and community rights.

Activists and some water-sector employees also considered concessions a serious problem. They complained of a lack of control over water-intensive private firms—such as hotels, dairy companies, and large breweries— that, once granted a concession, were allowed unlimited water usage without consequences.[59] Although rivers themselves were not granted in these concessions, rivers such as the Tempisque experienced excessive exploitation, and it was difficult for the state to regulate all concessions with limited personnel. There were also too many wells, and their drilling was virtually uncontrolled. Although the government proposed to increase fees for wells and concessions, the Movimiento Libertario and business groups fought against such moves, which they claimed would violate freedom.[60] Social movements remained alarmed by the continued emphasis on concessions in some versions of a proposed water bill that was in development,[61] as well as ongoing projects to "study" their possible expansion.[62]

Beneath concerns about concessions and environmental protection was the more fundamental issue of incompatible visions regarding water.[63] Unions, environmentalists, and social justice advocates rejected the idea of water as a private good to be exploited for personal gain. For one, they saw a deep contradiction between water as a human right and water as an economic good.[64] Under a private scheme, water rates would have to be set high enough to cover not only investment costs but also a profit margin: "the social ends are different."[65] Control over the resource was another

59. Alvaro Espinoza, representative, Association of AyA workers (ASTRA—Asociación de Trabajadores de Acuaductos y Acantarillados), interview with the author, 3 August 2006.

60. Gerardo Cascante Amador, Asesor Sindical—Sector AyA, National Association of Public and Private Employees (ANEP), interview with the author, 4 August 2006.

61. Alvaro Espinoza, ASTRA, interview with the author, 3 August 2006.

62. An earlier study of this sort was carried out by N + 1, a Spanish investment bank, and resulted in the privatization of the water system in Heredia. Some water sector officials believed this project to be financially infeasible without bankrupting AyA and that the state would end up subsidizing the private company. Heibel Rodriguez, AyA manager, interview with the author, 9 August 2006.

63. Osvaldo Durán Castro, "Davos del agua en México," *Ambientico* 152 (2006).

64. José María Villalta, lawyer, specialist in environmental rights, Foro Ambiental "No al TLC": "No hay ambiente para el TLC," 29 July 2006.

65. Gerardo Cascante Amador, ANEP, interview with the author, 4 August 2006.

issue. Even though water is a public good, water sources were on private property in many places, and because private property was considered increasingly sacred under neoliberalism, holistic public control became more difficult. Worse still were the regional plans like SIEPAC (Central American Electrical Interconnection System) and Plan Puebla Panama that sought the marketization and privatization of resources in the Central American region so that they might be used for large-scale development projects that served the interests of transnational corporations (TNCs).[66] This violated a basic premise of social democracy, where the national wealth was used for more egalitarian purposes.

CAFTA was seen as intimately linked to these regional plans, as it sought greater protections for private firms to claim discrimination when public firms and communities attempted to favor local control. Local elites with property or investments in areas slated for exploitation (e.g., Oscar Arias, Grupo Nación, the Pical family) supported this global strategy, opponents believed, because they stood to gain from their holdings. Moreover, the public would ultimately subsidize the costs of these private ventures: governments that borrowed to "develop" the water sector for export would be expected to pay back loans from general revenues. As one activist complained, "Water is the new way for countries to become indebted to TNCs. They move from being self-sufficient to dependent as a reward for granting TNCs the right to operate in their territory."[67] The fight against CAFTA was intricately tied to the fight to keep water public: "They are the same struggle."[68]

In response to the threats to public goods, activists pursued a vision of Costa Rica not simply as "a place to invest" but rather as a country with a proud history of progressive social policy and solidary development.[69] Unions, for example, put forward an alternative vision for development with their productive sector proposal entitled "Costa Rica: Toward the Third Republic vis-à-vis 21st Century National Challenges."[70] As ANEP put it, "Unions have been accused all these years by our detractors of having a

66. Osvaldo Durán Castro, Association of Alternative Projects for Social Development (PROAL—Asociación de Proyectos Alternativos para el Desarrollo Social), interview with the author, 7 August 2006.

67. Ibid.

68. Albino Vargas, secretary-general of ANEP, interview with the author, 2 August 2006.

69. Helio Gallardo, philosophy professor, University of Costa Rica, Foro Ambiental "No al TLC": "No hay ambiente para el TLC," 29 July 2006.

70. "Propuesta de los sectores productivos. Costa Rica: Hacia la tercera república, frente a los desafíos nacionales del siglo XXI," http://www.anep.or.cr/leer.php/748 (accessed 8 July 2009).

negative and intransigent, obstructionist attitude because we have resisted the onslaught of neoliberal fundamentalism. Today we show that, yes, we are proactive and have established our credentials as responsible actors for the future of the country."[71]

In the water sector, a number of organizations became involved in developing a complementary social agenda that would include, first and foremost, recognizing and respecting the requirements of healthy ecosystems, followed by focusing on water for human usage, agriculture, and other purposes.[72] They also sought to elevate the status of water to a good that is not constitutionally eligible for private control.[73] Centralized regulation would continue to be necessary but constrained by a healthy dose of local control.[74] Finally, water management would adhere to principles of inclusion for the whole of civil society.[75]

The revision of Costa Rica's water law brought together several of these groups in an inclusive process of debate, negotiation, and social learning.[76] In late 2001 and early 2002, three bills were presented to the Legislative Assembly, one by the acting government, one by the Costa Rican ombudsman, and one by deputy José Merino del Río, who, at the time, was a member of the progressive Democratic Force Party. The bills were brought before the Special Commission on the Environment, which carried out extensive consultations with civil society groups and organizations involved in water issues. After a lengthy and complex process of negotiations and debate, the bills were fused into one, Bill 14.585 (The Water Resources Law).[77] Social movements were happy both with the participative process and with the final text, in which the committee defined water clearly as a public good and excluded language referring to concessions on the grounds that there must be a separate law governing such complex and consequential instruments.[78]

---

71. The "Propuesta de los Sectores Productivos" listed a number of other organizations besides ANEP that were working together on this alternative, including the Costa Rican Chamber of Exporters (CADEXCO), the Movimiento Solidarista, the National Cooperatives Council (CONACOOP), the Mesa Nacional Campesina, and the School of Agricultural Engineers.

72. Osvaldo Durán Castro, PROAL, interview with the author, 7 August 2006.

73. Gerardo Cascante Amador, ANEP, interview with the author, 4 August 2006.

74. Osvaldo Durán Castro, PROAL, interview with the author, 7 August, 2006.

75. Working group on water, Foro Ambiental "No al TLC": "No hay ambiente para el TLC," 29 July 2006.

76. José María Villalta, lawyer, specialist in environmental rights and consultant for Legislative Deputy José Merino, interview with the author, 1 August 2006.

77. Ley de Recursos Hídricos.

78. Osvaldo Durán Castro, PROAL, interview with the author, 7 August 2006.

At this point, events took a turn. The collaborative version of the water bill was not compatible with CAFTA, especially regarding private involvement in the sector. It excluded, for example, the possibility of privatizing aqueducts and granting concessions for potable water provision. It also reversed earlier openings to the private sector in electricity generation, in particular as they related to hydroelectricity (see chapter 4).[79] Arias's party, the PLN (National Liberation Party), decided not to take the negotiated water reform text as its model and instead joined forces with the Libertarian Movement Party to freeze the project until it could be reworked to fit their vision for the sector. According to PLN deputy Maureen Ballestero, problems with the draft law included being "too statist and centralized," as well as being politically appealing but technically unviable because it "contained every single concern of everyone."[80] The acting government slowly altered the bill, thereby "showing its lack of respect for civil society and its willingness to make a joke of inclusive, deliberative processes."[81]

At present, struggles over the final contours of water reform remain to be seen. One thing is clear, however: CAFTA, Plan Puebla Panama, SEIPAC, and similar grand plans for submitting natural resources and public goods to market logics have polarized the region and thwarted efforts to implement alternatives. The CAFTA conflict in Costa Rica embodies many of the contradictions of market liberalization: conflicts between the ideals of commerce and the ideals of citizenship, technocratic arrogance that claims truth for economic precepts while giving more power to market actors, and polarization that undermines communication and closes debate. The question of whether services were a human right or something that should be allocated through the market ultimately did not incorporate the voices of everyone but rather favored those of economists and politicians. As a result, market liberalization was increasingly prioritized over traditional approaches to public goods. The ideology that considered water and electricity as mainly economic goods, and the sectoral policies that followed, created a gap between what Costa Ricans expected from their government and what their government provided. Declines in capacity to provide public goods, as well as institutional spaces for determining public goods policy, were thus consequences, not causes, of market-oriented reform.

79. José María Villalta, lawyer, specialist in environmental rights and consultant for Legislative Deputy José Merino, interview with the author, 1 August 2006.

80. Maureen Ballestero, deputy, National Liberation Party (PLN), interview with the author, 9 August 2006.

81. Albino Vargas, secretary-general of ANEP, interview with the author, 2 August 2006.

Despite institutionalized means for interest representation on joint commissions and negotiating committees in Costa Rica, citizen groups found it necessary to find other ways to promote their visions for public sector reform. Protest in Costa Rica emerged from the belief among "large sectors of society that the initiatives finally approved did not faithfully represent the agreements discussed during negotiations" (Gutiérrez-Saxe and Vargas-Cullell 2008). Rather than allowing marketization policies to retain the appearance of having emerged from consensus politics, they rebelled. Costa Ricans saw marketization as a radical assault on deep constitutional principles that many held dear: "We are not communist, but we believe in solidary development. What this means is that both communism *and* neoliberalism hold less appeal for us. There is no room for ideological extremists."[82] The loss of legitimacy of institutionalized spaces radicalized the opposition, making dialogue and deliberation more difficult.

Double movements in Costa Rica, then, were in part attempts to reinstitutionalize accountability in a country with a long history of solidary policies and democratic politics: "We don't want only to participate once every four years, or simply as complaining consumers."[83] It was not so much a question of an urgent need to find a new model, but a desire to recapture the one that already existed and had worked so well. As one activist argued, "Local movements do not need technical reasons for being against neoliberal policies, nor do they need to present alternatives. It is enough for them to say, 'We do not want our land and resources used for the benefit of business or elites.'"[84] Unfortunately, in most of these cases, the government did not heed the recommendations of citizen groups, despite painstaking efforts to come up with practical and just solutions for the challenges facing the country. It remains to be seen whether the ruling class will continue to ignore the barrage of critiques of neoliberal policy, or worse, its broader threat to social justice and sustainability.

Water Activism in El Salvador

In El Salvador, two distinct reactions to neoliberalism could be discerned: "reform," as evidenced by groups such as the National Development Foundation (FUNDE), and "resistance," the approach taken by the Center for

82. Albino Várgas, secretary-general of ANEP, interview with the author, 20 January 2003.

83. Working group on water, Foro Ambiental "No al TLC": "No hay ambiente para el TLC," 29 July 2006.

84. Osvaldo Durán Castro, PROAL, interview with the author, 7 August 2006.

Consumer Defense (CDC), as well as activist groups such as the Sinti Techan Network,[85] Pueblo Maiz, Bloque Popular Centroamericano, and Alianza Social Continental.[86] Reformers sought to capitalize on spaces opened by the peace process to confront the social and economic issues that had long plagued the country. Their primary focus was on carrying out and disseminating research to support public policies that contributed to social welfare. But government refusal to foster public discussion of privatization and other market-friendly policies frustrated some unions, academics, and activists, pushing them toward "resistance" in the form of strikes and protests. After twelve years of civil war, "revolution" might have lost some appeal, but these other forms of resistance continued.

Activists had been long concerned about the vision held by the ARENA government about water. Since the implementation of the first structural adjustment program (SAP) promoting "decentralization" as a solution to failing water provision, rural cooperatives, unions, and social movement organizations began to worry about its implications for water supply. As one prominent women's organization reported, neoliberal SAPs "did not consider the environmental costs of decentralizing public services related to natural resources, so vital in the case of water, much less measure the impact that this policy would have for the most vulnerable groups like women, children, and rural and marginalized urban residents" (Ortiz and Jarquín 2006, 81). There was no shortage of organizations working to improve water provision in El Salvador,[87] and over time, they brought a range of proposals to the public sphere for consideration, explicitly incorporating the principles discussed in chapter 1: environmental sustainability, human rights, and inclusion of marginalized populations.

Here, I will focus on one proposal, conceived by the Sinti Techan Network, which both reflected a range of perspectives from Salvadoran social organizations and reflected the concrete suggestions offered by these groups at various points in time. As early as 1995, a national Coordinating Commission for Hydrological Sector Reform began exploring the possibilities for modernizing the water company, ANDA (CDC 2005). ANDA's reform was shrouded in mystery, in part because eight distinct reform bills

85. Red Sinti Techan.
86. See www.asc-hsa.org.
87. A flyer advertising an upcoming "National Forum for the Defense of the Sustainability and Right to Water" (Foro Nacional por la Defensa de la Sustentabilidad y el Derecho al Agua) listed no less than seventy-five community, legal, religious, labor, women's, and solidarity organizations working toward a different kind of public goods policy in the water sector.

existed although none were formally debated or presented to the Legislative Assembly for apparently political reasons. Despite the insistence of ANDA officials that water would not be privatized, key aspects of the bill reflected greater marketization, rather than simply "decentralization," as proponents claimed.[88] Antiprivatization advocates believed that the government was postponing the public release of the bill until the last possible moment to head off debate and inevitable protest.[89]

ANDA's decentralization unit, UDES, claimed that municipalities were gaining capacity through the program and that financial shortcomings would be remedied by raised rates, with targeted subsidies for the poorest. But the capacity building that was to accompany decentralization was largely managerial and administrative.[90] UDES assisted local governments with the paperwork to transform decentralized systems into new legal entities and later with management issues, but "in the 2003–2004 period, few were the firms that actually received technical assistance" (CDC 2005). The bulk of the responsibility for day-to-day maintenance, infrastructure expansion, and long-term planning fell to the municipalities, without the concomitant borrowing capacity, tariff income, or human, technical, or administrative capabilities of the central government. Responsibilities were thus decentralized without the accompanying support. Municipalities were, in a sense, set up to fail.

Rather than wait for the formal draft water bill to materialize, social movement organizations took a proactive stance vis-à-vis the realities of UDES's program. The alternative started with a critique of the draft water law, from which the final law would presumably be derived. A number of provisions in the bill worried activists. For example, proposed concessions would be for up to thirty to fifty years, despite the issues discussed in chapter 4 about the unknowns and dangers of contracting. The bill also called for a water market, where water rights would be negotiated in terms of ability to pay. "Like King Midas," commented one of the network's economists, "capitalism is thought to convert everything it touches into commodities (a kind of capitalist gold); but water is not a commodity."[91] This market logic creates incentives for exclusionary policy and is potentially damaging to efforts at integrated water resources management. Subsidies in this case would be allowed only if they did not interfere with "financial equilibrium." The network activists expressed particular concern about the

88. Review of a draft bill by the author, June 2006.
89. Meeting of Red Sinti Techan, San Salvador, 30 June 2006.
90. Luis Trejo, ANDA-UDES, interview with the author, 19 July 2006.
91. Raúl Moreno, meeting of Red Sinti Techan, 30 June 2006.

increasing degeneration of water sources in El Salvador and the entire region. Unlike other countries in Central America, El Salvador did not exclude water from CAFTA consideration, and thus there would be no legal limits on water marketization and no obligation for corporations to keep water sales national.

The looming water reform spurred these organizations to create a "proposal of the people." The elements of their alternative proposal included values such as the centrality of sustainability; water as a human right, with priority given to people over corporations; basin management as an integral aspect of the framework; and the centrality of democratic participation.[92] With water provision, concessions would only be given when the people of a particular area chose to grant them, and only not-for-profit entities would be allowed to bid. The contracts would be short, evaluated, and renewed every one to two years. The alternative plan also proposed a hydrologic "plan from below" that incorporated local communities and a Project for the Recuperation of the Upper Lempa Basin.[93] Three micro-basin plans would shape the full basin plan, and basin committees and other mechanisms for citizen participation would be instituted at each level. At the national level, this mechanism would be the National Water Commission.[94] The goal of the participatory mechanisms would be to "achieve organized, permanent, and responsible participation of municipalities, communities, users, and other interested sectors; establish mechanisms for achieving agreement among particular concrete and perhaps contradictory interests; and give preference to decentralized and autonomous water management by municipalities and communities" (Ibarra, Campos, and Rivera 2002, 70).

The organizations proposed several guidelines for regulatory bodies: to consistently study and monitor water resources over time for impacts of use and contamination, as well as disseminate this information widely; to recognize and educate people about the social and cultural value of water, as well as collective and individual responsibility for its preservation; to

92. They explicitly incorporate the Dublin Principles for water reform (adopted at the International Conference on Water and the Environment in 1992), with an emphasis on giving preference to indicators of well-being and sustainability over economic efficiency. These four principles are (1) freshwater is a finite and vulnerable resource, essential to sustain life, development, and the environment; (2) water development and management should be based on a participatory approach, involving users, planners, and policy makers at all levels; (3) women play a central part in providing, managing, and safeguarding water; and (4) water has an economic value in all its competing uses and should be recognized as an economic good.

93. Proyecto de Recuperación de la Cuenca Alta del Río Lempa.

94. Comisión Nacional de Agua.

create clear usage guidelines that moderate among competing uses, with special attention to the reproductive needs of the Lempa River Basin and the ten other major river basins in the country; to establish ecological reserves when necessary to protect water resources; to ensure 100 percent access to potable water in both urban and rural areas at affordable prices, subsidized where needed; and to promote conservation. To achieve these goals, they proposed "a new institutionality for water management" in the form of a water authority that would work with basin and subbasin committees and where multiple uses and interests would be adjudicated. The social organizations recognized the difficulty of creating institutions that would meet these objectives but stressed that "the need for capacity-building" in this area "should not be used as an argument for privatization." For some business sectors and the ARENA government, this was seen "as a great opportunity to conduct juicy business deals at the expense of the quality of life for the population" (Ibarra, Campos, and Rivera 2002, 73). Instead of approving isolated and fragmented laws that ignored national strategies, they argued, a national water policy and plan must be discussed and adopted as a package, with a coherent legal basis for sustainable water management.

To ensure that municipalities had the financial capacity to make investments and meet demands, one prerequisite was adequate sources of funding. To achieve this in El Salvador would require loosening fiscal constraints and a greater political will to make it happen. However, instead of providing these needed resources, the ARENA government followed neoliberal precepts regarding fiscal austerity to an extreme. To address this, the organizations proposed the creation of a "national water fund" to coordinate an already-existing variety of state, donor, and lending sources. Pricing policy would need to be created that was not "unilaterally imposed from above" (Ibarra, Campos, and Rivera 2002, 71) but that addressed inequality in access and conservation. Proponents of this alternative conceived it to be participative and consensual and to account for conflicting uses, punish waste, stimulate conservation, protect water quality, protect basins, and collect fees or taxes that could be reinvested locally for protecting basins. An additional economic proposal included cross-subsidies—in a spirit of solidarity, conservation, and protection—to help the poor, initiate education campaigns, bring in new technologies, and carry out applied studies.

There is no way to know whether this or other alternatives would improve water management in El Salvador unless they are tested. But debates about alternative water reforms are absent in any formal institutional spaces, due in part to the long-term delay of releasing any kind of reform text on the part of the ARENA government or ANDA. Rumors constantly circulate regarding the expected release of the water bill, but it is difficult to have a meaningful public debate based on a protracted rumor. Many have spoken out against ANDA's water law on the basis that there has been a complete lack of consultation with the sector, as is common in El Salvador.[95] Instead, creeping "decentralization" continues to transfer water resources to private hands. Despite ANDA's claims that decentralization would be implemented only where it was requested (Ortiz and Jarquín 2006), the mayor of Santa Maria, Usulután, reported that his municipality was being forced to accept it.[96] As the municipality had no capacity to run the system without ANDA's assistance, he felt he had no choice but to take what ANDA offered: decentralization, like it or not.

Because accountability mechanisms are so vital in a context like this, ANDA's claims of community consultation are particularly in need of examination. The evidence indicates that rather than true consultation, where local populations could contribute their knowledge and express their concerns, ANDA hired a private consulting firm to visit communities and drum up support for decentralization. Locals criticized these public forums as a sham: "Meetings with ANDA and the government are just photo opportunities, and [ANDA's President Cesar] Funes does not even seem to know anything about water systems."[97] These kinds of public relations forums—where the entity promoting reform invites handpicked members of communities to attend a "discussion," only for them to find a preconceived agenda and a process of persuasion rather than a true dialogue about the pros and cons of the various options—are legendary in Central America. Many organizations, including the Center for Consumer Defense, criticized this approach as fundamentally undemocratic: "UDES . . . must ensure an adequate citizen consultation process so the population can be informed enough to say yes or no to decentralization. . . . It is not acceptable that they interpret citizen participation as just a few people. . . . If people want decentralization, they should choose it, accept it, and define it, then advance in that direction."[98]

95. "Ley de Agua con avance de un 80%, dice ANDA," *La Prensa Gráfica*, 28 May 2006.
96. Nicolas Castellón, mayor of Santa Maria, Usulután, meeting with the CDC and SETA (attended by the author), 18 July 2006.
97. Mercedes Serrano Gómez, municipal trustee of Berlín (Sindico Municipal of Berlín), interview with the author, 18 July 2006.
98. Danilo Pérez, Center for Consumer Defense (CDC), interview with the author, 19 July 2006.

Lack of accountability in reform processes—to local elected officials, much less to local communities—was worrisome in a sector as central to human well-being as water. To overcome obstacles to participation, some organizations took "consultation" into their own hands. Spearheading these efforts were the opposition FMLN at the national and local level, as well as SETA (the water union) and various nongovernmental organizations [the CDC, Caritas, the Salvadoran Ecological Union (UNES), the Foundation for the Study of Applied Law (FESPAD)], all of whom worked together to create new spaces for dialogue and coordination, as well as pry open existing channels of representation. SETA, for example, sent representatives to several forums sponsored by the Inter-American Development Bank, some to which they were not invited, to help raise consciousness about alternatives. They also organized a number of community discussion and consciousness-raising forums in villages across the country to discuss the unspoken trade-offs of, and alternatives to, what they saw as an inevitable slide toward total privatization of the sector. These meetings attempted to arm communities with information and prepare them for government "consultations." With these strategies, they hoped to force government accountability by helping communities to organize and protest against steps toward privatization.[99]

The purpose of contrasting the government and social movement approaches to "consultation" is to problematize the concept and pose the question of what is necessary for accountability in public goods sectors. The alternatives discussed earlier promised to bring sustainability and basin management to the center of the discourse and enshrine water as a human right, that is, water suitable for human consumption would be available to all. Democratic participation "from below" was central to these alternatives, as was continued national coordination. But when formal institutional spaces are closed to citizens, and when decision making takes place behind closed doors, with last-minute rush legislation, social conflict is likely, as are potentially devastating mistakes. Continued impunity in cases of repression adds to the complexity.[100] Since alternatives were not given a formal reception in El Salvador, social movements instigated their own double movements to carve out spaces for dialogue and struggle for embedded social policy.

---

99. Wilfredo Romero, secretary-general of SETA, meeting in San Augustín (attended by the author), 8 July 2006.

100. One of my interviewees, Moises Funes (the mayor of the usually peaceful village of Alegría), was murdered shortly after I interviewed him. Although the murder remains unsolved, there were clear indications that his policy positions, including opposition to the privatization of a local lagoon, were possible motivations.

Social movements in both Costa Rica and El Salvador, far from being ill-informed special interest groups that interfered with much-needed reforms, brought issues to public debates that had been excluded by strategies and processes of power (Lukes 1974, 2004b). They exposed naked exercises of power, decried agenda setting that excluded issues of concern, and presented counterhegemonic discourses for understanding the possibilities for public policy and visions of the public good. Although sometimes guilty of exaggerating the negative potential of neoliberal policies or the bad intentions of reformers, struggles to publicize alternative views and stem processes of privatization and marketization strengthened democracy by exposing contradictions between neoliberal claims and social justice outcomes.

CONCLUSION:
MARKET TRANSFORMATION OF PUBLIC GOODS

> It is not tyranny to stop someone from striking a match in the presence of gasoline fumes.
>
> —BARRINGTON MOORE, *Injustice:*
> *The Social Bases of Obedience and Revolt*

The main theoretical insight of this book is that multiple principles underlie public goods provision and that in order to provide public goods in ways that respond to these multiple ethics (including human rights and environmental sustainability), values other than cost and market efficiency must be included in conversations about reform. The main empirical finding is that neoliberal policy making of the past thirty years did not adequately incorporate these multiple ethics and, instead, imposed an economic and political project that weakened state structures and accountability mechanisms in public goods sectors while benefiting a small group of elites. Although institutions such as the World Bank recently softened their rhetoric toward alternative development approaches, in practice, most economists and many policy makers still see markets as the key to public goods troubles. Yet as this book shows, basic goods are far too complex and critical to be left up to markets.

Energy and water have become increasingly urgent topics in part because of rising costs of fossil fuel and the effect of global warming on water sources. Societies must find better ways to manage these resources by incorporating multiple ethics into decision-making processes. Those who advocate privatization speak as if market provision is a novel and exciting solution to an age-old problem. Many countries, in fact, tried market-based "solutions" in decades past; states and populations rejected them precisely because they failed to create broad-based access at affordable prices. But despite sometimes spectacular failures of market reforms, contemporary renationalization is politically thorny.[1] Contemporary trends in economic and social organization will profoundly influence who controls essential resources, who has access, and how decisions about them are made, all of which will affect their future availability and sustainability. These issues have potentially life and death consequences for the historically excluded—rural populations, landless peoples, marginalized urban communities, and women, who bear the brunt of shortfalls in public services. Market considerations are thus insufficient for judging the adequacy of reform.

Commodification and Threats to Citizenship

I have outlined some key concepts that a more substantive analysis (Polanyi 1957) of public goods might include: market, societal, political, and environmental organizing principles. Beneath this schema is a rights-based understanding of public goods, where the needs of the people are "determined not by how much money they can command but by transparent democratic processes, conducted in a spirit of pluralism, to which their full access is guaranteed by citizenship" (Martin 1993, 176). The key organizing principles that accompany the marketization of public goods (e.g., the profit motive and utility maximization) contradict such cooperative solutions by making self-interest the primary rational behavior. Personal choice is presented as a strategy to fight unfair constraints on individuals, while exclusionary institutional structures (i.e., private property and pricing mechanisms) promote an individualistic rather than a collective vision. The public good is eliminated in favor of answering to personal "preferences," and people are encouraged to think about their own desires instead of the deeper questions of who owns, operates, controls, or profits from public goods.

The meaning of citizenship itself changes when states grant "privileged rights of citizenship and representation to corporate capital, whilst constraining the democratization process that has involved struggles for representation for hundreds of years" (Gill 2003, 132). As private investors acquire the rights of citizens, they are not subsequently obliged to fulfill "the social responsibilities associated with citizenship" (Kohl 2003, 337). Private providers can thus invest or divest, based on their need to maintain

---

1. Juan Forero, "Latin America Fails to Deliver on Basic Needs," *New York Times*, 22 February 2005.

shareholder value rather than accountability to the larger population. The consequences include sectoral instability, as well as confusion regarding who is ultimately responsible for public goods. The shrinking of the state sphere creates the impression that citizens cannot turn to the state for public goods, destroying faith in public ethics or hope for good government (Lukes 2004a). Public servants vanish from the chain of responsibility connecting citizens to public goods. Citizens, who can mobilize around rights, are reframed as consumers acting outside the political sphere and are left with fewer channels of accountability: "While a political citizen is obliged to look for the best solution for society as a whole, a client, user or customer only has to take account of his own demands" (Oddvar Ericksen and Weigård 1999, 1).

As roll-back and commodification of highly necessary monopoly goods advances, those without exit options are forced to do business in the market, even at a high cost. This not only exacerbates inequality, as discussed in chapter 5, but also reduces *expectations* regarding equality in society. Inequality undermines social cohesion (ECLAC 2000), dismantles institutional arrangements for managing resources and binding people (Putnam 2000), weakens values beyond narrow self-interest, and has an overall deleterious effect on society (Pizzigati 2004). Distributive justice, however, can create conditions of stability, trust, and solidarity that make the promotion of other public goods possible.

In sum, the reversal under neoliberalism of gains made in the name of rights affect citizenship in several ways. Materially, the neoliberal turn is partly to blame for rolling back entitlements, destroying capacities, and making the state primarily accountable to capital and, secondarily, to the public. Procedurally, it is implicated in transforming citizens exercising rights into consumers exercising "choice" and closing off democratic spaces and channels of accountability in favor of market "voice." And ideologically, it puts into question faith in the public as an equalizing mechanism and reduces expectations for a just and equitable society. The result is exclusion, greater inequality, reduced expectations regarding social equality, and legitimized violations of social and economic rights. I summarize the discursive and political techniques that reconfigured the meaning of citizenship in table 17. This regime can be contrasted to that of social democratic states, which—while embracing the economic solvency of the state and supporting market activity—take seriously the role of the state in addressing its social and economic responsibilities, its legality, and its sovereignty. The objective of reform from this perspective would be "to restructure the state in order to strengthen it, not to make it weaker" (Bresser 1993, 1350).

Table 17 Citizenship under neoliberalism

Lens	(From): Postwar expectations rise	(Via): Neoliberal mechanisms	(To): Neoliberal citizenship
Public goods provision	Public goods provided primarily or exclusively by the state when markets fail	Privatization, "unbundling," competition policy, deregulation	Public goods rolled back; states geared to creating market conditions; state capacity challenged
View of "the public"	Faith in the state as an equalizing mechanism	Focus on state failure, fiscal crisis	Faith in the state, public service ethic damaged
View of solidarity	High expectations regarding equality	Individualism over community	Higher inequality, lower expectations regarding equality
Rights and state intervention	Protecting citizens' rights: states harnessed for protective "double movements"	Concentration of decision-making power/regulatory review in the executive, free trade	Protecting investors' rights: policy prevents states from "double movements"
Subjectivity	Subjects are citizens with rights	Individualistic consumerism	Subjects are consumers with preferences and "choices"
Voice	Economic voice primarily through the state	Accountability diffused; disconnect from policy makers	Economic voice primarily through the market

Commodification and Threats to the Environment

Just as applying market rationality to citizenship distorts the substantive relationship between the economy and society, subordinating the natural world to market principles perverts the relationship between humans and the environment, creating a situation in which land serves capitalist interests and not the needs of people or the earth. A memorable example of this distortion can be found in *The Grapes of Wrath* (Steinbeck 1939), where guards hold starving people at bay while bushels of perfectly edible but nonsaleable oranges are sprayed with kerosene and left to disintegrate in the California sun. Further, capitalism systematically "underproduces" nature (O'Connor 1988), and its expansion into public goods has led to increasing overexploitation of natural resources. Although water and electricity are not land, per se, they are akin to Polanyi's (1944) conception of land as a fictitious commodity, as their market price expressed through demand preferences may not reflect the full costs of their continued production or reproduction. Profit seekers often appropriate land and its associated natural endowments and productive capacities as gifts of nature, without considering their specific reproduction cycles, renewability, or capacity to absorb contamination.

Whether subsectors within the water and electricity fields are fictitious commodities in the Polanyian sense will vary. Water and rivers are not true commodities in that ecological, natural processes remain central to their reproduction, while the hydroelectricity that rivers make possible is a producible good that appears to be governable through pricing markets. But there is a difficulty in separating rivers from the electricity they generate, as harnessing this force changes fundamentally the life and reproduction of rivers and their surrounding basins. Similarly, though geothermal and nuclear power seem governable by market mechanisms, the consequences of harnessing these types of power are considerable for environmental sustainability and the health of humans and other living creatures. It is clear that there is some "public" aspect to these subsectors: commodification does not secure the necessary conditions for their reproduction, social contradictions arise from subjecting them to market logic, and state intervention is required to prevent harm to the natural environment, as well as to ensure they are responsive to social and economic rights.

At the root of this complexity is a deep contradiction between profit seeking and environmental conservation, the most obvious being that internalizing the costs of pollution damages profits. As governments compete to attract foreign direct investment, such costs are unlikely to be internalized, especially in sectors that rely on nonrenewable "dirty" energy such as electricity generation. A less obvious contradiction is that suppliers have every reason to stimulate demand so that it meets or exceeds supply and prices remain high. This translates into higher levels of consumption. Yet conservation requires a reduction, not an increase, in consumption. Another major incentive for overexploitation comes from the profits to be made from the private sale of goods extracted from common pool resources (Ostrom et al. 2002). Water bottled through concession agreements is one glaring example of the tremendous profit-making potential in this area.[2]

Proponents of market-based approaches routinely downplay their costs as minor compared with their benefits. Yet perhaps the most serious problem of increasing marketization of public goods is that *market failure is not the exception but the rule.* Examples can be found from Argentina to India to the Philippines to Atlanta, Georgia. When essential goods are involved, states must bail out private firms whose practices prove unsustainable (Rodríguez-Boetsch 2005). State regulation can alleviate negative outcomes in certain subsectors, but sometimes markets simply are not appropriate mechanisms for allocating these goods. Although governments are not immune to unsustainable practices—state policies in the former Soviet republics had a devastating effect on the environment, for example—they have fewer incentives for overexploitation and have been key players in regulatory efforts at conservation. As with imprudent marketization, state-led disasters were due in part to the subordination of broader societal goals to a single-minded objective (in the Soviet case, industrial development in a competitive Cold War context). This underscores the importance of social institutions that place democratic constraints on accumulation processes, whether they are capitalist or other (Streeck 1997) and the incorporation of multiple organizing principles in public goods policy decisions.

The Distinctiveness of Neoliberalism as a Political Project

It is important to avoid the mistake of attributing all the faults of a political system to whatever economic system happens to be in place at the time. As the Soviet case illustrates, accountability can be impeded not only by

2. "The Profits on Water Are Huge, but the Raw Material Is Free," *St. Petersburg Times,* 16 March 2008.

neoliberalism but also by bad governance. The key task here is to understand what, specifically, about neoliberal policies and practices was distinctive, and how those distinctive elements inherently disempowered certain
social groups and suppressed historical alternatives (Moore 1978) or paved
the way for elites to achieve this end. Of course, any transition presents
challenges and conflicts. But not all systems create impediments to alternative paths in the same way that neoliberal flanking mechanisms protect
markets and investors while silencing opponents and marginalizing nonmarket actors. More democratic systems leave open the possibility for citizens and workers to participate in decisions that matter for outcomes, as
well as to change paths and move forward with different plans. Social
democracy and corporatism, for example, have mechanisms for accountability and inclusion as an integral part of the system. Imperialism also
rules out alternative paths, but it requires a kind of brute force that neoliberalism does not.

Neoliberalism is not simply an ideology or set of economic policies. It
is a political project that actively stifles alternatives to its vision, using laissez-faire as an intellectual justification for the resulting power relations.
Although the moment of neoliberal roll-back is destructive, the moment
of roll-out is both creative (Brenner and Theodore 2002a) and preemptive.
It delimits the reach of states vis-à-vis markets and places the burden of
proof that intervention is justified on the former, thereby institutionalizing
neoliberal conceptions of the "proper" public–private split. This places
constraints on the double movement by "locking in future governments to
liberal frameworks of accumulation premised on freedom of enterprise"
(Gill 2002, 1). These preemptive restrictions on the state are justified not
because they protect against market failure but rather because they do not
impede or burden capital. This runs counter to the commonsense argument about why states should act: to promote the greater good and protect
society from harm.

It is true that the historically patrimonial states of Latin America were
not always effective conduits for accountability. State capture by vested
interests, which paid economic dividends for the ability to shape the policy
and legal environment in their favor, was a major target of World Bank
anticorruption activities and remains an integral part of international
financial institution (IFI) programs for "good governance." Yet *removing*
state action in public goods sectors via marketization went beyond simply
preventing its capture and severing patrimonial ties. It allowed unelected
third parties to operate in these fields, often with inadequate regulation,

capturing state *functions* rather than state actors. States and their laws and rules were just as surely wielded in the interests of a few rather than in the public interest, but this was considered the proper way for markets to function, unlike the dysfunction of a captured state. In this private realm, activities that would be allowed in the public sphere (e.g., reinvestment of profits for social ends, public awareness campaigns critical of a provider, on-site protests, or strikes) were potential violations of the "rights" of private property holders. Citizens were forced to stand alone and unprotected in the face of capital.

It is at this theoretical moment that the suppression of historical alternatives can give rise to potentially dangerous double movements. As Mahoney (2001) concluded, "If reactionary authoritarianism was historically a product of radical market policies, it is surely also possible that neoliberal reforms . . . carry the potential to create a new kind of class polarization and state control that could underpin highly repressive political systems in the decades to come" (281–82). My empirical data indicate that, notwithstanding the rather dramatic political shift away from neoliberal leaders and parties in recent years, economic structures and policies continue to limit the choices available to state actors. This does not bode well for countries with severe deficiencies in public goods sectors. Costa Rica shows more promise for success than many other countries in the region, but even here, the political compromise at the root of the model is in danger.

Isomorphism and the Suppression of Historical Alternatives

By now, it should be clear that neoliberalization was not a necessary outcome in public goods sectors. As Barrington Moore's (1978) historical account of injustice suggests, "particular historical events need not have turned out the way they did: history may often contain suppressed possibilities and alternatives obscured or obliterated by the deceptive wisdom of hindsight" (376). This book presents evidence regarding the closing of institutional paths to need-responsive public goods systems by neoliberal policies and the negative effect of such straitjacketing on these systems. But how do we know the alternative paths described in the narrative were truly available? Counterfactuals are important in providing an answer because they raise questions about why alternative outcomes did not come about. They elucidate hidden conflicts of interest and reveal power relations by showing *how* things might be different. To support the "suppression of alternatives" thesis, as well as to shed light on the limitations and possibilities of fighting for a more just society at particular historical junctures, Moore posits several questions:

1. Who does the suppressing of alternatives, and why?
2. What concrete steps would the alternative policy imply?
3. What were the obstacles to carrying it out? Were the obstacles real or imaginary? How can we tell?
4. On what resources in the existing social order could such an alternative draw? What about the functioning of institutional arrangements and the disposition of the population would enable us to draw tenable inferences about alternatives?
5. If alternatives appear feasible, why did they fail to be adopted? Were they not considered at all by those in power? If not, why not? If they were considered, why were actors unable to push for their adoption?

I attempted to address the questions posed by Moore throughout this book. To answer the first, I outlined the actors involved in attempting to create a neoliberal economic and social order in the public goods sectors of El Salvador and Costa Rica, as well as explored their stated and unstated motivations. I traced the origins of their ideas to an earlier century when the drive to liberalize was widely accepted, and when "no private suffering, no infringement of sovereignty, was deemed too great a sacrifice for the recovery of monetary integrity" (Polanyi 1944, 142). Defenders of this classical liberalism claimed that "the incomplete application of its principles was the reason for every and any difficulty laid to its charge" (143). Arguments supporting the continued application of structural adjustment, privatization, and other neoliberal policies were precisely and eerily the same. Just as liberals rewrote history, according to Polanyi, so neoliberals rewrote the history of development to exclude any positive role for an activist state (Chang 2003a). They were also resistant to evidence that contradicted their assumptions about markets, which explains in part their continued defense of market ideology. The evidence from both Costa Rica and El Salvador indicates that what drove market openings were actions of interested parties that stood to benefit, coupled with the efforts of people whose ideologies led them to believe that the market would provide public goods better than the state. What drove resistance, in turn, were actions of interested parties that stood to lose from privatization, coupled with the efforts of people who believed that greater reliance on the market would not produce better outcomes and would indeed threaten the basis of what they understood to be democracy, citizenship, and sustainability.

As for the second question: what concrete steps would alternative policies imply? In chapter 1, I outlined the principles that would need to be considered for public goods policies to incorporate not only market but also social, political, and environmental ideals. In chapter 2, I detailed the kinds of institutional, human, technical, and financial capacities that would be required for rights-based provisions of public goods (one alternative policy). I also discussed types of autonomy that states, public utilities, and regulatory agencies would need to carry out their mandates in public goods sectors. Finally, I examined the ties to both business and civil society that states would need to ensure accountable autonomy, allowing and obliging them to carry out their mandates in ways that reflected the principles discussed in chapter 1. These capacities are relatively complete in Costa Rica but would need to be built in El Salvador, where the Peace Accords presented opportunities for this kind of institution building.

The third set of questions draws our attention to the obstacles that neoliberal policy, discourses, and strategies presented for a rights-based vision of public goods. The debilitation of state institutions attempting to provide public goods, the excessive focus on market regulation, and the existence of fiscal constraints were obstacles that directly affected state capacity and autonomy, as discussed in chapter 4. Other autonomy deficits arose from investor protections and "preemptive" policies, which tied the hands of the state and shifted the target of social and economic rights claims to private sector actors, transforming citizens into consumers and alleviating pressures on the state for social justice. These obstacles were very real for Costa Rica and El Salvador, as evidenced by the disregard for rulings against harmful contracts, surplus expropriation and borrowing limitations on autonomous institutions, and increasing use of repression and deception rather than compromise in resolving conflicts of interest. Leaders did not exploit the opportunities for the development of more harmonious social relations in El Salvador—which were provided by restructuring the military at the end of the war and creating institutions to deal with economic and social injustices—because they did not have the institutional and political incentives to do so.

The fourth set of questions about resources brings our attention to a more pointed question: how could we know the alternatives would work? Most obviously, Costa Rica's solidary model is highly successful, and resources and political will in favor of state-led reform exist. Claims that this model is no longer possible are exaggerated and, in part, politically motivated. But in a country like El Salvador, where state-led development seems to be infeasible, it is important to ask whether alternatives to neoliberalism are real. I argued in chapter 5 that there are plausible alternatives and available resources in the existing social order, as well as internal groups ready to work for peace and social justice (e.g., progressive leaders; unions, both within and outside sectors slated for privatization; municipal and local organizations; certain NGOs, such as environmental, feminist, and development organizations; consumer and citizen groups; and university scholars). The United Nations and numerous international groups have also shown great interest in promoting peace in the region through expanding social and economic rights. Rights discourses and their attendant standards, such as accountability, could provide further leverage against neoliberal impediments to social justice (Nelson and Dorsey 2004). International bodies such as the UN play a key role in balancing the market fundamentalism that pervades so much IFI policy.

Numerous books and articles have been written that outline the contours of "another world" that might better reflect principles of justice, solidarity, and sustainability (e.g., Cavanaugh and Mander 2004). Building alternatives would require a dramatic shift in the distribution of power and wealth in society, so that existing alternatives are not pushed aside. This happened to some degree in El Salvador with the incorporation of opposition parties and the dismantling of the brutal military apparatus. The United Nations Development Programme (UNDP 2001) also suggested the development of new, nontraditional instruments to improve collective action within the public policy framework and recommended institutions that reward creativity, productivity, efficiency, responsibility, justice, transparency, participation, and solidarity. Independent media and active citizen participation in public policy, stronger regulation, and tax reform were among the concrete suggestions. As we saw in chapter 5, many Salvadorans continue proactively to resist the neoliberal model and work tirelessly for a more just society.

Although the Costa Rican model, like any model, is not perfect, it presents an interesting set of choices for how institution building might occur in other small, open nations at the periphery of the global economy, such as El Salvador. However, Salvadoran elites have remonopolized the spaces and opportunities opened by the Peace Accords, aided by neoliberal policies that give precedence to market conceptions of "optimal" social organization. Neoliberalism undermined alternatives by reproducing the social order that obstructed social justice in previous regimes. This is a fundamental problem that must be addressed. Market enthusiasts are not helping the situation when they reward El Salvador for following neoliberal precepts at the expense of all else. An awareness of the capacity, autonomy, and accountability requirements of a rights-based model could present a road map for the kinds of institution building that would be necessary to nurture an alternative model in such places as El Salvador. Without accountability to the wider society, however, it will fail.

This brings us to the fifth set of questions regarding the reasons alternatives have failed to date. As I showed in chapter 5, institutional strategies of agenda and process control, the creation of a technocratic "common sense" regarding "sound" policy, and the act of fostering feelings of inevitability regarding economic policy debilitated formal accountability mechanisms in Costa Rica and El Salvador. Coupled with a "preemptive movement" against those who might harness the state to implement protective, regulative, or redistributive measures, neoliberalism limited policy sovereignty, restricted development space (Wade 2003), and depoliticized economic policy. Elites in El Salvador rarely, if ever, considered non-neoliberal policy options. The lack of effective, formal horizontal and vertical accountability mechanisms made the "societal accountability" discussed by Smulovitz and Peruzzotti (2000) one of the few strategies left for opponents of neoliberal reform. In Costa Rica, alternatives had a fairer hearing, and indeed were implemented in a number of cases. But as argued above, these same horizontal and vertical mechanisms were attacked in a neoliberal offensive that placed market principles above most others for the management of economic policy.

The case regarding "the suppression of historical alternatives" in Latin America is compelling, as struggles for alternatives are visible in the present, not placed distantly in history. Later, however, if social movements and concerned citizens are unable to maintain control over development policy space, outcomes may appear to be the inevitable result of globalization. We must remain aware of these and other "stolen and betrayed alternatives," remembering that

> there were always alternatives to the free market . . . history didn't end. [Alternatives] were chosen, and then they were stolen. They were stolen by military coups. They were stolen by massacres. They were stolen by trickery, by deception. . . . We did not lose the battle of ideas. We were not outsmarted, and we were not out-argued. We lost because we were crushed. Sometimes we were crushed by army tanks, and sometimes we were crushed by think tanks. . . . These blueprints for another world . . . are popular because they have the

power to give millions of people lives with dignity, with the basics guaranteed. They are dangerous because they put real limits on the rich, who respond accordingly.[3]

Once we accept that market societies are, in fact, rather rare in history (Polanyi 1944), our minds are freed to seek more just, humane, and sustainable ways of organizing economies and societies.

Path Dependence

Despite the different political and institutional histories of El Salvador and Costa Rica, both saw the institutionalization of barriers to state-led development and the weakening of accountability mechanisms designed to make states respond to social and economic rights. It is important, however, not to make too much of these similarities. Although the evidence showed similar and consistent shifts across several countries undergoing neoliberal reform (Fourcade-Gourinchas and Babb 2002; Levi-Faur 2005), national political and institutional legacies remained central to the manner in which social actors adopted, adapted, or rejected them. Isomorphic pressures did not lead to policy convergence. In places like El Salvador, where power served to exclude rather than include and where the historical reality did not incorporate adequate public goods, the powerful co-opted market-friendly policies to serve their interests at the expense of other social groups. Market strengthening in a context of weak protections intensified and perpetuated elite control, dealing a long-term blow to both state capacity and social trust. Further, accountability was weakened when economic elites were allowed to pass as "experts" and when the interests of investors were presented and protected as if they represented the interests of all. This exacerbated social conflict and threatened the fragile Salvadoran peace. Despite otherwise dramatic postbellum reforms, the implementation of neoliberal policies represented a missed opportunity for more solidary forms of development.

It is ironic that the places most in need of reform seemed least likely to benefit because of capacity deficits and lack of responsiveness to nonmarket principles. But even those countries likely to benefit because existing

---

3. Naomi Klein, "Lost Worlds: Is Another World Possible?" Speech given at the 2007 American Sociological Association meetings, New York, N.Y., published 16 August 2007 by *Democracy Now!*

capacities and protections were strong, such as Costa Rica, faced reduced policy autonomy and a shift in power relations under neoliberalism. The institutionalization of a new model of economic management presented a structural change that challenged the status quo—in this case, of solidary national development—and provoked resistance and polarization, as policy spaces were attacked and contested. Robust institutional and political foundations, however, prevented the wholesale importation of neoliberal public goods models. Executive decisions were neither as uncompromising nor as insurmountable as in El Salvador, and Costa Rica's long history of stable institutions, political compromise, and socially minded policies (Morales-Gamboa and Baranyi 2003) afforded those opposed to liberalization the ability to present policy alternatives in institutional spaces that mattered for outcomes. The strength of educational institutions and a relatively high degree of public awareness were further reasons the more extreme manifestations of neoliberalism found limited success.

The argument is not that Costa Rica's social democratic characteristics are either necessary or sufficient conditions for preventing neoliberal reforms but, rather, that these characteristics slowed the spread of neoliberal policy and accounted for the selective manner in which it was accepted in Costa Rica (Clark 2001). Neoliberal attempts to privatize public goods have largely failed until now, in part because there is no genuine disaffection for state firms or ghastly experiences to justify rejecting them. Thus, pressures to privatize were not accompanied by widespread consumer demands for service improvements. Costa Rican gradualism, if it is able to overcome the obstacles presented by neoliberalism, shows promise for survival within the constraints of the global economy. Path impediments may be surmountable through alternative financial mechanisms and state capacity building, spearheaded by alternative political actors and social movements espousing counterhegemonic discourses of justice and inclusion. Costa Rica reminds us that there is hope that democracy can put limits on the power of capital in Latin America. But even here, the political compromise at the root of the model is in danger. A rather well-functioning model of public goods provision is slowly being weakened, and something must give: either neoliberalism will be checked—whether the double movement comes from the state or from the street—or the prospects for solidary social policy will dim.

Hope for the Future

The decline of the Costa Rican model would be unfortunate, as it is one of the few examples of a well-functioning social democracy in the developing world. Of course, reform in places like El Salvador will require more than simply emulating institutions from other settings. But the institutional model in Costa Rica may be more appropriate in the long run for ensuring social and economic rights in other developing countries than those presented by the neoliberal model. The goal is not to attempt to transform El Salvador into Costa Rica, but to be realistic about how to move from a situation in which basic needs are not met to one in which they are. Without a serious shift in the social bases of power, a healing of the historical wounds that make broad-based social partnership difficult, and institutional mechanisms to ensure rights and accountability, there will be no peaceful emergence of alternatives in El Salvador. The institutional variation that makes societies and polities healthy should be encouraged, not reduced: "The robustness of institutions often depends on multiple and diverse principles and logics of action" (Hollingsworth 2002, 9). The goal is a more just world, where the logic of markets and capital accumulation does not subordinate organizing principles of fairness and social and economic rights. Countries will always have their own styles and histories, but convergence on the axis of justice would be a welcome isomorphism.

Overcoming institutional legacies and power relations put into place by neoliberalism will not be easy and will require resources, capacities, and state efforts for a new round of reconstruction. Newly elected leftist leaders in Latin America, including Salvadoran president Mauricio Funes, will face formidable obstacles as they try to reorient their economies in the post–Washington Consensus era. Yet historical causation is not deterministic. At critical junctures, there are struggles, and outcomes depend not only on the structural leverage people possess but also on "political will and political intelligence [that] make a very powerful difference" (Moore 1978, 393). This book attempts to give voice to those who have found themselves thwarted and silenced by policies, discourses, and practices accompanying the establishment of a market-friendly order in public goods sectors. I hope it will serve to keep alive doubts about the inevitability of neoliberal globalization, as well as reilluminate dimly lit paths leading away from domination of the earth's resources and people toward sustainability, solidarity, and social justice.

APPENDIX: METHODOLOGICAL NOTES

The research presented in this book demonstrates how principles regarding public goods emerge in discourses and are concretized in institutions, promoted by a range of actors with varied interests, as well as how these manifestations promote or hinder the realization of alternative models for achieving development goals in water and electricity sectors. Comparative-historical analysis (CHA) is used to help clarify the ways in which different articulations prioritize one set of principles or another (e.g., market or social), as well as the consequences of these different articulations. This approach addresses a common critique of Polanyi's concept of embeddedness: that there is no existing self-regulating market with which to compare more "socially embedded" arrangements. Market- and state-led development projects both rely on embedding, but the institutional forms associated with each have distinct underlying guiding principles and ramifications for public goods provision. This research shows how embedding organized according to market principles creates obstacles for organizational principles that are more responsive to democratic or environmental concerns, and this, in turn, "suppresses historical alternatives" (Moore 1978) to neoliberalism that might more effectively address deep-rooted problems of securing social and economic rights and sustainability.

Like all CHA, this book is concerned with causal analysis, processes over time, and systematic, contextualized comparisons (Mahoney and Rueschemeyer 2003). This methodology is driven by certain assumptions "about the nature of the social and political world and especially about the nature of causal relationships within that world," which are not understandable using inferential techniques that assume linear causation, unit homogeneity, independence of cases, and ability to include all relevant variables (Hall 2003). This underlying ontology recognizes that early causal developments can have delayed and cumulative effects and that actors make choices based on iterated rounds of interaction. "Multiple conjunctural causation" approaches of CHA thus more adequately decipher the complexity of social phenomena than many of the common methods in economics and political science.[1]

For example, policy makers in international financial institutions and think tanks tend to assume that certain key policies (like privatization) are fundamentally sound and will lead to greater efficiency in the long run (e.g., Williamson 2004). Setting aside the problem regarding the meaning of "efficiency" discussed elsewhere in this book, from the perspective of CHA, it is too simplistic to assume that any one-size-fits-all policies are going to lead to desired outcomes across all settings. In path-dependent models, interaction effects have a cumulative nature, leading down such different roads that "it becomes unreasonable to suppose that an x occurring today has the same effect, y, across all settings" (Hall 2003).[2] Although international financial institutions give lip service to the idea that timing and sequence of reforms, as well as institutional setting, influence outcomes, the assumptions underlying classical models and the (often quantitative) methodologies employed collide with the more complicated, conjunctural ontological assumptions discussed earlier.

Tools of CHA

Proposed remedies within the comparative-historical tradition to the disconnect between ontology and methodology have concentrated on moving away from grand theory and abstract modeling. Small-N studies allow scholars to ask big questions—such as why things happen when they do, or how they do—by exploring cases more deeply than would otherwise be possible (Amenta 2003). The emphasis is on both institutional and "social mechanisms," that is, "basic forms of human behavior or recurrent forms of collective action that are constitutive components of the causal chains leading to broader political outcomes" (Hall 2003). CHA also provides innovative tools for linking structure and agency, showing how people are swayed by institutions, or how institutions structure choices, distribute

1. In recent years, rational choice models have paid more attention to issues mentioned herein. However, even iterated game modeling misses out on a host of institutional and social factors that influence outcomes, such as cumulative causation, critical junctures, and feedback effects.

2. The definition of path dependence adopted for this discussion is that of James Mahoney (2000): "historical sequences in which contingent events set into motion institutional patterns or event chains that have deterministic properties." The claim is not that history is wholly contingent, nor that the processes under study wholly determine outcomes: seemingly random "critical junctures" can be considerably determined by structure, while actors or exogenous shocks may disrupt seemingly inexorable causal sequences (Thelen 2003).

resources (money, information, access, etc.), and create categories and realities that seem "natural." Institutional analysis, in particular, can provide a useful bridge "by stressing the formation of institutions at critical junctures, by designating the substantive choices they embody, and by highlighting their distributive qualities, networks, flows of information, and framing capacities" (Katznelson 2003). Bayesian analysis, for its part, uses simple probability rules to test a priori beliefs about theories (Western 2001). It asks, "Given strong prior beliefs about the relation between two variables, does new data shift that belief?" (Goldstone 2003). The question is not, "what do I need to show to believe that something is true x percent of the time?" as in probabilistic methods. A small number of facts can cast doubt on a previously held belief by showing that there is an important causal relationship where the tested theory does not see one, that the claims a theory makes cannot be substantiated by the evidence, or that the theory predicts one thing and something else happens.

Process tracing, a methodological strategy that examines a sequence of events, demonstrates how events are plausibly linked, given the interests and situations faced by groups or individuals. If causal mechanisms can be identified throughout a string of variables, this is likely a causal path. This tool is especially useful in studies in which the cause and effect are separated in time (Mahoney 2003), as with the Latin American debt crisis in the early 1980s and the near-complete neoliberalization of policy a decade later. Another type of within-case analysis is causal narrative, which uses comparisons of within-case chronologies across cases as a basis for causal inference. These "strategic narratives" can contribute to theoretical development by presenting evidence to clarify or debunk previous theories (Goldstone 2003).

CHA is also concerned with institutional transformation. Static portrayals of capitalist "models" in comparative political economy have given way to more nuanced analyses of "timing, sequence and the determinants of seismic institutional change" (Hay 2004a). "Punctuated equilibria" approaches, for example, argue that such change follows from exogenous shocks that open spaces for innovation by disrupting stable institutional arrangements. The primary focus is the institutional or political context of crisis periods and the effect of shocks on existing institutional and political arrangements. This approach is useful, though it does not adequately explain institutional arrangements that are resilient vis-à-vis exogenous shocks. For example, "punctuated equilibrium" does not well describe the resilience of Costa Rican social democracy vis-à-vis economic crisis and the neoliberal sea-change throughout Latin America. It also does not explain well the cumulative effect over time of small institutional changes. So, for example, it would have no way of measuring the effect of incremental neoliberal reforms on institutional capacities or the debilitation of publicly owned utility sectors evident in many places. Turning points can be endogenous to institutional arrangements, sometimes resulting from earlier (exogenous or endogenous) developments.

Kathleen Thelen (2003) introduces another useful concept, "layering," for interpreting institutional innovation and reproduction.[3] Layering entails renegotiating certain aspects of institutions while leaving other aspects intact. For example, implementing a private system on top of an existing public system, as has occurred in electricity and water systems globally, affects the interests of key stakeholders and affects the trajectory of future policies: "The growth of private alternatives can undermine support for universal programs among the middle class, on whose 'contingent consent' the whole public system rests" (Thelen 2003, 227). This could be an unintended consequence of privatization or an intentional strategy; the outcome is the same. Costa Rica is instructive in showing how such layering can debilitate and transform an incumbent system without the political difficulties of outright dismantling. This perspective clarifies how institutions can serve ends that diverge from their original intent and how institutional change can affect the relative power of social groups, as well as pinpoints the mechanisms and logics that induce institutional change over time.

Employing the Tools of CHA

To answer the questions posed in this book, I utilize a number of comparative-historical strategies for both within- and between-case analysis. The case studies of Costa Rica and El Salvador were carefully chosen as "most likely" and "least likely" scenarios with which to test economic theories regarding marketizing reforms using Bayesian analysis. In the Costa Rican context, I address why privatization policy was so widespread, as well as whether neutral technocrats were the main supporters—and special interest groups the main resistors—of privatization. I pinpoint alternative causal factors implicated in the pervasiveness of privatization policy, document how interested actors fought for privatization, regardless of the

---

3. The other conceptual tool proposed by Thelen, conversion, is not used in this analysis.

objective need for it, and show that resistance to privatization occurred because people were convinced that it was not beneficial for them. This analysis leads me to conclude that distributional analyses (Schamis 1999) are more convincing explanations of both the promotion of and the resistance to privatization than arguments regarding efficiency or technical necessity. In the Salvadoran context, I address a key assumption of arguments favoring privatization: that private provision will improve services where public systems have fallen short. Again, the evidence weighs heavily against classical predictions, thus casting doubt on the theories that have driven public goods sector reform for two decades.

The main substance of the book concerns the cumulative and path-dependent effects of neoliberal governance of public goods. To demonstrate cumulative effects, I use process tracing to link early causes (neoliberal attacks on the state combined with strict macroeconomic policy in the 1980s) with later effects (public sector debilitation and widespread privatization in the 1990s and beyond). I argue that early neoliberal strategies created a context that facilitated the suppression of historical alternatives (Moore 1978), undermining the continued viability of the successful Costa Rican state-led model of development, as well as the promise of the Salvadoran Peace Accords for economic and social rights. Similar neoliberal economic globalization processes were thus causing some level of convergence in these two very different contexts.

Yet there remained a great deal of divergence regarding the manner in which neoliberalism was adapted to each context. In my analysis, I use causal narrative to show how similar processes operate quite differently in Costa Rica and El Salvador because of the inherited institutional landscape on which these processes take place. For example, in Costa Rica it was harder for privatization advocates to implement reform than in El Salvador because public goods had a long and successful institutional history in the former. This afforded resistors with ideological and material resources with which to argue against privatization, despite the multiple pressures to liberalize its public goods sectors. In El Salvador, where state autonomy, capacity, and embeddedness were sorely lacking, privatization policies in sensitive sectors were built atop already shaky foundations. Although the causal narratives for the cases presented in this book are partial, they provide evidence for how neoliberal reforms created surprisingly similar policy constraints via discourses and practices, as well as how the inherited institutional and political landscapes shaped outcomes in divergent ways.

Duration and timing were important variables for explaining these outcomes. In El Salvador, democratization came after neoliberalization, thus allowing the latter to preempt the development of state-led public goods sectors. In Costa Rica, however, neoliberalization entered the scene after democracy had already been well established, making it more difficult for neoliberal reformers to make headway but also undermining to some degree the institutional pillars of Costa Rican democracy. Policies have feedback effects as well. The manner in which they are institutionalized affects later policy. For example, I show that in Costa Rica, the population benefited from an effective public sector and thus was not willing to give it up. Successful public goods created their own "interest group": content citizens. In El Salvador, by contrast, people were more willing to risk the private sector under conditions in which the state proved negligent. This did not prevent some from protesting against the privatization of essential services, but it did make privatization more broadly palatable. Breaking down the privatization process of two sectors in two countries over time allows me to isolate how institutions are important in the process— democratic, regulatory, political, or other.

REFERENCES

Abers, Rebecca, and Margaret Keck. 2006. "Muddy waters: The political construction of deliberative water basin governance in Brazil." *International Journal of Urban and Regional Research* 30 (3): 601–22.

AFL-CIO and UNITE. 2003. Testimony of the American Federation of Labor and Congress of Industrial Organizations and Union of Needletrades, Industrial and Textile Employees before the Congress. "Central America: Labor rights and child labor reports." Pursuant to the Trade Act of 2002, Section 2102(C)(8)–(9), 5 June.

Albiac, María Dolores. 1998. *Los ricos más ricos de El Salvador*. San Salvador: Fundación Heinrich Böll.

Albouy, Yves. 1999. "Taking stock of progress: The energy sector in developing countries." In *Energy and Development Report: Energy After the Financial Crises*. Washington, D.C.: World Bank.

Alvarez Basso, Carmen C. 1992. *Recuperar la importancia de los derechos económicos, sociales, y culturales*. San Salvador: Fundación Nacional para Desarrollo (FUNDE).

Amenta, Edwin. 2003. "What we know about the development of social policy: Comparative and historical research in comparative and historical perspective." In *Comparative Historical Analysis in the Social Sciences*, ed. James Mahoney and Dietrich Rueschemeyer, 91–130. New York: Cambridge University Press.

Amsden, Alice H. 2001. *The Rise of the Rest: Challenges to the West from Late-Industrializing Economies*. Oxford: Oxford University Press.

ANEP (Asociación Nacional de la Empresa Privada). 2001. "Propuesta para la construcción de un NUEVO El Salvador." *II ENADE: Encuentro Nacional de la Empresa Privada*. San Salvador: ANEP.

———. 2002. *III ENADE: Encuentro Nacional de la Empresa Privada*. San Salvador: ANEP.

Anner, Mark. 2008. "Meeting the challenges of industrial restructuring: Labor reform and enforcement in Latin America." *Latin American Politics and Society* 50 (2): 33–65.

Arriola Palomares, Joaquín. 1993. "Critica a la lógica neoliberal." Documento de Trabajo No. 50. San Salvador: Fundación Nacional para Desarrollo (FUNDE).

Asamblea Legislativo. 1992. Ley de la Procuraduría para la Defensa de los Derechos Humanos. El Salvador.

Aslanbeigui, Nahid, Steven Pressman, and Gale Summerfield, eds. 1994. *Women in the Age of Economic Transformation: Gender Impact of Reforms in Post-Socialist and Developing Countries*. London: Routledge.

Avritzer, Leonardo. 2006. "New public spheres in Brazil: Local democracy and deliberative politics." *International Journal of Urban and Regional Research* 30 (3): 623–37.

AyA (Instituto Costarricense de Acueductos y Alcantarillados). 2002. *Agua potable y saneamiento de Costa Rica*. San José, Costa Rica: AyA.

Bachrach, Peter, and Morton Baratz. 1962. "The two faces of power." *American Political Science Review* 56 (4): 947–52.

———. 1970. *Power and Poverty: Theory and Practice*. New York: Oxford University Press.

Balanyá, Belén, Brid Brennan, Olivier Hoedeman, Satoko Kishimoto, and Philipp Terhorst. 2005. *Reclaiming Public Water: Achievements, Struggles and Visions from Around the World*. Amsterdam: Transnational Institute and Corporate Europe Observatory.

Baldry, Eileen. 2006. "The social justice aspect of a social justice–human rights–community development approach to practising social development." Working paper, School of Social Work, University of New South Wales.

Barry, Norman. 1990. "Markets, citizenship and the welfare state: Some critical reflections." In *Citizenship and Rights in Thatcher's Britain*, ed. Raymond Plant and Norman Barry, 34–77. London: Institute of Economic Affairs.

Bauer, Carl J. 1997. "Bringing water markets down to earth: The political economy of water rights in Chile, 1976–1995." *World Development* 25 (5): 639–56.

Beatty, Sam. 1999. *Power Generation and Distribution in Central America*. Washington, D.C.: Trade Information Center, United States Department of Commerce. http://www.ita.doc.gov/td/energy/centpd.html. Accessed 23 June 2008.

Bellamy Foster, John. 2002. *Ecology Against Capitalism*. New York: Monthly Review Press.

Bentham, Jeremy. 2005. *Theory of Legislation*. Translated by Richard Hildreth from the French of Etienne Dumont. London: Elbrion Classics. Reprint of 1896 edition by Kegan Paul, Trench, Trübner.

Beyer, Harald. 1999. "La modernización del estado." *Boletín Económico y Social*, no. 160. San Salvador: Fundación Salvadoreña para el Desarrollo Económico y Social. March.

Biersteker, Thomas J. 1995. "The 'triumph' of liberal economic ideas in the developing world." In *Global Change, Regional Response: The New International Context of Development*, ed. Barbara Stallings, 174–96. New York: Cambridge University Press.

Block, Fred. 2003. "Karl Polanyi and the writing of the great transformation." *Theory and Society* 32:275–306.

Blyth, Mark. 2002. *Great Transformations: Economic Ideas and Institutional Change in the Twentieth Century*. New York: Cambridge University Press.

Bockmann, Johanna, and Gil Eyal. 2002. "Eastern Europe as a laboratory for economic knowledge: The transitional roots of neoliberalism." *American Journal of Sociology* 108:310–52.

Bourdieu, Pierre. 1977. *Outline of a Theory of Practice*. Cambridge: Cambridge University Press.

Bowman, Kirk S. 2002. *Militarization, Democracy, and Development: The Perils of Praetorianism in Latin America*. University Park: Pennsylvania State University Press.

Boyer, Robert. 2000. "The political in the era of globalization and finance: Focus on some *Régulation* School research." *International Journal of Urban and Regional Research* 24 (2): 274–322.

Brenner, Neil, and Nik Theodore. 2002a. "Cities and the geographies of 'actually existing neoliberalism.'" *Antipode: A Radical Journal of Geography* 34:349–79.

———, eds. 2002b. *Spaces of Neoliberalism: Urban Restructuring in Western Europe and North America.* Cambridge, Mass.: Blackwell.

Bresser Pereira, Luiz Carlos. 1993. "Economic reforms and cycles of state intervention." *World Development* 21:1337–53.

Bresser Pereira, Luiz Carlos, José María Maravall, and Adam Przeworski. 1993. *Economic Reforms in New Democracies: A Social Democratic Approach.* Cambridge: Cambridge University Press.

Bulmer-Thomas, Victor. 1987. *The Political Economy of Central America Since 1920.* New York: Cambridge University Press.

Burawoy, Michael. 2001. "Transition without transformation: Russia's involutionary road to capitalism." *East European Politics and Societies* 15:269–90.

Call, Charles T. 2003. "Democratisation, war and state-building: Constructing the rule of law in El Salvador." *Journal of Latin American Studies* 35:827–62.

Cardoso, Fernando Henrique, and Enzo Faletto. 1979. *Dependency and Development in Latin America.* Berkeley and Los Angeles: University of California Press.

Casteñeda, Jorge G. 1996. "Democracy and inequality in Latin America: A tension of the times." In *Constructing Democratic Governance: Latin America and the Caribbean in the 1990s—Themes and Issues,* ed. Jorge I. Domínguez and Abraham F. Lowenthal, 42–63. Baltimore: Johns Hopkins University Press.

Cavanagh, John, and Jerry Mander. 2004. *Alternatives to Economic Globalization: A Better World Is Possible.* San Francisco: Berrett-Koehler.

CDC (Centro para la Defensa del Consumidor). 1997. *Ley de protección al consumidor: Explicada, y su reglamento.* San Salvador: CDC.

———. 2005. *El vaivén de la (des) centralización del agua en El Salvador 1999–2005.* San Salvador: CDC; Fundación Heinrich Böll; Novib; y Desarrollo y Paz.

CEDAW. 1979. *United Nations Convention on the Elimination of All Forms of Discrimination Against Women.* New York: United Nations.

CEPAL (Comisión Económica para América Latina). 2003. *Evaluación de diez años de reformas en la industria eléctrica del istmo centroamericano.* Cuidad de México: CEPAL.

Cerny, Philip G. 1999. "Globalization and the erosion of democracy." *European Journal of Political Research* 36:1–26.

CESCR (United Nations Committee on Economic, Social, and Cultural Rights). 1976. *International Covenant on Economic, Social, and Cultural Rights.* New York: United Nations Committee on Economic, Social, and Cultural Rights.

———. 2002. *General Comment No. 15 on the Right to Water.* New York: CESCR.

CESPAD (Centro de Estudios para la Aplicación de Derecho). 1991. *Información legal para la obtención de los servicios básicos.* Memoria de la Jornada. San Salvador: CESPAD.

Chang, Ha-Joon. 2002. *Kicking Away the Ladder: Development Strategy in Historic Perspective.* London: Anthem Press.

———. 2003a. *Globalisation, Economic Development and the Role of the State.* Penang, Malaysia: Third World Network; London: Zed Books.

———, ed. 2003b. *Rethinking Development Economics.* London: Anthem Press.

Chang, Ha-Joon, and Peter Evans. 2005. "The role of institutions in economic change." In *Reimagining Growth: Institutions, Development, and Society*, ed. Gary Dymski and Silvana de Paula, 99–140. New York: Edward Elgar.

Chase-Dunn, Christopher. 2002. "Globalization from below: Toward a collectively rational and democratic global commonwealth." *Annals of the American Academy of Political and Social Science* 581:48–61.

Chibber, Vivek. 2002. "Bureaucratic rationality and the developmental state." *American Journal of Sociology* 107 (4): 951–89.

———. 2003. *Locked in Place: State-Building and Capitalist Industrialization in India, 1940–1970*. Princeton: Princeton University Press.

Clark, Mary A. 2001. *Gradual Economic Reform in Latin America: The Costa Rica Experience*. Albany: State University of New York Press.

Clayton, Andrew. 1999. *Contracts or Partnerships: Working Through Local NGOs in Ghana and Nepal*. London: WaterAid.

Cline, William R. 1989. "The Baker Plan and Brady Reformulation: An evaluation." In *Dealing with the Debt Crisis*, ed. Ishrat Husain and Ishac Diwan, 176–93. A World Bank Symposium. Washington, D.C.: World Bank.

Cordero, José Antonio. 2000. *El crecimiento económico y la inversión: El Caso de Costa Rica*. Santiago, Chile: Economic Commission for Latin America and the Caribbean (ECLAC).

Cornick, Jorge, Leonardo Garnier, Jorge Guardia, Jaime Ordóñez, Adrián Torrealba, Francisco Villalobos, and Juan Manuel Villasuso. 2004. "Estabilidad, control del gasto y desarrollo: Este tríptico debe ser el complemento de la reforma tributaria." In *Reforma fiscal en Costa Rica: Aportes a una agenda inconclusa*, ed. Manuel Barahona and Yajaira Ceciliano. San José, Costa Rica: FLACSO.

Cornwall, Andrea. 2008. "Unpacking 'participation': Models, meanings, and practices." *Community Development Journal* 43 (3): 269–83.

Corona, Rossana. 1996. "Impact of privatization in Mexico on economic efficiency and market structure: Analysis of five companies." In *Bigger Economies, Smaller Governments: Privatization in Latin America*, ed. William Glade and Rossana Corona, 247–76. Boulder, Colo.: Westview Press.

Cortés Ramos, Alberto. 2001. "Cultura política y sistema de partidos en Costa Rica: ¿Nuevas tendencias en el 2002?" In *La democracia de costa Rica ante el siglo XXI*, ed. Jorge Rovira Más, 233–54. San José: Editorial de la Universidad de Costa Rica.

Crouch, Colin. 2000. *Coping with Post-democracy*. London: Fabian Society.

Dahl, Robert. 1961. *Who Governs? Democracy and Power in an American City*. New York: Doubleday.

———. 1999. "The shifting boundaries of democratic governments." *Social Research* 66:915–31.

Dezalay, Yves, and Bryant Garth. 2002. *The Internationalization of Palace Wars: Lawyers, Economists and the Contest to Transform Latin American States*. Chicago: University of Chicago Press.

Dicken, Peter. 1998. *Global Shift: Transforming the World Economy*. 3rd ed. New York: Guilford Press.

DiMaggio, Paul J., and Walter W. Powell. 1983. "The iron cage revisited: Institutional isomorphism and collective rationality in organizational fields." *American Sociological Review* 48:147–60.

Dubash, Navroz K. 2002. *Power Politics: Equity and Environment in Electricity Reform*. Washington, D.C.: World Resources Institute.

Duménil, Gérard, and Dominique Lévy. 2001. "Costs and benefits of neoliberalism: A class analysis." *Review of International Political Economy* 8:578–607.

ECLAC (Economic Commission for Latin America and the Caribbean). 2000. *Equity, Development, and Citizenship*. Santiago, Chile: ECLAC.

———. 2007. *Statistical Yearbook for Latin America and the Caribbean*. Santiago, Chile: ECLAC.

Esping-Andersen, Gøsta. 1990. *The Three Worlds of Welfare Capitalism*. Princeton: Princeton University Press.

Evans, Peter B. 1995. *Embedded Autonomy: States and Industrial Transformation*. Princeton: Princeton University Press.

———. 1996. "Government action, social capital and development: Reviewing the evidence on synergy." *World Development* 24:1119–32.

———. 2004. "Development as institutional change: The pitfalls of monocropping and the potentials of deliberation." *Studies in Comparative International Development* 38 (Winter): 30–52.

Fischer, Ronald, Rodrigo Gutiérrez, and Pablo Serra. 2003. *The Effects of Privatization on Firms and on Social Welfare: The Chilean Case*. Latin American Research Network. Washington, D.C.: Inter-American Development Bank.

Foster, Christopher D. 1992. *Privatization, Public Ownership and the Regulation of Natural Monopoly*. Oxford: Blackwell.

Fraser, Nancy. 1989. *Unruly Practices: Power, Discourse, and Gender in Contemporary Social Theory*. Minneapolis: University of Minnesota Press.

Fung, Archon, and Erik Wright. 2003. *Deepening Democracy: Institutional Innovations in Empowered Participatory Governance*. London: Verso.

FUSADES (Fundación Salvadoreña para el Desarrollo Económico y Social). 1992. "¿Cómo está nuestra economía?" In *Departamento de Estudios Económicos y Sociales*. San Salvador: FUSADES.

———. 1999. "La modernización del estado." *Boletín Económico y Social*, no. 160. San Salvador: FUSADES. Marzo.

García, Luis E., Diego J. Rodriguez, and Lorena Rossi. 2000. *Dams, Development, and the Environment in Latin America and the Caribbean: Some Experiences of the Inter-American Development Bank*. Sustainable Development Department. Washington, D.C.: Inter-American Development Bank.

Garrett, Geoffrey. 1998. *Partisan Politics in the Global Economy*. New York: Cambridge University Press.

Gereffi, Gary, and Miguel Korzeniewicz, ed. 1994. *Commodity Chains and Global Capitalism*. Westport, Conn.: Praeger.

Gill, Stephen. 2000. "The constitution of global capitalism." Paper presented to "The Capitalist World, Past and Present" panel at the International Studies Association Annual Convention, Los Angeles. www.theglobalsite.ac.uk. Accessed May 2008.

———. 2002. "Constitutionalizing inequality and the clash of globalizations." *International Studies Review* 4:47–65.

———. 2003. "Globalization, market civilization, and disciplinary neoliberalism." Chap. 7 in *Power and Resistance in the New World Order*, ed. Steven Gill. New York: Palgrave Macmillan.

Goitia, Alfonso. 1994. "La modernización del Estado: El papel del estado en la sociedad." *Alternativas para el Desarrollo* 18:7–14. San Salvador: Fundación Nacional de Desarrollo (FUNDE).

Goldstone, Jack A. 2003. "Comparative-historical analysis and knowledge accumulation in the study of revolutions." In *Comparative Historical Analysis in the Social Sciences*, ed. James Mahoney and Dietrich Rueschemeyer, 41–90. New York: Cambridge University Press.

Gómez, Ileana. 1997. *Estado, actores sociales y medio ambiente urbano en El Salvador.* San Salvador: Salvadoran Investigative Program on Development and the Environment (PRISMA).

Grabher, Gernot, ed. 1993. *The Embedded Firm: On the Socioeconomics of Industrial Networks.* London: Routledge.

Graham, Carol. 2002. *Strengthening Institutional Capacity in Poor Countries: Shoring Up Institutions, Reducing Global Poverty.* Washington, D.C.: Brookings Institution.

Gramsci, Antonio. 1971. *The Prison Notebooks.* New York: Columbia University Press.

Granovetter, Mark. 1985. "Economic action and social structure: The problem of embeddedness." *American Journal of Sociology* 91 (3): 481–510.

Green, Donald P., and Ian Shapiro. 1994. *Pathologies of Rational Choice Theory: A Critique of Applications in Political Science.* New Haven: Yale University Press.

Green, Duncan. 2003. *Silent Revolution: The Rise and Crisis of Market Economics in Latin America.* New York: Monthly Review Press.

Grindle, Merilee S. 1996. *Challenging the State: Crisis and Innovation in Latin America and Africa.* New York: Cambridge University Press.

Grindle, Merilee S., and John W. Thomas. 1991. *Public Choices and Policy Change: The Political Economy of Reform in Developing Countries.* Baltimore: Johns Hopkins University Press.

Guasch, J. Luis. 2004. *Granting and Renegotiating Infrastructure Concessions: Doing It Right.* Washington, D.C.: World Bank Institute.

Gutiérrez-Saxe, Miguel, and Jorge Vargas-Cullell. 2008. "Selección de textos de los informes *Estado de la Nación y de la Región Centroamericana,* y documentos de los autores para valorar procesos nacionales de concertación." Paper given at the annual meeting of the Society for the Advancement of Socio-Economics (SASE), panel on "Concertación in Central America." University of Costa Rica, 22 July.

Hachette, Dominique. 1996. "Fiscal aspects of privatization." In *Bigger Economies, Smaller Governments: Privatization in Latin America,* ed. William Glade and Rossana Corona, 137–62. Boulder, Colo.: Westview Press.

Haggard, Stephan, and Robert R. Kaufman. 1992. *The Politics of Economic Adjustment: International Constraints, Distributive Conflicts, and the State.* Princeton: Princeton University Press.

Haglund, LaDawn. 2006. "Hard-pressed to invest: The political economy of public sector reform in Costa Rica." *Revista Centroamericana de Ciencias Sociales* 3 (1): 5–46.

Hahnel, Robin. 2005. "What mainstream economists won't tell you about neoliberal globalization." Keynote address at the *Socialist Studies* launch ceremony. Annual Conference of the Canadian Federation for the Humanities and Social Sciences. London, Ontario, 3 June.

Hall, Peter A. 2003. "Aligning ontology and methodology in comparative politics." In *Comparative Historical Analysis in the Social Sciences*, ed. James Mahoney and Dietrich Rueschemeyer, 373–404. New York: Cambridge University Press.

Hamilton, Nora. 1982. *The Limits of State Autonomy: Post-revolutionary Mexico*. Princeton: Princeton University Press.

Haney, Lynne. 2000. "Global discourses of need: Mythologizing and pathologizing welfare in Hungary." In *Global Ethnography: Forces, Connections, and Imaginations in a Postmodern World*, ed. Michael Burawoy, 48–73. Berkeley and Los Angeles: University of California Press.

Hansen-Kuhn, Karen. 1993. *Structural Adjustment in Central America: The Case of Costa Rica*. Washington, D.C.: Development Gap.

Hardin, Garrett. 1968. "The tragedy of the commons." *Science* 162:1243.

Harper, Krista, and S. Ravi Rajan. 2004. *International Environmental Justice: Building the Natural Assets of the World's Poor*. Amherst: University of Massachusetts, Political Economy Research Institute (PERI).

Harvey, David. 2003. "The 'new imperialism': Accumulation by dispossession." In *The New Imperial Challenge: Socialist Register 2004*, ed. Leo Panitch and Colin Leys, 63–87. New York: Monthly Review Press.

Hawken, Paul, Amory Lovins, and L. Hunter Lovins. 2000. *Natural Capitalism: Creating the Next Industrial Revolution*. Boston: Back Bay Books.

Hay, Colin. 2004a. "Ideas, interests and institutions in the comparative political economy of great transformations." *Review of International Political Economy* 11:204–26.

———. 2004b. "The normalizing role of rationalist assumptions in the institutional embedding of neoliberalism." *Economy and Society* 33:500–527.

Hayek, Friedrich A. 1944/1976. *The Road to Serfdom*. Chicago: University of Chicago Press.

Heilbroner, Robert L., and Peter Bernstein. 1989. *The Debt and the Deficit: False Alarms/Real Possibilities*. New York: W. W. Norton.

Hemispheric Energy Regulatory Assistance (HERA). 2002. "Best practices guide: Electricity regulation in Latin America." The Energy Group of the Institute of International Education. HERA Project. New York: IIE.

Hirst, Paul, and Grahame Thompson. 1996. *Globalization in Question: The International Economy and the Possibilities of Governance*. Malden, Mass.: Polity Press.

Hollingsworth, J. Rogers. 2002. "Some reflections on how institutions influence styles of innovation." Paper presented to the Swedish Collegium for Advanced Study in the Social Sciences (SCASSS), 26 September.

Humphreys, David. 2006. "Public goods, neoliberalism and the crisis of deforestation." Paper presented to the Annual Conference of the British International Studies Association. University of Cork, Ireland, 18–20 December.

Hunt, Alan. 1990. "Rights and social movements: Counter-hegemonic strategies." *Journal of Law and Society* 17 (Autumn): 309–28.

Ibarra Turcios, Angel María, Ulises Campos Jarquín, and Francisco Javier Rivera. 2002. *Hacía la gestión sustentable del agua en El Salvador: Propuestas básicas para elaborar una política nacional hídrica*. San Salvador: UNES (Unidad Ecológica Salvadoreña), Federación Luterana Mundial, Foro Regional de Gestión de Riesgos.

IEA (International Energy Agency). 2002. *World Energy Outlook 2002.* Paris: IEA.

Jayasuriya, Kanishka. 2001. "Globalization and the changing architecture of the state: The regulatory state and the politics of negative co-ordination." *Journal of European Public Policy* 8:101–23.

Jessop, Bob. 1990. *State Theory: Putting the Capitalist State in Its Place.* University Park: Pennsylvania State University Press.

———. 2001. "Regulationist and autopoieticist reflections on Polanyi's account of market economies and the market society." *New Political Economy* 6:213–32.

Jiménez, Ronulfo, ed. 2000. *Los retos políticos de la reforma económica en Costa Rica.* San José, Costa Rica: Academia de Centroamérica.

Johnstone, Nick, Elisabeth Wood, and Robert Hearne. 1999. "The regulation of private sector participation in urban water supply and sanitation: Realising social and environmental objectives in developing countries." Discussion Paper 24142. International Institute for Environment and Development, Environmental Economics Programme, London.

Kahler, Miles. 1992. "External influence, conditionality, and the politics of adjustment." In *The Politics of Economic Adjustment: International Constraints, Distributive Conflicts, and the State,* ed. Stephan Haggard and Robert R. Kaufman, 89–136. Princeton: Princeton University Press.

Kalecki, Michal. 1939. *Essays in the Theory of Economic Fluctuations.* London: Allen and Unwin. Reprinted in Jerzy Osiatynski, ed. 1990. *Collected Works of Michal Kalecki,* 231–318. Oxford: Clarendon Press.

Katznelson, Ira. 2003. "Periodization and preferences: Reflections on purposive action in comparative-historical social science." In *Comparative Historical Analysis in the Social Sciences,* ed. James Mahoney and Dietrich Rueschemeyer, 270–301. New York: Cambridge University Press.

Kaul, Inge. 2003. *Public Goods: A Positive Analysis.* Office of Development Studies. New York: United Nations Development Programme.

Kessides, Ioannis N. 2004. *Reforming Infrastructure: Privatization, Regulation, and Competition.* Policy Research Group. Washington, D.C.: World Bank.

Khor, Martin. 2001. *Rethinking Globalization.* London: Zed Books.

King, Lawrence P. 2002. "The emperor exposed: Neoliberal theory and de-modernization in postcommunist society." Manuscript, Yale University.

Klasen, Stephan. 2008. "The efficiency of equity." *Review of Political Economy* 20 (2): 257–74.

Kohl, Benjamin. 2003. "Restructuring citizenship in Bolivia: El Plan de todos." *International Journal of Urban and Regional Research* 27:337–51.

Kothari, Miloon. 2001. "Statement by the United Nations special rapporteur on adequate housing, appointed under the Commission on Human Rights resolution." Preparatory Committee for the International Conference on Financing for Development. New York.

Krippner, Greta R. 2001. "The elusive market: Embeddedness and the paradigm of economic sociology." *Theory and Society* 30:775–810.

Lanzara, Giovan Francesco. 1998. "Self-destructive processes in institution building and some modest countervailing mechanisms." *European Journal of Political Research* 33:1–39.

Lara López, Edgar. 2006. *Social and Economic Impacts of the Privatization of Electricity Distribution in El Salvador.* San Salvador: Fundación Nacional para Desarrollo (FUNDE).

Lefeber, Louis, and Thomas Vietorisz. 2007. "The meaning of social efficiency." *Review of Political Economy* 19 (2): 139–64.

Leftwich, Adrian. 1993. "Governance, democracy and development in the Third World." *Third World Quarterly* 14 (3): 605–24.

Lemos, Maria Carmen, and João Lúcio Farias de Oliveira. 2004. "Can water reform survive politics? Institutional change and river basin management in Ceará, Northeast Brazil." *World Development* 32 (December): 2121–37.

Levi-Faur, David. 2005. "The global diffusion of regulatory capitalism." *ANNALS of the American Academy of Political and Social Science* 598:12–32.

Levine, Peter, and Lars Hasseblad Torres. 2008. *Where Is Democracy Headed? Research and Practice on Public Deliberation.* Washington, D.C.: Deliberative Democracy Coalition.

Loftus, Alexander J. 2001. "Of liquid dreams: A political ecology of water privatization in Buenos Aires." *Environment and Urbanization* 13 (2): 179–99.

Lukes, Steven. 1974. *Power: A Radical View.* London: Macmillan.

———. 2004a. "Invasions of the market." In *From Liberal Values to Democratic Transition: Essays in Honor of Janos Kis,* ed. Ronald William Dworkin, 57–78. Budapest: Central European University Press.

———. 2004b. *Power: A Radical View.* 2nd ed. London: Palgrave Macmillan.

Lukes, Steven, and LaDawn Haglund. 2005. "Power and luck." *European Journal of Sociology* 46 (1): 45–66.

Lungo, Mario, and Francisco Oporto. 1995. *La infraestructura y los servicios en El Salvador: La situación en momentos de su modernización y privatización.* Avances 7 (May). San Salvador: Fundación Nacional para Desarrollo (FUNDE).

MacLeod, Dag. 2004. *Downsizing the State: Privatization and the Limits of Neoliberal Reform in Mexico.* University Park: Pennsylvania State University Press.

———. 2005. "Privatization and the limits of state autonomy in Mexico: Rethinking the orthodox paradox." *Latin American Perspectives* 32 (4): 36–64.

Mahoney, James. 2000. "Path dependence in historical sociology." *Theory and Society* 29:507–48.

———. 2001. *The Legacies of Liberalism: Path Dependence and Political Regimes in Central America.* Baltimore: Johns Hopkins University Press.

———. 2003. "Knowledge accumulation in comparative-historical research: The case of democracy and authoritarianism." In *Comparative Historical Analysis in the Social Sciences,* ed. James Mahoney and Dietrich Rueschemeyer, 131–74. New York: Cambridge University Press.

Mahoney, James, and Dietrich Rueschemeyer, eds. 2003. *Comparative Historical Analysis in the Social Sciences.* New York: Cambridge University Press.

Malkin, Jesse, and Aaron Wildavsky. 1991. "Why the traditional distinction between public and private goods should be abandoned." *Journal of Theoretical Politics* 3 (4): 355–78.

Mann, Michael. 1984. "The autonomous power of the state: Its origins, mechanisms, and results." *Archives Européennes de Sociologie* 25:185–213.

Manzetti, Luigi. 1999. *Privatization South American Style.* Oxford: Oxford University Press.

Marshall, T. H. 1949. "Citizenship and social class." In *Class, Citizenship, and Social Development,* ed. T. H. Marshall. 1964. New York: Doubleday.

Martin, Brendan. 1993. *In the Public Interest? Privatisation and Public Sector Reform.* London: Zed Books.

Moore, Barrington. 1978. *Injustice: The Social Bases of Obedience and Revolt.* White Plains, N.Y.: M. E. Sharpe.

Morales-Gamboa, Abelardo, and Stephen Baranyi. 2005. "Costa Rica: State-building, national leadership, and 'relative success.'" In *Making States Work: State Failure and the Crisis of Governance,* ed. Simon Chesterman, Michael Ignatieff, and Ramesh Thakur, 234–51. Tokyo: United Nations University Press.

Moreno, Raúl. 2000. *Reforma fiscal en El Salvador: Una exigencia impostergable.* San Salvador: Fundación Nacional para Desarrollo (FUNDE).

Mosk, Sanford A. 1950. *Industrial Revolution in Mexico.* Berkeley and Los Angeles: University of California Press. Quoted in Rosemary Thorp. 1998. *Progress, Poverty, and Exclusion: An Economic History of Latin America in the 20th Century.* Washington, D.C.: Inter-American Development Bank; Baltimore, Johns Hopkins University Press.

Moyers, Bill. 2003. Text of speech at the "Take Back America" Conference, 4 June, Washington, D.C.

Muhairwe, William T. 2005. "Performance improvement programmes: The case of National Water and Sewerage Corporation, Uganda." Presentation: "Managing Water Supply and Sanitation Services in Large Cities and Urban Areas." Karachi, Pakistan.

Musgrave, Richard A. 1969. "Provision for social goods." In *Public Economics,* ed. Julius Margolis and Henri Guitton, 124–44. London: Macmillan.

Nancarrow, Blair E., and Geoffrey J. Syme. 2001. "Challenges in implementing justice research in the allocation of natural resources." *Social Justice Research* 14 (4): 441–52.

Nelson, Joan M. 1990. *Economic Crisis and Policy Choice: The Politics of Adjustment in the Third World.* Princeton: Princeton University Press.

Nelson, Paul, and Ellen Dorsey. 2004. "New rights advocacy: Origins and significance of a partial human rights–development convergence." International Studies Association Meetings, Montreal, Quebec.

North American Congress on Latin America. 2003. "Privatization and its discontents." In *NACLA Report on the Americas.* New York: NACLA.

Nozick, Robert. 1974. *Anarchy, State, and Utopia.* New York: Basic Books.

Nussbaum, Martha C. 2003. "Capabilities as fundamental entitlements: Sen and social justice." *Feminist Economics* 9 (2–3): 33–59.

O'Connor, James. 2001. "Introduction to 2001 edition of fiscal crisis of the state." *Capitalism, Nature, Socialism* 12:99–114.

Oddvar Ericksen, Erik, and Jarle Weigård. 1999. "The end of citizenship? New roles challenging the political order." ARENA Working Papers No. 26.

O'Donnell, Guillermo. 1999. "Horizontal accountability in new democracies." In *The Self-Restraining State,* ed. Andreas Schedler, Larry Diamond, and Marc F. Plattner, 29–52. Boulder, Colo.: Lynne Rienner.

OLADE (Organización Latinoamericana de Energía. Energy Economic Information System). 2007. *Energy Statistics.* Quito, Ecuador: OLADE. Version 18, November.

Olivera, Oscar, and Tom Lewis. 2004. *¡Cochabamba! Water War in Bolivia.* Cambridge, Mass.: South End Press.

Ó Riain, Seán. 2000. "States and markets in an era of globalization." *Annual Review of Sociology* 26:187–213.

Orloff, Ann. 1993. "Gender and the social rights of citizenship." *American Sociological Review* 58 (3): 303–28.

Ortiz Gómez, Ana Silvia, and Aura Cecilia Jarquín Castro, consultoras. 2006. *Diagnóstico del impacto del proceso de descentralización del sistema de agua potable en el bienestar de las mujeres de Berlín, Usulután.* San Salvador: Las Dignas: Asociación de Mujeres por la Dignidad y la Vida.

Osiatynski, Jerzy, ed. 1990. *Collected Works of Michal Kalecki.* Oxford: Clarendon Press.

Ostrom, Elinor. 2005. *Understanding Institutional Diversity.* Princeton: Princeton University Press.

Ostrom, Elinor, Thomas Dietz, Nives Dolšak, Paul C. Stern, Susan Stonich, and Elke U. Weber, eds. 2002. *The Drama of the Commons.* Washington, D.C.: National Academy Press.

Paniagua Serrano, Carlos Rodolfo. 2002. "El bloque empresarial hegemónico salvadoreño." *ECA: Estudios Centroamericanos* año LVII:609–93.

Peck, Jamie, and Adam Tickell. 2002. "Neoliberalizing space." *Antipode: A Radical Journal of Geography* 34:380–404.

Pickhardt, Michael. 2006. "Fifty years after Samuelson's 'The pure theory of public expenditure': What are we left with?" *Journal of the History of Economic Thought* 28 (4): 439–60.

Pierson, Paul. 1994. *Dismantling the Welfare State? Reagan, Thatcher, and the Politics of Retrenchment.* Cambridge: Cambridge University Press.

———. 2003. "Big, slow-moving, and . . . invisible: Macro-social processes in the study of comparative politics." In *Comparative Historical Analysis in the Social Sciences,* ed. James Mahoney and Dietrich Rueschemeyer, 177–207. New York: Cambridge University Press.

Pinheiro, Armando Castelar, and Ben Ross Schneider. 1995. "The fiscal impact of privatisation in Latin America." *Journal of Development Studies* 31 (5): 751–85.

Pitsch, Mark, and Robert Ritzenthaler. 2001. "The autonomy tale." Report from Bluefields, Nicaragua. Resource Center of the Americas.

Pizzigati, Sam. 2004. *Greed and Good.* New York: Apex Press of the Council on International and Public Affairs.

Polanyi, Karl. 1944. *The Great Transformation.* Boston: Beacon Press.

———. 1957. "The economy as instituted process." In *Trade and Market in the Early Empires: Economies in History and Theory,* ed. Karl Polanyi, Conrad M. Arensberg, and Harry W. Pearson, 243–70. Glencoe, Ill.: Free Press.

Polsby, Nelson. 1980. *Community Power and Political Theory: A Further Look and Problems of Evidence and Inference.* New Haven: Yale University Press.

Portes, Alejandro. 1997. "Neoliberalism and the sociology of development: Emerging trends and unanticipated facts." *Population and Development Review* 23:229–59.

———. 2006. "Institutions and development: A conceptual reanalysis." *Population and Development Review* 32 (2): 233–62.

Power, Michael, and Lynn Scott McCarty. 2006. "Environmental risk management decision-making in a societal context." *Human and Ecological Risk Assessment* 12:18–27.

Przeworski, Adam. 1991. *Democracy and the Market: Political and Economic Reforms in Eastern Europe and Latin America*. New York: Cambridge University Press.

Przeworski, Adam, and Henry Teune. 1970. *The Logic of Comparative Social Inquiry*. New York: Wiley.

Public Citizen. 2001. *Water Privatization Case Study: Cochabamba, Bolivia*. Washington, D.C.: Public Citizen.

———. 2005. *NAFTA Chapter 11 Investor-State Cases: Lessons for the Central America Free Trade Agreement*. Publication No. E9014. Washington, D.C.: Public Citizen.

———. 2009. *Table of NAFTA "Chapter 11" Foreign Investor-State Cases and Claims*. Washington, D.C.: Public Citizen.

Putnam, Robert D. 2000. *Bowling Alone: The Collapse and Revival of American Community*. New York: Simon and Schuster.

Ragin, Charles. 1989. *The Comparative Method: Moving Beyond Qualitative and Quantitative Strategies*. Berkeley and Los Angeles: University of California Press.

Rawls, John. 1971. *A Theory of Justice*. Cambridge, Mass.: Belknap Press.

Reding, Andrew. 1986. "Voices from Costa Rica." *World Policy Journal* 3 (2): 317–45.

Roberts, Bryan R. 1995. *The Making of Citizens: Cities of Peasants Revisited*. London: Arnold.

Rodríguez, Leopoldo. 2006. "Aguas turbias: The privatization of water and sewage services in Argentina." Paper presented at the Latin American Studies Association conference, San Juan, Puerto Rico.

Rodríguez Argüello, Percy. 2000. *Desarrollo y regulación de los servicios públicos en Costa Rica*. San José: Autoridad Regulador de los Servicios Publicos.

Rodríguez-Boetsch, Leopoldo. 2005. "Public service privatisation and crisis in Argentina." *Development in Practice* 15 (3–4): 302–15.

Rodríguez-Clare, Andrés. 1998. "Internal debt in Costa Rica: An alternative focus." In *Revista Acta Académica*, 95–101. San José, Costa Rica: Universidad Autonoma de Centro América (UACA).

Rojas Bolaños, Manuel. 2000. "Política y concertación en Costa Rica." *Espacios: Revista Centroamericana de Cultura Política* 12:14–21.

Rose, Nikolas. 1993. "Government, authority, and expertise in advanced liberalism." *Economy and Society* 22:283–99.

———. 1999. *Powers of Freedom: Reframing Political Thought*. Cambridge: Cambridge University Press.

Rose-Ackerman, Susan. 1997. "The political economy of corruption." In *Corruption and the Global Economy*, ed. Kimberly Ann Elliott, 31–60. Washington, D.C.: Institute for International Economics.

Rowden, Rick, and Vicki Gass. 2003. *Investor Rights or Human Rights? The Impacts of the FTAA*. Washington, D.C.: ActionAid USA and Washington Office on Latin America (WOLA).

Rubio, Roberto. 1997. "A siete años de la estabilización y el ajuste en El Salvador." *Alternativas para el Desarrollo* 47. San Salvador: Fundación Nacional para Desarrollo (FUNDE).

Ruggie, John Gerard. 1982. "International regimes, transactions, and change: Embedded liberalism in the post-war economic order." *International Organization* 36:379–415.

Salamon, Lester M. 2002. "The new governance and the tools of public action: An introduction." In *The Tools of Government: A Guide to the New Governance*, ed. Lester M. Salamon, 1–47. New York: Oxford University Press.

Sanchez Ancochea, Diego. 2005. "Domestic capital, civil servants, and the state: Costa Rica and the Dominican Republic under globalization." *Journal of Latin American Studies* 37:693–726.

Sandbrook, Richard. 2000. "Review of *Development as Freedom* by Amartya Sen." *Third World Quarterly* 21:1071.

Sandler, Todd. 1999. "Intergenerational public goods." In *Global Public Goods: International Cooperation in the 21st Century*, ed. Inge Kaul, Isabelle Grunberg, and Marc A. Stern, 20–50. New York: Oxford University Press.

SAPRIN (Structural Adjustment Participatory Review International Network Secretariat). 2001. *The Policy Roots of Economic Crisis and Poverty: A Multi-Country Participatory Assessment of Structural Adjustment*. Washington, D.C.: SAPRIN.

Schamis, Hector. 1999. "Distributional coalitions and the politics of economic reform in Latin America." *World Politics* 51:236–68.

———. 2002. *Re-forming the State: The Politics of Privatization in Latin America and Europe*. Ann Arbor: University of Michigan Press.

Schipke, Alfred. 2001. *Why Do Governments Divest? The Macroeconomics of Privatization*. Heidelberg: Springer.

Schneider, Ben Ross. 1998. "Elusive synergy: Business-government relations and development." *Comparative Politics* 31 (1): 101–22.

Schneider, Elizabeth M. 1986. "The dialectic of rights and politics: Perspectives from the women's movement." *New York University Law Review* 61:589.

Sclar, Elliott D. 2000. *You Don't Always Get What You Pay For: The Economics of Privatization*. Ithaca: Cornell University Press.

Scott, James C. 1998. *Seeing Like a State: How Certain Schemes to Improve the Human Condition Have Failed*. New Haven: Yale University Press.

Searle, John R. 1998. *Mind, Language and Society*. Basic Books, New York.

Segovia, Alexander. 2002. *Transformación estructural y reforma económica en El Salvador: El funcionamiento económico de los noventa y sus efectos sobre el crecimiento, la pobreza y la distribución del ingreso*. Guatemala City: F and G Editores.

Segura Ballar, Ricardo. 1999. *National Resistance to the Implementation of the Neoliberal Economic Model in Costa Rica*. San José: Union of ICE Engineers and Professionals (SIICE).

Seligson, Mitchell A. 2002. "Trouble in paradise? The erosion of system support in Costa Rica, 1978–1999." *Latin American Research Review* 37:160–85.

Sen, Amartya K. 1970. *Collective Choice and Social Welfare*. San Francisco: Holden-Day.

———. 1999. *Development as Freedom*. New York: Alfred A. Knopf.

Shapiro, Ian. 2006. "On the second edition of Lukes' third face." *Political Studies Review* 4:146–55.

Silver, Beverly J., and Giovanni Arrighi. 2003. "Polanyi's 'double movement': The belle époques of British and U.S. hegemony compared." *Politics and Society* 31:325–55.

Skocpol, Theda. 1985. "Bringing the state back in: Strategies of analysis in current research." In *Bringing the State Back In*, ed. Peter Evans, Dietrich Rueschemeyer, and Theda Skocpol, 3–43. New York: Cambridge University Press.

Smulovitz, Catalina, and Enrique Peruzzotti. 2000. "Societal accountability in Latin America." *Journal of Democracy* 11:147–58.

Sojo, Carlos. 2004. *Líneas de tensión: Gestión política de la reforma económica. El Instituto Costarricense de Electricidad (ICE) y la privatización de empresas públicas.* Santiago de Chile: CEPAL.

Special Mixed Commission on ICE. 2000. "Contingency plan for strengthening ICE." Report of the Social Movement Delegates, Special Mixed Commission on ICE. San José, Costa Rica.

Spence, Jack. 2004. *War and Peace in Central America: Comparing Transitions Toward Democracy and Social Equity in Guatemala, El Salvador, and Nicaragua.* Brookline, Mass.: Hemisphere Initiatives.

Stallings, Barbara, ed. 1995. *Global Change, Regional Response: The New International Context of Development.* New York: Cambridge University Press.

Stark, David Charles. 1998. *Postsocialist Pathways: Transforming Politics and Property in East Central Europe.* New York: Cambridge University Press.

Steinbeck, John. 1939/2002. *The Grapes of Wrath.* Repr., New York: Penguin.

Stiglitz, Joseph. 2002. *Accounting Tricks Around the Globe.* Project Syndicate. New York: Global Policy Forum.

Strange, Susan. 1998. *States and Markets.* New York: St. Martin's Press.

Streeck, Wolfgang. 1997. "Beneficial constraints: On the economic limits of rational volunteerism." In *Contemporary Capitalism: The Embeddedness of Institutions,* ed. J. Rogers Hollingsworth and Robert Boyer, 197–219. New York: Cambridge University Press.

Swyngedouw, Erik, and Nikolas C. Heynen. 2003. "Urban political ecology, justice, and the politics of scale." In "Justice and Urban Political Ecology." Special issue, *Antipode* 35 (5): 898–918.

Syme, Geoffrey J., Elisabeth Kals, Blair E. Nancarrow, and Leo Montada. 2006. "Ecological risks and community perceptions of fairness and justice: A cross-cultural model." *Human and Ecological Risk Assessment* 12:102–19.

Syme, Geoffrey J., Blair E. Nancarrow, and J. A. McCreddin. 1999. "Defining the components of fairness in the allocation of water to environmental and human uses." *Journal of Environmental Management* 57: 51–70.

Tangermann, Klaus-Dieter. 1995. "La democracia Centroamericana en la discusión." In *Ilusiones y dilemas: La democracia en Centroamérica,* ed. Klaus-Dieter Tangermann, 15–61. San José, Costa Rica: Facultad Latinoamericana de Ciencias Sociales (FLACSO).

Taylor, Lance, ed. 1993. *The Rocky Road to Reform: Adjustment, Income Distribution, and Growth in the Developing World.* Cambridge, Mass.: MIT Press.

Tendler, Judith. 1997. *Good Government in the Tropics.* Baltimore: Johns Hopkins University Press.

Terry, Donald F., and Steven R. Wilson. 2005. *Beyond Small Change: Making Migrant Remittances Count.* Washington, D.C.: Inter-American Development Bank.

Thelen, Kathleen. 2003. "How institutions evolve: Insights from comparative-historical analysis." In *Comparative Historical Analysis in the Social Sciences,* ed. James Mahoney and Dietrich Rueschemeyer, 208–40. New York: Cambridge University Press.

Thorp, Rosemary. 1998. *Progress, Poverty, and Exclusion: An Economic History of Latin America in the 20th Century.* Washington, D.C.: Inter-American Development Bank; Baltimore: Johns Hopkins University Press.

Torres-Rivas, Edelberto. 1996. "Democracia y mercado." *Tendencias* 54:37–39.

———. 1997. "Las aporías de la democracia al final de siglo." In *Democracia para una nueva sociedad: Un modelo para armar*, ed. Helena González and Heidulf Schmidt, 213–27. Caracas, Venezuela: Nueva Sociedad.

———. 2001. "La sociedad civil en la construcción democrática." *Espacios: Revista Centroamericana de cultura política* 14:3–16.

Toye, John. 2003. "Changing perspectives in development economics." In *Rethinking Development Economics*, ed. Ha-Joon Chang, 21–40. London: Anthem Press.

Tsakalotos, Euclid. 2004. "Market constraints, economic performance and political power: Modernizers versus leftists." *Socio-Economic Review* 2 (3): 415–24.

Tyler, Tom R., and Peter Degoey. 1995. "Collective restraint in social dilemmas: Procedural justice and social identification effects on support for authorities." *Journal of Personality and Social Psychology* 69 (3): 482–97.

Udayagiri, Mridula, and John Walton. 2002. "Global transformation and local counter movements: The prospects for democracy under neoliberalism." Paper presented at "The Next Great Transformation? Karl Polanyi and the Critique of Globalization" conference, University of California, Davis, 12–13 April.

UNDP (United Nations Development Programme). 2001. *Informe sobre desarrollo humano: El Salvador*. San Salvador: Programa de las Naciones Unidas para el Desarrollo.

———. 2002a. *Deepening Democracy in a Fragmented World*. New York: Oxford University Press.

———. 2002b. *El gasto público en servicios sociales básicos en El Salvador: Iniciativa 20/20*. San Salvador: Programa de las Naciones Unidas para el Desarrollo.

———. 2003. *Millennium Development Goals: A Compact Among Nations to End Poverty*. New York: Oxford University Press.

UNIMER Research International. 2000. *Fourth Annual Opinion Poll*. San José, Costa Rica: UNIMER.

United Nations General Assembly. 1986. *Declaration on the Right to Development*. A/RES/41/128.

———. 2000. *United Nations Millennium Declaration*. A/RES/55/2.

Vargas Solís, Luis Paulino. 2007. *Soñar con los pies en la tierra*. Document for Citizen Dialogue. San José: Fundación PROCAL (Promoción, Capacitación y Acción Alternativa).

Veltmeyer, Henry, James Petras, and Steve Vieux. 1997. *Neoliberalism and Class Conflict in Latin America: A Comparative Perspective on the Political Economy of Structural Adjustment*. New York: St. Martin's Press.

Vilhena Vieira, Oscar. 2007. "Inequality and the subversion of the rule of law." *Sur—Revista Internacional de Direitos Humanos* 6:29–51.

Vlachou, Andriana. 2004. "Capitalism and ecological sustainability: The shaping of environmental policies." *Review of International Political Economy* 11:926–52.

Vogel, Steven K. 1996. *Freer Markets, More Rules: Regulatory Reform in Advanced Industrial Countries*. Ithaca: Cornell University Press.

Von Ungern-Sternberg, Thomas. 2004. *Efficient Monopolies: The Limits of Competition in the European Property Insurance Market*. Oxford: Oxford University Press.

Wade, Robert. 1998. "The coming fight over capital flows." *Foreign Policy* 113:41–54.

———. 2003. "What strategies are viable for developing countries today? The World Trade Organization and the shrinking of 'development space.'" *Review of International Political Economy* 10:621–44.

WEDO (Women's Environment and Development Organization). 2003. *Diverting the Flow: A Resource Guide to Gender, Rights, and Water Privatization.* Privatization Working Group. New York: WEDO.

Western, Bruce. 2001. "Bayesian thinking about macrosociology." *American Journal of Sociology* 107:353–78.

Whaites, Alan. 2008. "States in development: Understanding state-building." A DFID working paper, Governance and Social Development Group, Policy and Research Division, Department for International Development, London.

WHO (World Health Organization). 2002. "Water, sanitation and health: The current situation." *Joint Monitoring Programme for Water Supply and Sanitation.* Geneva: World Health Organization and UNICEF.

Wilder, Margaret, and Patricia Romero Lankao. 2006. "Paradoxes of decentralization: Water reform and social implications in Mexico." *World Development* 34 (11): 1977–95.

Williamson, John. 1990. "What Washington means by policy reform." In *Latin American Adjustment: How Much Has Happened?* ed. John Williamson, 7–20. Washington, D.C.: Institute for International Economics.

———. 1994. *The Political Economy of Policy Reform.* Washington, D.C.: Institute for International Economics.

———. 2004. "Discussion of 'After the Washington Consensus.'" Ford Foundation's "Leading Edge Roundtable." New York City.

Wilson, Bruce M. 1994. "When social democrats choose neoliberal economic policies: The case of Costa Rica." *Comparative Politics* 26:149–68.

Wing, Adrien Katherine, ed. 2000. *Global Critical Race Feminism: An International Reader.* New York: New York University Press.

Wolfram, Catherine D. 1998. "Increases in executive pay following privatization." *Journal of Economics and Management Strategy* 7 (3): 327–61.

Wood, Elisabeth. 2000. *Forging Democracy from Below: Insurgent Transitions in South Africa and El Salvador.* Cambridge: Cambridge University Press.

Woods, Ngarie. 2003. "Unelected government: Making the IMF and World Bank more accountable." *Brookings Review* 21 (2): 9–12.

World Bank. 1995. *Bureaucrats in Business: The Economics and Politics of Government Ownership.* Washington, D.C.: World Bank.

———. 2001. *Development Debates: Latin America and the Caribbean.* Bolivia, Dominican Republic, Guatemala, and Nicaragua: World Bank Group.

———. 2004. *World Development Report: Making Services Work for Poor People.* Washington, D.C.: World Bank.

Yashar, Deborah J. 1997. *Demanding Democracy: Reform and Reaction in Costa Rica and Guatemala, 1870s–1950s.* Stanford: Stanford University Press.

Yergin, Daniel, and Joseph Stanislaw. 1998. *The Commanding Heights: The Battle Between Government and the Marketplace That Is Remaking the Modern World.* New York: Simon and Schuster.

Zamora, Rubén. 1997. "Una cuestion de modelos o un problema de poder?" In *Gobernabilidad y desarrollo democrático en América Latina y el Caribe,* ed. Fondo Fiduciario. España: PNUD.

Zibechi, Raúl. 2005. "New challenges for radical social movements." *North American Congress on Latin America (NACLA): Report on the Americas* 38 (5): 14–21.

Zysman, John. 1985. *Governments, Markets, and Growth: Financial Systems and the Politics of Industrial Change.* Ithaca: Cornell University Press.

INDEX

Pages in *italics* indicate references that appear in tables.